OPENING DOORS

Participants at the 1988 conference, "Opening Doors: An Appraisal of Race Relations in America," University of Alabama. The picture projected in the background is of George Wallace's historic "stand in the schoolhouse door."

OPENING DOORS

Perspectives on Race Relations
in Contemporary America

To Greg

*Best wishes from
your friend and
Colleague*

Harry

EDITED BY

HARRY J. KNOPKE

ROBERT J. NORRELL

RONALD W. ROGERS

The University of Alabama Press
Tuscaloosa and London

Library of Congress Cataloging-in-Publication Data

Opening doors : perspectives on race relations in contemporary America
/ edited by Harry J. Knopke, Robert J. Norrell, Ronald W. Rogers.
p. cm.
Includes bibliographical references and index.
ISBN 0-8173-0497-5 (alk. paper)
1. United States—Race relations. 2. Racism—United States.
I. Knopke, Harry J., 1946– . II. Norrell, Robert J. (Robert
Jefferson) III. Rogers, Ronald W., 1944– .
E185.615.064 1991
305.8′00973—dc20   90–36167

British Library Cataloguing-in-Publication Data available

CONTENTS

ACKNOWLEDGMENTS

The idea for a national symposium on contemporary race relations grew out of discussions among a number of University of Alabama faculty and staff members concerning the then impending twenty-fifth anniversary of Governor George C. Wallace's "stand in the schoolhouse door" at the University. These discussions began in the spring of 1987 and centered, either explicitly or implicitly, on both the need to recognize this occasion in the most appropriate way and the desire to realize the best possible outcome of observing an event that was one of the most deleterious in the University's history. This book indicates quite clearly that these early discussions, and the work that followed, were highly productive. The national symposium held June 11–13, 1988, was an unqualified success, not only in terms of attendance but, more importantly, for the positive effects it generated for participants, observers, and the University through the informed, sensitive discussions that were generated by the speakers whose essays appear in this volume.

A core group of University of Alabama faculty and staff provided the initial directions for recognizing the Wallace stand. Harry Knopke, John Blackburn, Malcolm MacDonald, Cully Clark, Mike Ellis, Dale Allison, Stan Murphy, Jeff Norrell, and Ron Rogers contributed their time and energies to conceptualizing and developing the symposium. Their discussions were supported by the initial research conducted by Brenda Burns and Jerry Oldshue, and by the institutional memory of Thelma Allen. Once the structure and content of the symposium was established, Carol Duncan worked with seemingly unceasing energy and good cheer to facilitate the speakers' participation and to organize their manuscripts. Roxanne Gregg demonstrated the same characteristics as she assisted with those efforts and played the additional critical role of supervising the computer processing of this manuscript. Jeanie Weaver's marketing and organizational skills were important to the success of the symposium itself; her efforts were enhanced by Jan Pruitt's artistic contributions. Finally, three University of Alabama students assisted in the final phases of research for this manuscript: Steve Griffith, Karen Singleton, and Carla Shows helped assure the accuracy and integrity of the manuscript of this book.

PREFACE

On June 11, 1963, The University of Alabama provided the backdrop for what would become a lasting symbol in U.S. civil rights history. With his stand in the schoolhouse door staged at Foster Auditorium on the University's campus, Governor George C. Wallace attempted to defy a federal mandate by blocking the admission of two black students to the University. Overruled by the highest levels of federal government, Wallace relented; the major university of the last Southern state to integrate its educational institutions then went about enrolling Vivian Malone and James Hood as it had planned to do for some time.

In the intervening twenty-five years considerable progress has been made toward ensuring equal rights for all Americans. Yet, even today, racial incidents continue to make headlines, not just on college campuses or in the South, but in major northern cities and, indeed, nationwide.

The nature of racial prejudice and discrimination—its causes, its history, and its impact on society—was the focus of a national symposium hosted by The University of Alabama to mark the twenty-fifth anniversary of the stand in the schoolhouse door. On this anniversary occasion the major participants in the Wallace stand reconvened to reflect on the issues and circumstances surrounding that event. In addition, because of the original event's central place in civil rights history, and because of the myriad racial disturbances and difficulties that exist today, scholars from across the country were asked to contribute to an extensive examination of racial prejudice and discrimination. They addressed themselves to three levels or dimensions of experience: the individual, institutional, and sociocultural levels. These different dimensions served as specific and collective focal points of the conference because traditions, values, beliefs, and behavior patterns differ at each level; yet each level is practically and conceptually interrelated with the others.

This book, which contains the set of papers commissioned for the symposium is divided into three sections: historical context, current psychosocial-cultural assessments of prejudice and discrimination, and strategies for change. The chapters of each section revolve around the Wallace stand in different ways and, by using the analytic tools of historians and behavioral and social scientists, endeavor to add to our understanding of prejudice, discrimination, and race relations. The diversity in viewpoint and level of analysis that each represents contribute to both the uniqueness and the immediacy of this book.

In the book's first section, "Historical Perspectives," four quite different yet complementary papers set the historical context for considering U.S. race relations on the twenty-fifth anniversary of the desegregation of The University of Alabama. Each takes a distinct vantage point for explaining how human relations in the South reached the moment of crisis in 1963, and, in turn and together, for describing some of the roots of the progress and the conflicts that mark contemporary human relations. The multiple perspectives are intended to deepen our historical understanding of a storied, almost mythic event on the one hand, and our appreciation of its broader context on the other. How did George Wallace's stand in the schoolhouse door come to be? What were the social, political, and institutional forces that let events like it happen? What in fact was its effect in Alabama, the South, the country?

Leon F. Litwack, Morrison Professor of History at The University of California at Berkeley, opens with a richly textured portrait of the U.S. black experience during the first generation of freedom. Professor Litwack explores how the freedmen and freedwomen coped with the continuing exploitation and discrimination of blacks by white supremacists in the postwar South. New forms of discrimination replaced slavery as the means of racial control, yielding a post-Civil War South that had many characteristics of a horror story—terrorism, violence, and hopelessness. But Professor Litwack's chapter is also an inspiring story of courage and determination, one in which blacks developed cultural forms like the blues, partly as a means of dealing with the troubles of an oppressed existence. Using the examples of a number of remarkable individuals, he details blacks' determination to persevere. He also vividly recounts the survival strategies they employed that enabled their descendants to live for increasingly better days as the twentieth century moved to maturity.

Fannie Allen Neal, a former executive with the American Federation of Labor–Congress of Industrial Organizations, brings a personal perspective to the history of black Southerners in the mid-twentieth century. Mrs. Neal tells the story of her life and, with it, the experience of black Alabamians whose forebears are the subjects of Professor Litwack's chapter. She presents a unique historical portrait of social and political events that occurred in Alabama and the South and the effects they generated for countless individuals. In doing so she describes the many hardships encountered by both blacks and whites and identifies the great obstacles to civil rights for blacks. But she also recounts joyously the triumphs, not least of which was securing the right to vote. Mrs. Neal reveals one of what must certainly be thousands of personal sagas of protest and progress among blacks in the modern South and demonstrates quite clearly the mutual gains that can be realized by blacks and whites working together. Her experiences and observations point the way to future human rights activism.

E. Culpepper Clark, Chairperson and Professor of Speech Communication at The University of Alabama, delves deeply into the institutional history of the University and the circumstances that would capture the nation's attention in 1963. Professor Clark shows that The University of Alabama had been contemplating the possibility of desegregation since the 1940s. Successive presidents of the University encountered a very powerful board of trustees dominated by elderly white men whose racial attitudes had been formed largely in the previous century. Time and again, and most notably with the Autherine Lucy situation in 1956, the board had opportunities to accept a token desegregation that would have forestalled the dramatic moments of June 1963. But until the Kennedy administration showed its determination to force the University's desegregation, the board of trustees fought a sometimes unscrupulous war against prospective black students. In this chapter Professor Clark describes the underpinnings of institutional responses to such compelling mid-century issues as desegregation and, in doing so, explains how we came to the historic event staged at the schoolhouse door.

Dan T. Carter, Mellon Professor of American History at Emory University, offers a characterization of the dominant historical figure in the schoolhouse door stand, Governor George C. Wallace. Professor Carter places Wallace's actions in the context of an emerging national political career, one that capitalized on the fears of white Americans about changes in race relations. Wallace gave voice to the alienation that many whites, Southern and Northern, felt from a national government that finally demonstrated some concern for blacks. In Tuscaloosa, Wallace learned how to gain the attention of the nation by taking a defiant pose, and, as Professor Carter explains, he went on to learn other lessons in other places, such as at Harvard University, about developing a following of angry Americans who assumed a vocal, demonstrative position in the United States in the sixties and seventies.

These chapters develop individual, institutional, and broader sociopolitical contexts related to the Wallace stand at The University of Alabama. These contexts serve to focus the status and condition of race relations in the South, and, indeed, in the nation through the decade of the sixties and beyond. They also help clarify further our understanding of many of the roots of contemporary race relations in the United States.

In the second section of the book, "Current Psycho-Socio-Cultural Assessments of Prejudice and Discrimination," our attention turns from assessments of particular historical events and circumstances that helped shape contemporary relations between the races to social scientists' study of the basic nature of prejudice and discrimination. The three chapters in this section present current psychological and social-psychological perspectives on prejudice and discrimination.

In the first chapter Dr. Mortimer Ostow examines prejudice from the perspective of a practicing psychoanalytic therapist. Although psychoanalysis has not been used extensively to explicate the dynamics of prejudice, Dr. Ostow uses the cases of two of his own patients to present the etiology and manifestation of prejudice at the level of the individual. Even though these patients are mentally ill, Dr. Ostow argues that we may still draw inferences about the development of prejudice in normal individuals, because prejudice, in the psychoanalytic or Freudian view, is just one manifestation of the psychodynamics of intrapsychic and interpersonal relations.

The two case histories presented concern antisemitism; Dr. Ostow maintains that the roots of antisemitism do not differ essentially from the roots of prejudice toward any other group of people, and that prejudice is simply one mechanism for resolving intrapsychic conflicts acquired early in life. Dr. Ostow investigates prejudice as both an individual phenomenon and the interplay of the individual and the group. The origins and sequelae of prejudice are illuminated with the traditional psychoanalytic emphasis on the role of early experiences, particularly the resolution of the Oedipal conflict and sibling rivalry. Dr. Ostow shows that those traits, feelings, and thoughts that are undesirable within the individual are projected onto other people, and the selection of the target of prejudice is guided by society toward its scapegoats and outgroups.

In contrast to the psychoanalytic emphasis on case studies, the next two chapters present the work of social scientists whose methods and concepts of evidence are quite different. In his chapter, Professor Walter Stephan uses quantitative techniques in a systematic search for answers to questions about the effects of school desegregation. On the one hand, George Wallace believed desegregation would corrode race relations, while on the other hand, the Supreme Court and social scientists believed it would improve race relations. Who was right? Professor Stephan shows how relevant legal, political, and ethical issues can be transformed into variables to be studied by the methods of social science.

Professor Stephan reports the short-term effects of desegregation on self-esteem, achievement, and race relations, using the school to represent modern U.S. institutions. He then describes the long-term effects on educational attainment, occupational choice, and voluntary interracial contact. Next, he informs us of the conditions necessary to improve intergroup relations. Although these conditions have rarely been implemented in any school system, he argues persuasively that if and when these conditions are met in our schools, there is hope for race relations to improve.

Professors John Dovidio and Samuel Gaertner approach the study of prejudice at the societal level from a direction very different from that of the psychoanalyst Ostow, but they reach one similar conclusion: prejudice is rooted in normal human functioning. That is, prejudice can be a product of our normal cognitive operations and our normal motivational processes.

Professors Dovidio and Gaertner review the changes in racial attitudes that have occurred in this country from the 1930s through the present. They report that whites are more tolerant of blacks and less likely to express negative attitudes. Unfortunately, this decrease in the overt expression of negative attitudes has been replaced by a subtle and indirect form of racism. Drawing on their own experimental research, as well as that of other investigators, they discovered that although whites do not discriminate against blacks if situational norms are clear, discrimination can occur if norms governing appropriate behavior in a situation are ambiguous or conflicting. This modern form of racism is a product of our attitudes having grown more complex and ambivalent, largely by incorporating the principle of egalitarianism into our conscious decision-making about the treatment of minority groups. The authors conclude there is room for hope if the new tolerance residing in our consciousness can become fully integrated into our subconscious.

A common theme running through all the chapters in the second section is that race relations must still be viewed through a Janus mask, one face focusing grimly on the past, but the other face looking optimistically forward. The final section, "Strategies for Change," takes this forward looking stance. The chapters it contains consider a number of ways to deal effectively with the causes and effects of prejudice and discrimination as they take place at the individual, institutional, and sociocultural levels of human interaction.

In the first chapter, Rhoda Johnson, Chair and Associate Professor of Women Studies at The University of Alabama, describes a set of strategies for empowering individuals to change their own behavior and that of relevant groups to which they belong. It is based on her ongoing research agenda, which aims to understand how the average person is enabled to recognize the need for change and then empowered to effect it. Part of the rationale for her strategies centers on the concept of oppression; she develops this concept by noting that meaningful change must address economic, psychological, sexual, and physical oppression as well as legal oppression. This approach is especially needed in a society where subtle forms of racism have replaced most legal forms.

The concept of oppression also contributes in several ways to the basis for a training process she has developed and utilized that is aimed at empowering individuals to assist in the elimination of racism, classism, sexism, and other forms of domination. The workshop process she explicates in the chapter is organized to help participants move from understanding oppression in its various forms, to understanding personal feelings about that oppression, to establishing individual and common goals for the group to both make a commitment to change and to take specific actions toward making change. The sequence she describes is applicable to a wide variety of groups and settings.

Thomas Pettigrew, Professor of Social Psychology at the University of California, Santa Cruz, and the University of Amsterdam, provides a thoughtful assessment of some of the institutional changes that have occurred over the past twenty-five years and utilizes this historical perspective to predict additional changes that are likely to occur in the future. He notes the irony emanating from the fact that, while the South still has miles to travel before it has fully shed its burden of racial injustice, the past twenty-five years have witnessed far greater racial change in the South than in other regions. These changes, he points out, did not result from initial attitude changes of white Southerners but, on the contrary, were largely imposed on the unwilling white South. The changes were structural and altered permanently the region's basic institutions. These alterations, in turn, began to reshape the behavior of Southerners which led to reshaping both black and white racial thinking.

In Pettigrew's view, the Southern process of initial structural change followed by new racial behavior and attitudes is the key lesson of the past quarter century that should guide future racial action. The many remaining institutional barriers to full black participation in U.S. society must be addressed directly and must result in structural changes occurring throughout the nation that compare with those that have begun to transform the South. Professor Pettigrew is convinced that these needed institutional alterations will evolve more rapidly in the South than elsewhere.

In the final chapter James Jones, Executive Director for Public Interest at the American Psychological Association and Professor of Psychology at the University of Delaware, develops a sociocultural context for change strategies. The thesis of his chapter is that we have broken the color line but have not yet broken the culture line. He reiterates the quintet of cultural concepts he calls TRIOS that suggests that black is more than a color and that adaptation to continuing racism in American society requires a bicultural approach.

In developing his argument, Professor Jones first recalls the concept of Cultural Racism he posited several years ago which specifies that when groups differ in their cultural heritage and when one group uses its power advantage to exploit the disadvantage of the other group, then cultural racism is an appropriate explanation for the results. This concept both acknowledges the overlap and confusion of race and culture and suggests that the notion of a color blind society necessarily is one in which standards of competence and appropriateness are subtly linked to cultural styles that are Anglo-Saxon and cultural in origin. After explicating his concept of TRIOS, an acronym standing for five dimensions of human experience, Time, Rhythm, Improvisation, Oral expression, and Spirituality, he considers two means for coping with prejudice and racism and for joining the European and African traditions. One is the central tendency approach, represented by the melting pot concept, while the second is the variance approach and is represented by the ethnicity concept. He shows how the former approach devolves to a majority rule strategy by which normative expectancy often defines acceptability. The second, in contrast, identifies the aspects of traditional culture or ethnicity as those which are expressive of one's identity, and at the same time takes into account those features of a broader society that consistently get rewarded and hence define meritocracy. The broad strategies he proposes arise from this latter approach.

The chapters of this book describe the progress that has been made in this country in the relationships between and among the races since a sneering Governor George C. Wallace told bystanders to "come back and see us in Alabama" as he left The University of Alabama following his futile stand in the schoolhouse door. They also shed some new light on our understanding of prejudice and discrimination and serve to broaden our current perspectives on the traditions, values, attitudes, and behavior patterns that contribute to and reflect these negative components of race relations. At the same time, by recounting historical issues associated with prejudice, racism, and discrimination, by offering current analyses of these concepts, and by suggesting strategies for effecting appropriate and meaningful change, they also lead to a clear understanding of the nature and extent of progress yet to be realized before we are able to engage in harmonious race relations and enjoy the benefits of a more just society.

SECTION I
Historical Perspectives

1

HELLHOUND ON MY TRAIL

Race Relations in the South from Reconstruction to the Civil Rights Movement

Leon F. Litwack

When the United States chose in 1898 to liberate the dark-skinned people of Cuba, Puerto Rico, and the Philippine Islands, black U.S. troops were among the liberators. But when the black regiments returned home, after demonstrating their courage, patriotism, and loyalty, they encountered a far more formidable and devious enemy—white-skinned Americans. No sooner had the 10th Cavalry been dispatched to a camp in Alabama, for example, than clashes broke out between white and black troops, and between black troops and white civilians. In May 1899, the regiment returned to Cuba as part of the occupation army—an order the black soldiers welcomed with unconcealed enthusiasm.[1]

Nothing could wipe from the memories of black veterans the treatment accorded them in the country that had sent them to war, and in particular the humiliation to which they were subjected after the troop trains crossed into the South—the segregated waiting rooms, the restaurants, cafes, and saloons that refused them service, the contemptuous stares, the racial epithets, the hateful letters and editorials in the Southern press. On June 22, 1899, a black sergeant stationed in Gibara, Cuba, recorded his thoughts. He had enlisted as a private some six years earlier, and when ordered into action in Cuba he had thought himself as patriotic as any soldier in the army.

> I believed the achievements of the black soldiers were destined to advance our cause many years; but now . . . the silence of the government on the recent murders of our people, and the unconcealed determination of those in authority not to allow our soldiers to share any of the fruits of victory,

3

have taken from me every spark of patriotism, every vestige of loyalty which I once possessed and have left me a man without a country, a mere soldier of fortune serving a flag I may be destined to hate; and in place of this patriotism there has come again my old dream of a great Negro republic built up out of the ruins of certain southern states, where Negroes make their own laws, sit as Judge and jurors in their own courts, levy their own taxes, build their own schools, and raise and officer their own armies. . . . Our aims might not be fulfilled in our day, but would it not be better to leave to our posterity the legacy of names made great by their association with freedom's battles than to leave to them a fortune gained by cringing and truckling to white men? Why should our men continue to apologize for the Government's failure to protect us? I have done that too long and am now forced to say that a government that cannot or will not protect its most loyal citizens is no government for me.[2]

From the American Revolution to World War II, blacks fought to create and preserve this nation in the belief that their proven patriotism would force white Americans to recognize their equality and humanity. Ned Cobb, an Alabama sharecropper, could only shake his head at such naïveté.

I've had white people tell me, "This is white man's country, white man's country." They don't sing that to the colored man when it comes to war. Then it's all *our* country, go fight for the country. Go over there and risk his life for the country and come back, he ain't a bit more thought of than he was before he left.[3]

Three wars waged by the United States to make the world safe for democracy—the Spanish-American War, World War I, and World War II—ended with struggles waged by black Americans to make the United States safe for themselves.

Narrow Boundaries, Limited Options

Racial privilege remains a pervasive reality in the United States, deeply rooted in this nation's history, traditions, and institutions. For two centuries, African-Americans, by their sheer presence, have held a mirror to this nation; they have been the severest test of American ideals, of the quality and depth of America's loyalty to its professed and often proclaimed values. That unique position has afforded black Americans a very different perspective on this country and its most cherished beliefs and institutions.

The destruction of the Confederacy brought to some four million black men and women the promise of freedom; emancipation and Reconstruction revolutionized black expectations, introduced into black lives the excitement of anticipation, the prospect of far-reaching change. There was bold talk of new ways of living and working, and a newly freed people found reasons to be optimistic, to think they could aspire to the same goals, possessions, and prospects as white Americans. But that optimism proved short-lived, and expectations were quickly disappointed if not betrayed. The dreams and aspirations inspired by freedom and the brief experiment in biracial democracy would be twisted and tortured toward increasing hopelessness and despair.

Generations of black youths came to appreciate the terrible unfairness of the world into which they were born: the narrow boundaries, the limited options, the need to curb ambitions, to weigh carefully every word, gesture, and movement when in the presence of whites. A black woman born into an impoverished family in Durham, North Carolina, remembered a childhood in which she was admonished to contain her feelings. "My problem started when I began to comment on what I saw. I insisted on being accurate. But the world I was born into didn't want that. Indeed, its very survival depended on not knowing, not seeing—and, certainly, not saying anything at all about what it was really like."[4]

Whatever aspirations black youths entertained, they would have to face a moment of truth and be forced to undergo the rites of racial passage; they would come to understand, early in their lives, that color marked them as inferior in the eyes of whites, no matter how they conducted themselves. By the turn of the century, no one pretended to take seriously the Supreme Court order commanding separate but equal facilities for blacks and whites, and by the time Pauli Murray reached public school in North Carolina around World War I, the separate and inferior facilities she encountered prepared her for the adult world she would soon enter.

Our seedy run-down school told us that if we had any place at all in the scheme of things it was a separate place, marked off, proscribed and unwanted by the white people. We were bottled up and labeled and set aside—sent to the Jim Crow car, the back of the bus, the side door of the theater, the side window of a restaurant. We came to know that whatever we had was always inferior. We came to understand that no matter how neat and clean, how law abiding, submissive and polite, how studious in school, how churchgoing and moral, how scrupulous in paying our bills and taxes we were, it made no essential difference in our place.[5]

Generations of black youths shared a common training and education based upon their early racial experiences, their initial racial awakening. The first time she was addressed as "nigger" a Mississippi girl listened without satisfaction to her parents' explanation:

I could not understand my overwhelming sense of shame, as if I had been guilty of some unknown crime. I did not know why I was suffering, what brought this vague unease, this clutching for understanding. . . . [T]here is a difference in knowing you are black and in understanding what it means to be black in America. Before I was ten I knew what it was to step off the sidewalk to let a white man pass.[6]

James Weldon Johnson remembered, the first time he was ordered out of the railroad coach reserved for whites, the smug look on the faces of the white passengers. "If their satisfaction rose from any idea that I was having a sense of my inferiority impressed upon me, they were sadly in error; indeed, my sensation was the direct opposite; I felt that I was being humiliated."

For some blacks, the initial shocks of racial recognition came in the terror visited upon black homes during and after Reconstruction, in the inferior schooling available to them, or, more commonly, in the schooling unavailable to them and in the need to labor in the fields—even as children—alongside their families. After a "two-day education," Richard Manuel Amerson, born on a farm near Livingston, Alabama in 1885, went to work. "And I says I is educated, yassum, to hard work . . . I write wid a hoe and reads wid a plow."[7]

The White South at the Turn of the Century

No matter what whites did, they never achieved the racial security they so desperately sought. What Ralph Ellison said of the black presence in the South half a century later was no less true of the late nineteenth century: "Southern whites cannot walk, talk, sing, conceive of laws or justice, think of sex, love, the family or freedom without responding to the presence of Negroes."[8] Not only did whites remain obsessed with the subject of Negroes, they focused their concern on certain Negroes in particular, the children and grandchildren of the former slaves, the first post-emancipation generations, to whom (said W. E. B. Du Bois) "War, Hell, and Slavery were but childhood tales, whose young appetites had been whetted to an edge by school and story and half-awakened thought," those who with alarming regularity in the late nineteenth and early twentieth century were letting the old customs slip by. "The new negro," a prominent Georgia editor told a Northern audience in 1904, "is killing the relation established by the old negro."[9]

Even as many whites embraced the New South, they chose to romanticize the old Negro, the rapidly disappearing Negro. Between 1890 and World War I, white southerners went to extraordinary lengths to mythologize the past, to fantasize an Old South, a Civil War, and a Reconstruction that conformed to the images they preferred, images that comforted and reassured them. "We know and remember, as our children cannot, the brighter side of Negro character," an Alabamian observed.[10] Stories told by former slaves, in dialect, usually collected, edited, and published by a former mistress or master, the newspaper tributes to "the old slavery-time Negroes," the much publicized reunions of former slaves with former masters and mistresses, and the statues and monuments erected to honor those who had stood by beleaguered white families in the Civil War—these but suggest the dimensions of an almost ritualistic white nostalgia at the turn of the century. The fantasies of whites knew few if any restraints. For the World's Columbian Exposition of 1893 in Chicago, Rebecca Felton, an outspoken Georgia feminist and political activist, suggested that the Southern exhibit feature "two darkies of the old regime . . . Every body says it will be splendid. [We] don't want any educated negroes—simply the old ones who were real slaves—and contented."[11]

The idealization of the "old Negro" underscored and exaggerated generational differences. To listen to whites, the New Negro, born in freedom, was devoid of the habits of diligence, order, morality, and faithfulness taught by slavery; young blacks possessed neither the temperament, demeanor, nor humility of their elders, and they were said to be more restless, less deferential, and still worse, less fearful of whites. If most of them conformed to the prevailing racial etiquette, they did not do so with the same conviction; they did not play their roles with the same cheerfulness. "They don't sing as they used to," an Atlanta white woman told a Northern visitor. "You should have known the old darkies of the plantation. Every year, it seems to me, they have been losing more and more of their care-free good humor. I sometimes feel that I don't know them any more. Since the riot [1906] they have grown so glum and serious that I'm free to say I'm scared of them!"[12]

The contrast between "old time darkies" and the New Negro suggested to many a graver threat to white supremacy than Reconstruction itself—the need to impress upon a new generation of blacks who had never known the discipline of slavery, who had not learned to curb their ambitions, that there were substantial restraints on their freedom and clear limits to their aspirations. By the 1890s, with the first generation of post-emancipation blacks reaching maturity, custom and etiquette no longer provided whites with adequate protection, they were no longer deemed reliable mainstays of racial supremacy. All too often, or so it seemed, especially in the towns and cities to which they were flocking, young blacks ignored the etiquette and violated the customs. "The alienation is going on, widening, deepening and intensifying," a native white conceded. "The white man is losing his sympathy and the negro his feeling of dependence."[13] The situation demanded vigilance. If black people had become a source of social danger and contamination, the need to control, contain, and quarantine them could hardly be questioned. "[W]e whites," a Memphis merchant explained to an English visitor in 1909, "have learnt to protect ourselves against the negro, just as we do against the yellow fever and the malaria—the work of noxious insects."[14]

The disease demanded extraordinary measures, and whites went about applying them systematically. Between 1890 and 1915, the racial creed of the white South manifested itself in the systematic disfranchisement of black men, in rigid patterns of racial segregation, in unprecedented violence and brutality, and in the dissemination of dehumanizing racial caricatures. Disfranchisement came to the South because the issue of political participation remained linked in the white mind with social equality. If blacks gave up their political aspirations, they would abandon any hopes of achieving social equality. That was the premise on which the white South acted: disfranchisement was a way to maintain the integrity of the white race, while reducing the self-esteem and political aspirations of blacks. If the freed slaves had been less than manageable in their exercise of the vote, even worse might be expected of a new generation of assertive blacks. "Any way they could deprive a Negro was a celebration to em," an Alabama black recalled. "White man revealed in that he was afraid the nigger was gettin to be too smart to just follow his way of votin like sheep."[15]

The efforts to quarantine black Southerners extended beyond the polling places. Custom and etiquette had previously defined the social relations between the races. Between 1890 and 1915, however, the white South moved to write those customs into the statute books, to extend segregation to almost every conceivable situation in which the two races might come into contact. Jim Crow came to the South in an expanded and more rigid form, in response to perceptions of a new generation of blacks unschooled in racial etiquette, in response to growing doubts that this generation could be trusted to stay in its assigned place without legal compulsions, and in response to economic and social changes that introduced new sources of inter-racial contact and potential conflict.

Black Reality in the White South

Thirty years after the Civil War, Booker T. Washington, articulating the Gospel of Success to an overwhelmingly propertyless black laboring class, emerged as the pre-eminent black spokesman. He grounded his advice to blacks on the proposition: "It is not within the province of human nature, that the man who is intelligent and virtuous, and owns and cultivates the best farm in his county, shall very long be denied the proper respect and consideration," and he insisted as well, "The Negro merchant who owns the largest store in town will not be lynched." W. E. B. Du Bois, whatever his differences with Washington, articulated much the same position: "The day the Negro race courts and marries the savings-bank will be the day of its salvation."[16] Teachers and primers alike—not only the McGuffey Reader but black variants—assured a generation of black youths that success came ultimately to the hard-working, the sober, the honest, the frugal, and the educated, to those who led moral, virtuous, Christian lives.[17]

But Washington and Du Bois were wrong, tragically mistaken, as were the success manuals and school primers. The experience of black men and women contradicted a fundamental assumption and promise of the

American dream: that material success was the direct result of hard work. For the first post-emancipation generation, as for their parents, faithful adherence to the work ethic brought most of them nothing. No matter how hard they labored, no matter how fervently they prayed, the chances for making it were less than encouraging. A native Mississippian described the people with whom he grew up as "hard-working, God-fearing, church-going folk who prayed trustingly to an Almighty God. Six days a week most of them toiled like beasts of burden—but to little avail. Their lives did not change materially; they simply got older, grew weary, took sick and died."[18]

The obstacles black people faced were exceptional and formidable, shaped profoundly by the ways in which white men and women perceived and acted upon racial differences. Even as whites scorned black incompetence, they feared evidence of black competence. Even as whites derided blacks for their ignorance and lack of foresight, they resented educated, literate, and ambitious blacks. "We, the Southern people, entertain no prejudice toward the ignorant per se inoffensive Negro," a Huntsville, Alabama editor explained. "It is because we know him and for him we entertain a compassion. But our blood boils when the educated Negro asserts himself . . . ."[19] Among some whites, it had long been an article of faith that an educated black man was a useless black man, subversive of good race relations. The trouble with "these young niggers," a white Alabama preacher remarked, is that once they "get a little learnin . . . thar ain't no gittin' along with 'em."[20] Education—like the ownership of land—spoiled the Negro as a laborer, developed in him wants that could never be satisfied, expectations that could never be realized. When the "new negro" reaches for "higher and better things than the old attained," a white woman warned, he gives up those very qualities that made "the dear old darkey" such a superior menial.[21] Inevitably, an educated Negro was bound to become a discontented Negro, a resentful Negro, and hence a "dangerous nigger." "Education brings light," an Atlanta newspaper editor observed, "and light perception, and with quickened faculties the negro sees the difference between his real and his constitutional status in the republic. He sees that neither worth nor merit nor attainment can overcome the world-wide repulsion of type and color; and, seeing this, he is moved to rebellious protest and sometimes to violent revenge." Frustrated in his ambitions, denied a social elevation commensurate with his education, the New Negro, warned a white psychologist, is apt to visit his resentment on the most prized possession of white men—their women. "The crime of [sexual] assault is the crime of the 'New Negro'—not of the slave nor of the ex-slave."[22]

Even as Washington articulated his self-improvement creed, the violence inflicted upon his people was often selective, aimed at those who had succeeded, those in positions of leadership, those who owned the best farm in the county and the largest store in town, those perceived as having stepped out of their place. Washington had only to read his own mail to gain a sense of what was happening. Back in 1890, Isaiah Montgomery, the only black delegate to the Mississippi Constitutional Convention, proclaimed his faith in economic and educational progress as the key to race progress. He approved a reduction in black voting, based on literacy and a poll tax, convinced such qualifications would encourage blacks to improve themselves. By obtaining property and knowledge blacks would win back the vote and gain acceptance by whites. Some fourteen years later, an obviously shaken Montgomery wrote to Washington. He cited several recent incidents in his home county to illustrate "the depths to which Mississippi has descended."

> Rev Buchanan has the best appointed printing establishment of any colored man in the State, and conducts a Baptist newspaper . . . , and was no doubt prospering, his daughter was his cashier and Bookkeeper, they kept a Horse and Buggy, which the young woman used frequently in going to and from work; they kept a decent house and a Piano; a mass meeting of whites decided that the mode of living practiced by the Buchanan family had a bad effect on the cooks and washerwomen, who aspired to do likewise, and became less disposed to work for the whites. [A mob subsequently forced Buchanan and his family from the town, not even permitting them to remove their possessions.]

> Thomas Harvey runs a neat little Grocery, he kept a Buggy and frequently rode to his place of business, he was warned to sell his Buggy and walk. Mr. Chandler keeps a Grocery, he was ordered to leave, but was finally allowed to remain on good behavior. Mr. Meacham ran a business and had a Pool Table in connection therewith, he was ordered to close up and don overalls for manual labor. Mr. Cook conducted a Hack business between the Depots and about town, using two Vehicles, he was notified that he would be allowed to run only one and was ordered to sell the other. . . .[23]

The same fears of black success and assertiveness that provoked much of the violence of Reconstruction proved no less pervasive in the early twentieth century when blacks no longer posed a political threat. A black newspaper voiced despair over the "daily examples" of white men singling out for harassment "the black man who has something, who knows something and who stands for something. . . . Appeals to leading whites are of no avail, for they are aiding and abetting the whole thing."[24] The belief grew among many blacks, documented in their day-to-day lives, that education could bring them only frustration and disappointment and that it was futile to work hard and obtain wealth and property because the "man" will somehow find a way to deprive them of their gains, whether by fraud, intimidation, or violence. The examples abounded.

Black Success and Its Effects

The Class of 1886 at Tuskegee Institute felt sufficiently optimistic about their prospects to adopt as their motto, "There Is Room at the Top." But in the town of Tuskegee, the danger of success was readily acknowledged by a black resident: "I know men who won't keep a horse. If they get one they will sell it. If you ask such a one why he sold his horse he very likely will say 'A white man see me in dat 'ere horse, he look hard at me. I make [up] my min' a mule good 'nugh for a ole nigger like me.'" A black farmer in Alpharetta, Georgia knew that he "better not accumulate much," because, he explained, "no matter how hard and honest you work for it, they . . . well you can't enjoy it."[25] Fannie Lou Hamer, born in 1917 to a Mississippi sharecropper family, recalled how her father kept cropping until he saved enough to purchase some wagons, plow tools, and mules. But a white man came to his lot and poisoned the mules. "It killed everything we had. . . . That poisoning knocked us right back down flat. We never did get back up again. That white man did it just because we were getting somewhere. White people never like to see Negroes get a little success."[26]

Throughout the South, white farmers terrorized black farmers off land they rented or had purchased with money they had saved as tenants; the more fortunate blacks lost only their lands and crops. Whitecapping (vigilante raids) might be used to terrorize the entire black population of a county but more often than not it was directed against successful black farmers who worked land coveted by whites. The testimony, much of it collected by Congress and by the Department of Justice, is strikingly similar: "They wanted to run me off . . . on account of my crop," a Mississippi farmer testified. "They took everything I had, and all my wife had, and broke us teetotally up."[27] Incidents of white violence, in fact, had a way of increasing in the summer months, after blacks had planted their crops. "Now is the season," explained a Georgia editor, "when the tenant with the best crop gets run off the place."[28]

Few understood better than Ned Cobb, the Alabama sharecropper born in 1885, how evidence of black success often aggravated white fears and anxieties. Through persistence and hard work, and by drawing on his inner strength and refusing to submit to the whims of white men, Cobb managed to accumulate some property. But to keep the property was a continual struggle, demanding more resourcefulness and energy than he had expended to acquire it: "I had men to turn me down, wouldn't let me have the land I needed to work, wouldn't sell me guano, didn't want to see me with anything. Soon as I got to where I could have somethin for sure and was makin somethin of myself, then they commenced a runnin at me."

Nor did local whites appreciate the sight of Ned Cobb driving about town in a buggy. It infuriated them. That was because, Cobb explained, white people "hated to see niggers livin like people." It remained an article of faith in the white South that a poverty stricken black laborer was a more manageable laborer, a more manageable black man. For blacks to accumulate property or money was to make them independent, and whites feared the consequences.

Afraid a nigger might do somethin if he got the money in his own hands, do as he please; might hold on to it if he wanted to hold it, might spend it accordin to his pleasure. The white people was afraid—I'll say this: they was afraid the money would make the nigger act too much like his own man. Nigger has a mind to do what's best for hisself, same as a white man. If he had some money, he just might do it.

For some blacks, the way to survive was not to accumulate enough to arouse white resentment and invite retaliation. The unsuccessful black man posed no threat; he knew his place. Cobb described his own father as such a man.

He had money but—whenever the colored man prospered too fast in this country under the old rulins, they worked every figure to cut you down, cut

your britches off you. So, it might have been to his way of thinkin that it
weren't no use in climbin too fast; weren't no use in climbin slow, neither,
if they was goin to take everything you worked for when you got too high.

Ned Cobb's brother seemed to have adopted that lesson as a way of life.
"He made up his mind that he weren't goin to have anything and after
that, why, nothin could hurt him."[29]

Physical, Moral, Legal Violence

Neither accommodation nor economic success guaranteed blacks their
civil rights, not even physical survival. The quality of the racial violence
that gripped the South between the 1880s and World War I made it distinctive in this nation's history. How many black Southerners were
lynched, beaten, mutilated, or quietly murdered in order to enforce deference and submission to whites will never be known. (Conservatively, in
the first two decades of the twentieth century, some two to three lynchings occurred every week, and in many instances extra-legal lynchings
were averted only by legal lynchings—rapid trials and executions.) Even
an accurate body count would fail to reveal how hate and fear transformed ordinary white Americans into mindless murderers and sadistic
torturers, the savagery that, with increasing regularity, characterized assaults on black men and women. The offenses which precipitated the
violence related less to sex-related crimes (as reported or misreported in
the press) than to questions of racial etiquette and economic competition—and in some regions, an observer concluded, "There was just an
assumption . . . that you had to have a lynching every now and then to
preserve equitable race relations."[30] The victims tended to be the sons
and daughters of the former slaves, those said by whites to have been
born into the false teachings of Reconstruction. If the violence impressed
upon blacks their vulnerability, it also exposed the moral character of the
white community. "The lynch mob came," a Mississippi woman recalled. "I ain't ever heard of no one white man going to get a Negro.
They're the most cowardly people I ever heard of."[31]

To count the lynchings and burnings, to detail the savagery, the me-
thodical torture prolonged for the benefit of the spectators is to under-
score the cheapness of black life, the degree to which many whites by the

early twentieth century had come to think of black men and women as less than human. "Back in those days," remembered a black Mississippian, "to kill a Negro wasn't nothing. It was like killing a chicken or killing a snake. The whites would say, 'Niggers jest supposed to die, ain't no damn good anyway—so jest go on an' kill 'em.'"[32] What was new, what was different this time around was the voyeurism and sadism that characterized these ritualistic murders. The usual modes of violence no longer satisfied the emotional needs of the crowd. Newspapers supplied the lurid details, photographers captured the carnival-like atmosphere, the expectant mood of the crowd, the men and women hoisting their children on their shoulders. To dismiss the atrocities as the work of crazed fiends or to attribute the brutality to the lower orders of white society is to miss how terrifyingly normal these people were, the class and racial solidarity they displayed, the frequency with which lynchings took place in the most churchified communities, and the self-righteousness which animated the lynchers—the conviction that they had participated in a necessary act, a rite of racial self-preservation. No wonder grand juries refused to indict, newspapers refused to name names, and townspeople closed ranks—all becoming partners in the crime. After a brutal lynching in Little Rock, the local newspaper observed, "This may be 'Southern brutality' as far as the Boston Negro can see, but in polite circles we call it Southern chivalry, a Southern virtue that will never die."[33]

No matter how many whites publicly deplored lynching and terrorism, the dominant racial views which fed the violence remained unchanged. The press, the schools, the church stood mostly silent in the face of the ugliest atrocities; they preached a morality that ignored the most immoral and uncivilized conduct in their very midst. The newly emerging social sciences validated theories of black degeneracy and inferiority, providing scholarly footnotes to traditional racist assumptions and helping to justify on "scientific" grounds a complex of racial laws, practices, and beliefs. The *Encyclopaedia Britannica*, in its American edition of 1895, drew on the most recent scientific scholarship to assert that "the inherent mental inferiority of blacks" was "an inferiority which is even more marked than their physical differences."[34] Historians miseducated several generations of Americans. School textbooks glorified Anglo-Saxon achievements, taught the superiority of the white race, superior to all others in intellectual and moral development and in physical beauty;

the same texts disparaged blacks as primitive and inferior, the most degraded, the least civilized of the races.[35] Even so, blacks were expected to pay obeisance to the same patriotic and moral values as whites, to share in the same love of God and country. It was difficult if not impossible for some to assimilate such obvious contradictions.

> In school we too sang the National Anthem, we too saluted and pledged allegiance to the flag. But in my heart and mind I knew the pledge was a lie—there was no "liberty and justice for all." Even then I suspected the American Democracy so gallantly depicted in my history books was a pageant of myths, tall-stories told by men contaminated with white supremacy.[36]

Popular fiction (such writers as Thomas Nelson Page and Joel Chandler Harris), the dialect stories, the cartoons, the anecdotes, the caricatures that appeared regularly in newspapers and magazines reinforced the familiar image of the shiftless, improvident, irresponsible, immoral, and occasionally dangerous and threatening Negro. The minstrel show and vaudeville depicted a race of buffoons and half-wits, addicted to simple pleasures and given to the use of words they neither understood nor could properly pronounce. And the cinema, particularly "Birth of a Nation" in 1915, did more than any historian to explain the "Negro problem" to the American people, did more than any novel or tract to impress upon Americans the dangers posed by a race freed from the restraints of slavery and rapidly retrogressing toward bestiality. It proclaimed the belief that the American Nation had been born (or reborn) only after the superior white race regained total, undisputed control, effectively nullifying the Fourteenth and Fifteenth Amendments.

With equal forcefulness, dehumanizing images of black men and women were imprinted on the white mind in the commerical products sold to white America, in those crude caricatures and objects which exaggerated and distorted the physical appearance of black people and mocked their lives and aspirations. The "picturesque Negro," slow, stupid, and easily frightened, replete with banjo eyes, saucer lips, and an obsequious or leering grin was packaged and marketed as a suitable household or yard adornment: the hitching post, a lawn ornament in the form of a grinning black stable boy; the doll, milk pitcher, or ceramic cookie jar fashioned after the image of a smiling, heavy set, aproned and turbaned black mammy; the bottle opener in the shape of a gaping minstrel; the white haired, toothless Uncle Remus smiling on the label of a can of syrup bearing his name and his testimonial; the salt and pepper shakers in the shape of black children; the ashtrays in the shape of Ubangi lips; the pencil sharpener shaped like an alligator's mouth, the figure of a black child on the end of the accompanying pencil; a children's bank, called "The Jolly Nigger," in the shape of a grinning black man, whose eyes rolled when a coin was placed in his mouth. Golly-wogs and pick-a-ninnies, Mammies, Aunt Jemimas, and Uncle Bens, crap shooting, minstrel tapping, watermelon eating, hallelujah-shouting black caricatures—these were the white dreams and images of which black nightmares were made. But in their efforts to dehumanize black men and women, whites succeeded in the end in dehumanizing only themselves.

Race relations in the South, a visitor declared in 1909, had become a "state of war."[37] It was a war black men and women were losing. The odds were formidable. The political system denied them a voice; the judicial system evinced no respect for law, order, or justice but functioned largely to advance and reinforce their economic and social repression. The history of race relations is a history of *legal* violence, violence sanctioned by the law; it is the dreary story, fully documented but not yet fully told, of the perversion of justice and the deep complicity of law enforcement agencies, the courts, and the legal profession in that perversion. For many blacks, understandably, the distinction between the law and lawlessness became so blurred as to be indistinct.

Who can say, in the end, what kind of violence took the largest toll in black minds and bodies—the violence inflicted by lynch mobs or the violence meted out by the landlord, the merchant, the banker, the judge, the sheriff, the newspaper editor, the school superintendent, the politician, the scholar, the entertainer. Born in Natchez in 1908, Richard Wright spent his childhood in Mississippi, Tennessee, and Arkansas. He came to be deeply impressed with the mechanisms and pervasivenss of white repression and control, with the extraordinary ways those mechanisms shaped his day-to-day behavior. He remembered most vividly the fear of making the wrong move, the "sustained expectation of violence" that forced him to curb his impulses, speech, manner, and expression. "Tension would set in at the mere mention of whites and a vast complex of emotions, involving the whole of my personality, would be aroused. It was as though I was continuously reacting to the threat of some natural force whose hostile behavior could not be predicted."[38]

Black Folklore and Songs

For scores of black men and women, remaining inoffensive in the eyes of whites became a way of life and survival. But even as they made their peace with the dominant society, even as they learned to accommodate, to mask their feelings in the presence of whites, they found ways to impart meaning to their lives. Excluded from the white world, blacks would seek refuge in their own institutions, in their own schools, churches, and businesses, in their own increasingly separate society—a nation within a nation; they would expend their energies on shaping a separate community and culture that would impart some measure of dignity and self-respect, that would provide the inner resources necessary for survival.

Numbers of young blacks, however, opted to live by their wits on the fringes of society, mostly in the cities and towns, where they would seek alternative ways to survive, often outside the law, carrying on what one observer described as "unceasing psychological scrimmage with the whites."[39] From the late nineteenth century, in fact, black folklore and song accorded an increasingly prominent place to black desperados, outlaws, and killers, loners who had fallen away altogether from society, who were arrogant and defiant, who flouted the legal and moral code.

> I'm so bad, I don't ever want to be good, uh, huh;
> I'm going to de devil and I wouldn't go to heaven, uh, huh,
> No I wouldn't go to heaven if I could.

As he was about to be hanged, in 1894, black outlaw John Hardy was asked if he wanted to pray. He replied, "Just give me time to kill another man, Lord, Lord/Just give me time to kill another man." No less defiant, folk hero Stagolee went to his death anticipating new triumphs: "Stagolee took de pitchfork an' he laid it on de shelf/'Stand back, Tom Devil, I'm gonna rule Hell by myself.'" John Hardy, Stagolee, Railroad Bill, Aaron Harris, Po' Lazarus, Billy Bob Russell, Bad Lee Brown, all of them loners, heroes, legends in their time, men whose reputations and popularity in the black community often exceeded those of white-recognized black leaders.[40]

In life as in song and lore, they forfeited their lives for their arrogance and rebellion. As a child in Mississippi, Richard Wright watched with awe black men who cursed and violated the laws, sneered at the customs and taboos, mimicked the antics of white folks, and prided themselves on outwitting them. But eventually, Wright observed, they paid a terrible price for their freedom. "They were shot, hanged, maimed, lynched, and generally hounded until they were either dead or their spirits broken." Charles W. Chesnutt, twenty-two years old in 1880, a teacher in Fayeteville, North Carolina, confided to his journal that his generation was faring badly. "[O]f all the young men who grew up along with me, there were a hundred of them I suppose, three-fourths of them have died, have been killed by liquor, or by something . . . Some from consumption . . . ; some have been killed in drunken brawls."[41]

Nowhere perhaps in these decades did black Southerners pour out their concerns, frustrations, and bitterness with such feeling as in the music they created. It was in these years, in the 1890s and 1900s, in the Mississippi Delta, for example, that the blues began to be heard—on street corners, in the train stations, in the cafes, jook joints and brothels, at house parties and picnics, in the boarding houses, work camps, and crossroads stores. It was played and sung by men and women who disengaged themselves from the norms and values of conventional society, mostly poor, illiterate, propertyless, but they felt freer than most, they prided themselves on being masterless, on being independent of a system that tied others to the land through violence, coercion, and the law. Charley Patton's niece said of her bluesman uncle, "He just left when he got ready, because he didn't make no crops. . . . He was a *free man*."[42]

The first blues performances astonished the audiences. It was unlike anything they had experienced before—"the weirdest music I had ever heard," remembered W. C. Handy. It was intensley personal music, more often than not about travel and drink, love and loss, droughts and floods, whoring preachers, sadistic sheriffs, and insensitive judges, personal catastrophes and betrayed expectations, the best of times and the worst of times. It exuded little confidence in the ability of people to effect changes in how they lived or in their future prospects, as in Willie Brown's lament:

Can't tell my future, I can't tell my past.
Lord, it seems like every minute sure gon' be my last.
Oh, a minute seems like hours, and hours seems like days.
And a minute seems like hours, hour seems like days.[43]

The blues had its roots in the field hollers, shouts, chants, and work songs of black field hands and roustabouts. But it was profoundly different—deeper, more personalized, more immediate, more intense, more gripping, more painful: "Blues grabbed mama's child, and it tore me all upside down./The blues is a low down aching old heart disease/And like consumption, killing me by degrees."[44] It was more violent, more subversive, more threatening, as in the chilling fantasy described by Furry Lewis, born in 1900, and raised in the Delta at Greenwood:

> I believe I'll buy me a graveyard of my own,
> I believe I'll buy me a graveyard of my own,
> I'm goin' kill everybody that have done me wrong.[45]

It had a language of its own, and it captured the consciousness of a new generation. The blues answered the need of that generation to work a lot of frustration, bitterness and disappointment out of their systems; it was a way to deal with personal betrayals. "Blues," writes Greil Marcus, "grew out of the need to live in the brutal world that stood ready in ambush the moment one walked out of the church. Unlike gospel, blues was not a music of transcendence; its equivalent to God's Grace was sex and love. Blues made the terrors of the world easier to endure, but blues also made those terrors more real."[46] One can hear it in the bluesy dirge sounded by Charley Patton, born near Edwards, Mississippi in the early 1880s:

> Ev'ry day, seems like murder here
> Ev'ry day, seems like murder here
> I'm gonna leave tomorrow, I know you don't want me here.[47]

in the desperation voiced by blueswoman Bertha "Chippie" Hill:

> I'm gonna lay my head on a lonesome railroad line
> And let the 219 pacify my mind.[48]

in the defiance articulated by an anonymous Memphis bluesman:

> I feel my hell a-risin', a-risin' every day;
> I feel my hell a-risin', a-risin' every day;
> Someday it'll burst this levee and wash the whole wide world away;[49]

and in the plaintive, tormented cry of Robert Johnson, born in 1911, who spent his youth in the upper Mississippi Delta and left this epitaph:

You may bury my body, down by the highway side
Baby, I don't care where you bury my body when I'm dead and gone
You may bury my body, ooooo, down by the highway side
So my old evil spirit can get a Greyhound bus, and ride.[50]

Eloquent black spokesmen in their own right, yet none of them—Robert Johnson, Charley Patton, Son House, Willie Brown, Tommy Johnson, Skip Janes—are to be found in the dictionaries of American or African-American biography, the histories of Southern literature, or the encyclopedias of Southern history. But to listen to them is to feel more vividly, more intensely than any mere poet, novelist, or historian could convey them—the terrors, the tensions, the quiet despair that pervaded the lives of blacks coming to adulthood in the early twentieth century in the rural South—and later in the urban North.

Well, I drink to keep from worrying and I laugh to keep from crying,
Well, I drink to keep from worrying and I laugh to keep from crying,
I keep a smile on my face so the public won't know my mind.

Some people thinks I am happy but they sho' don't know my mind,
Some people thinks I am happy but they sho' don't know my mind,
They see this smile on my face, but my heart is bleeding all the time.[51]

Accommodation Without Submission

"Few men," wrote W. E. B. Du Bois, "ever worshipped Freedom with half such unquestioning faith as did the American Negro for two centuries."[52] In one decade, however, black Southerners moved from a hopeful freedom to a circumscribed and inferior citizenship, from heightened expectations to betrayal and disillusionment. Reconstruction had promised to bring black people fully within the meaning and protection of the Constitution, to end the violence, robbery, humiliation, and exploitation associated with enslavement. But for the nearly 8 million blacks who lived and worked in the South in 1900 (90 percent of the nation's black population), that promise had been forcibly betrayed. The decision handed down by the Supreme Court in 1896 in *Plessy* v. *Ferguson* did not proclaim a new racial order; it reinforced what state and federal courts had consistently upheld and it confirmed what most black people already knew from personal experience: that the quality of life and freedom they could enjoy depended upon local option—the will of the majority of whites in a state or locality. The decision reflected popular thought, scholarly opinion, bipartisan politics, North and South. Once a symbol of sectional strife, the Negro by 1900 had become a symbol of national reconciliation on the basis of white supremacy. When President Theodore Roosevelt wrote in 1906 "that as a race and in the mass they [Negroes] are altogether inferior to the whites," he articulated a belief embraced by most Americans.[53]

Black leaders, editors, and preachers thrashed about with their programs, manifestos, and sermons. But the mass of black men and women sensed they had been done in. Few blacks could maintain a faith in progress, trapped as they were in a web of controls and an exploitative system that encouraged neither initiative nor hope. Perhaps the real story lies not in their repression, but in how they survived, how they established communities, and how so many families managed to maintain stable homes. Ralph Ellison once suggested that any people who could endure so much brutalization and keep together and endure "is obviously more than the sum of its brutalization. Seen in this perspective, theirs has been one of the great human experiences and one of the great triumphs of the human spirit in modern times."[54]

If most blacks were forced to accommodate, they did not necessarily submit. There was a difference. Like many children of former slaves, Ned Cobb learned to obey whites and to avoid trouble. That was the legacy he inherited. But in the 1930s he joined the Alabama Sharecroppers Union.

> I thought this: a organization is a organization and if I don't mean nothin by joinin I ought to keep my ass out of it. But if I'm sworn to stand up for all the poor colored farmers—and poor white farmers, if they'd takin a notion to join—I've got to do it. Weren't no use under God's sun to treat colored people like we'd been treated here in the state of Alabama.[55]

Charles Wingfield grew up in Lee County, Georgia, a few miles from Albany. Like Ned Cobb, he came to learn that his people lived and acted by different rules from those of whites, that self-preservation dictated a measured response to the world around him.

I wondered what it was like to live. . . . Countless nights I cried myself to sleep. . . . I must have asked God why a thousand times but I never got an answer. Was nine of us kids in the family and we all had to work. I stayed out of school a lot of days because I couldn't let my mother go to the cotton field and try to support all of us. I picked cotton and pecans for two cents a pound. I went to the fields six in the morning and worked until seven in the afternoon. When it came time to weigh up, my heart, body, and bones would be aching, burning and trembling. I stood there and looked the white men right in their eyes while they cheated me, other members of my family, and the rest of the Negroes that were working. There were times when I wanted to speak, but my fearful mother would always tell me to keep silent. The sun was awful hot and the days were long. . . . The cost of survival was high. Why I paid it I'll never know.[56]

Generations of black youths paid the same price. When Charles Wingfield pronounced that judgment about his life in 1963, he was sixteen years old, Ned Cobb was nearing eighty, the Emancipation Proclamation was one hundred years old. Ned Cobb had known when to "fall back," but he had refused to demean himself; he had refused to become one of the "white men's niggers." For that refusal, and for his efforts to organize and protect Alabama sharecroppers, he spent twelve years of his life in an Alabama prison. Charles Wingfield organized a protest at the Lee County Training School, where he was an honors student. He was immediately expelled. He enlisted in SNCC—the Student Non-Violent Coordinating Committee.

The Civil Rights Movement

The white racial attitudes that demanded and sanctioned an inferior place for black Americans survived World War II. But that war, in so many ways, marked a turning point in the black American's relationship to this society, and in the 1950s and 1960s a new climate of political necessity and a new generation of black Americans helped to restructure race relations. The civil rights movement, which Ned Cobb watched with fascination from his Alabama farm, and which Charles Wingfield joined, struck down the legal barriers of segregation and disfranchisement in the South, changed profoundly the unwritten protocols and daily practice of social custom, and challenged the economic and educational barriers that had crippled black aspirations in the North. Hundreds, thousands took to the streets, mostly young people, defying the laws, defying the apathy of their elders, disciplined by nonviolence, insisting on bringing the Constitution and the nation's professed values into closer harmony, embracing the promise of a new reconstruction, more sweeping, more enduring than the last.

Even today, more than two decades later, the scenes remain vivid in the memories of those who experienced them and who watched them as they were flashed on TV screens across the country and throughout the world: the black students barred at the entrances to schools and colleges; the beatings in the train and bus stations and in the jails; the black churches burned to the ground; the thousands of arrests; the police dogs, the fire hoses, the electric cattle prods; the bombings, the murders, the assassinations. Few could forget as well the songs, the speeches, the heightened expectations.

What they achieved was impressive, far-reaching in the ways it changed the face of the South—if not the nation. But it was revealing, too, for the paradoxes and contradictions it exposed. Perhaps the Civil Rights Movement accomplished all that street marches and demonstrations reasonably could accomplish. Perhaps it reached the limits of its ability to effect change. For all the political gains, the dismantling of Jim Crow, the mass marches, the optimistic rhetoric, many of the same tensions and anxieties persisted and festered. Even as the civil rights movement struck down legal barriers, it failed to dismantle economic barriers. Even as it ended the violence of segregation, it failed to diminish the violence of poverty. Even as it ended school segregation by law, it failed to end segregation by income and tradition. Even as it transformed the face of Southern politics, it did nothing to reallocate resources, to redistribute wealth and income. Even as it entered schools and colleges, voting booths and lunch counters, it failed to penetrate the corporate boardrooms and federal bureaucracies where the most critical decisions affecting American lives were made. Even as it increased the black middle class (the principal beneficiaries of the Civil Rights Movement), it left behind a greater number of black Americans to endure lives of quiet despair and hopelessness. "For years I labored with the idea of reforming the existing institutions of the society, a little change here, a little change there," Martin Luther King, Jr., confided to a journalist less than a year before his assassination. "Now I feel quite differently. I think you've got to have a reconstruction of the entire society, a revolution of values."[57]

The brutalizing effects of more than two centuries of slavery and another century of enforced segregation and miseducation continue to shape race relations, continue to hold up a mirror to Americans, to test the democratic experiment, the principles and values Americans embrace. Twenty years have passed since the Kerner commission warned that the United States was "moving toward two societies, one black, one white—separate and unequal." That process continues. The barriers to racial justice today fail to provoke the same moral outrage; they are more subtle, far more elusive than a "red neck" sheriff or a demagogic governor. But no matter how it is measured—by where most blacks live, their income, the schools they attend, or their future prospects—this nation remains in critical ways two societies, separate and unequal, racism remains deeply embedded in our culture, and the consequences spill over into almost every facet of American life. The victims threaten to become, if tens of thousands have not already become, a large shadow population of interior exiles, aliens in their own land, locked into a cycle of deprivation and despair, empty of belief or hope, volatile and combustible.

From the Mississippi Delta, in the early twentieth century, bluesman Robert Johnson articulated a lonely and terrifying sense of personal betrayal and anguish that transcended time and region. He suggested a society impossible to overcome—or to escape. There was no way to assimilate. There was no way to separate.

> I got to keep moving, I got to keep moving
> blues falling down like hail
> blues falling down like hail
> Uumh, blues falling down like hail
> blues falling down like hail
> and the days keeps on 'minding me
> there's a hellhound on my trail,
> hellhound on my trail,
> hellhound on my trail.[58]

2

CONFRONTING PREJUDICE AND DISCRIMINATION
Personal Recollections and Observations

Fannie Allen Neal

Origins

I have been asked to share some of my personal recollections and experiences of what it has meant to be born and to grow up as a black citizen in Alabama. My recollections span a period of at least the past sixty years. The place to start is at the very beginning, for it was early in my life that my frustrations and resentment of existing conditions began to grow. These frustrations were continually nourished through my maturing years, until I became interested in the labor movement, which first gave me a way of realizing my own dreams and desires.

My story is not uncommon. I grew up pretty much like most black Alabamians. I am the great granddaughter of Washington McCloud who was born into slavery in Pike County, Alabama. His daughter, Mary McCloud, was my maternal grandmother, and she exerted a major influence on my life. Her daughter (my mother) was conceived under a chinaberry tree in the pasture where a white man (the master's son) forced his will on her late one afternoon while she was driving the milkcows from the pasture up to the barn to be milked.

My paternal great grandfather, Willis Allen, was also a slave who was owned by a white man named Andrew Allen. My great grandfather Allen was born in southeast Georgia, near Savannah, and my great grandmother, Esther Allen, a Cherokee, was born in South Carolina.

Racism had its first major impact on my life when my father died. He was a sharecropper in Montgomery County, Alabama. I was eight years old at the time. There were ten children in our family, and six of us were under fifteen years of age at the time of my father's sudden death. After the funeral, the white man who was the overseer of the land and the house where we were living came to see my mother. He did not linger long in expressing his sorrow about my father's death but very quickly got down to the business at hand. He reminded my mother about the cotton that we had made, the corn that had been harvested and stored in the barn, the hay and the cattle that my father had raised. He recounted the fact that the peanuts and sweet potatoes had also been harvested and stored. It sounded almost as though he was going to say what a prudent manager and good farmer my father had been. Instead, he came quickly to the point: he said, to my mother, "You are very fortunate. In fact your husband made ALMOST enough to pay the debt he owed me for advancing him money to make the crop."

But that was not the end of his message. He told my mother that he was willing to let us remain on the farm, but he presented her with a contract that he wanted her to sign. He handed the paper to my mother, and when she glanced at it she saw the names of my brothers listed in the body of the contract. Her immediate reaction was, "He's trying to get me to sign my boys into slavery," and she handed the contract back to the overseer and told them that she would find some other place for us to live. She was not going to sign over her children to slavery again.

So as a child I learned very early that injustice existed. I knew that my mother had been treated unfairly. Every person old enough in our household had worked in the fields every day helping my father, and he had not been dead a week when the overseer showed up to claim almost everything we owned. I did not know then how I was going to deal with such injustices, but I knew, very early in life, that I had to find a way to make some changes.

My formal education began in the "separate but equal" schools of Montgomery County. I walked ten miles a day to and from school and I saw the white children being bused to school. Sometimes the children would throw trash at us from the windows and call us all kinds of names. When we moved to Montgomery, I enrolled in school there and completed grammar school and junior high school. This was in 1935, and in Montgomery County, when you finished the ninth grade, if you were black, you couldn't go to high school unless you could get $12.50 every three months to go to Alabama State, which at that time was a state normal school. There was no public high school for blacks anywhere in

Montgomery County. So, I enrolled at Alabama State and eventually, with the help of my brothers, I completed high school in 1940.

Before I finished high school, I married, into a relationship that was not a lasting one, continued going to school with the help of my family supporting the child I bore, and at the same time got a job working for a well-known white family in Montgomery. It was a typical domestic job; I went to work every morning at 7:00 A.M., and would leave around 2:30 P.M. to go to school. I walked approximately five miles from our house to my job; then I walked from my job some two and one-half miles to attend school; and then, on most nights, I would walk four miles home because I did not have bus fare. I did not know it then, but that walking proved in time to be good training for taking part in the most famous walk of all, the Montgomery bus protest in 1955–56.

After completing high school, I worked for a white Montgomery family for two years. It was not a matter of choice for me, for there simply were no other jobs available to black women unless one was fortunate enough to go to college and become a teacher. To illustrate how typical the jobs of domestic work and teaching were for black women, I recall several years ago going into a Montgomery department store to open a charge account. I was dressed to catch the airplane from Montgomery to Washington, and in asking me the questions necessary for approval of the charge account, the clerk looked at me and said: "Now, Fannie, where do you teach school?" I took great pleasure in telling her that I was an executive with the labor movement, the national AFL-CIO, but it came as a shock to her to learn that a black woman, dressed well, could be anything other than a school teacher! Since I was dressed up, the clerk knew that I couldn't be a domestic worker!

The white family for whom I had worked offered to pay my tuition and expenses if I would go to college. I considered it very seriously, and talked to one of my brothers about it. He said to me: "I want you to go to school, but you aren't going to take any handouts." He recommended that I get a job and save some money and send myself to school.

Work

When I started looking around Montgomery for some job other than domestic work, I decided to apply for a job at the Reliance Manufacturing Company. This New York firm had negotiated with Tuskegee Institute in the early 1930s to get a plant in Montgomery specifically to hire black women. The plant made men's shirts.

When I applied, I was told that there were no jobs, but I persisted by saying, "I need a job very badly." So the manager agreed to let me come by in the afternoon after my domestic job to learn to turn pockets. Then I learned to turn cuffs. I did this for several days, and then I was shifted around to other operations. A job came open where they needed a printer to print the labels for size tabs, and I got that job. The pay was fifteen cents an hour for the first forty hours, and then we were paid the minimum wage of twenty-five cents an hour. I caught on to the work quickly, so the foreman of the cutting department let me learn to tie the different parts of the shirt. We called it "bundling" and then we would send the bundles over to the stitching room to be assembled into the garment.

The office workers at the plant were all white people; the operators in the stitching room and in the shop were black, except for a few blacks who were called floor walkers and were in charge of machine operators. But the supervisor of the stitching room was white. The man in charge of the cutting department was white, as well as the person in charge of the shipping department. Anybody who was in charge of *anything* or *anybody* was white.

Shortly after I went to work at Reliance, the man who had the job of head "marker" left the plant. In 1942, men were being drafted into the armed services, and this had created a shortage of workers. The assistant superintendent told the superintendent that he wanted to try me out to see if I could learn how to mark. This was after several white women had tried and quit. The superintendent said that I couldn't learn that job because I was "colored." When I heard this, I knew that I had to learn the job. The assistant superintendent had faith in me and took the time to teach me the job in the evenings when I would stay and work late in order for him to show me different things about the job. For a week, I worked two hours overtime every day, and I learned that job inside out. I subsequently held that job from late 1942 until the plant closed in 1959. I mastered it. In order to keep it, I made a point of not teaching my job to anyone else. My job was critical to the operation of the factory, and it had to be performed with skill and precision. This gave me considerable leverage later on when we decided to organize a union and affiliate with the Amalgamated Clothing Workers of America.

Although my own working conditions at the plant had continually improved, there were injustices that many other workers suffered. Wages were low since the vast majority of the workers were not only women but also black.

We reported for work at seven o'clock every morning to do our jobs. If there was a slowdown in operations—and for certain workers there was no work to be done that day, the management would sometimes keep the workers waiting until twelve o'clock—only to tell them there was no work and that they could go home and come again tomorrow. This happened to some of the workers almost every day. Many of them rode to work in car pools, and usually had to wait until everyone in the pool completed work. This created great frustration and it inspired me more than anything else to want to join the union. When we finally got our union, the first contract we negotiated provided that, if a worker showed up for work and was told there was no work, the Company had to pay the worker for four hours. This was called reporting time. Very soon no one had to wait because they were told the day before not to come in to work.

And then there was the matter of wages. In my job, I earned fifty-six cents an hour; the white man who held the job before me was paid one dollar an hour. My supervisor had a way of harassing me by saying things like, "You've got a white man's job." Finally, I confronted him one day by telling him that the job belonged to the person who was doing it. I said "This is not a white man's job, it's my job!" We had serious words about it and if it had been in his power to fire me, he would have done so right on the spot.

In the late 1930s and 1940s, the CIO was organizing extensively in the South. An organizer out of Birmingham came to Montgomery to talk with some of us who worked at Reliance Manufacturing. At that time, the Union had not been able to organize Reliance plants in the South, although both the AFL and the CIO (before the merger into one organization) had made overtures to the workers of Reliance.

I was one of five people that CIO organizer Carey Haigler talked to on his first visit with us in Montgomery. Since we were black, there was no public meeting place we could use, so we met in private homes for the first few times. At that first meeting, Haigler gave us a copy of the Wagner Act, and explained to us that under this Act we had the right to organize and bargain for our wages and working conditions. He left us some cards for collecting signatures which was the procedure used for workers who wanted to join a union.

Before he got back to Birmingham, we had signatures on every one of the cards he had left with us. He said that he would see us again in about a week, and in the meantime, we were to select carefully workers in the plant to come with us to the next meeting. Haigler returned the next week as promised. We asked for more cards, and he told us to start bringing others whom we could trust to attend our meetings. At the third meeting, our group had really expanded, and we had signed up so many people we had to move out of private homes and meet at a Montgomery night club.

This activity became known to the superintendent, and he started calling us in for talks, one by one. Some were not strong enough to stand up to him and admit that they had signed the cards, but others of us were able to compensate for their fears. The superintendent offered to give me the supervisor's job in the stitching room and said that it would pay $200 a month (which in those days sounded to me almost like a million dollars would today). I knew that I knew absolutely nothing about running the stitching room, but I did not say that. I told him that I did not want that job since it would mean that I could not be a member of the union.

The superintendent reminded me that if I persisted in supporting the union, I might lose my job. I was ready for that bluff, because I knew that no one else could do my job, and for that reason they could not afford to fire me. Not teaching my job to somebody else was the best job security I ever had. Whatever else they might have said about me, they could not say that I did not do my work well. I was dependable, on time, and I performed my job in a very responsible manner. So I said to the superintendent, a white man, that he was not going to fire me for union activities. And then I pulled from my apron pocket a worn out copy of the Wagner Act and said to him: "We're not going to go by what you say and not by what I say but by what this law says!" I think that was the first time he had ever seen a copy of the Wagner Act, but we had been reading it and talking about it in our union meetings at nights and had worn the paper out.

The union election was held August 14, 1945. It was a very exciting day for us because V-J Day occurred on the same day that we voted to have the Amalgamated Clothing Workers Union represent us, the first ACWU to be organized in the South in a Reliance Manufacturing plant. The vote was overwhelming: 298 for the union, and only 28 against.

Now that we had won the union, there was so much to be learned. I was elected shop steward, which meant that I was involved in all the grievances. We had to learn how to negotiate our contract and what to ask for. We had to elect officers. We held classes and training sessions at least twice a week. We met in private homes for these meetings. In the meantime our president negotiated with the Lutherans and got permission to meet at the Lutheran school. We would sing union songs—songs about cooperation, and rolling the union on. We often sang "Solidarity Forever":

> When the union's inspiration through a worker's blood shall run
> There will be no power greater anywhere beneath the sun;
> Yet what force on earth is weaker than the feeble strength of one;
> But the union makes us strong! Solidarity forever!

Another favorite was the old spiritual "We shall not be moved:" Just like a tree that's planted by the waters, / We shall not be moved!"

We had learned to work as a team to get our union organized, and immediately the international union advised us to become a part of the state CIO Council. This was a statewide body located in Birmingham and was the umbrella of all CIO unions in the state. Shortly after we affiliated with the state body, several of us from Montgomery were elected to attend the state CIO convention.

When we arrived at the convention site, we went into the auditorium and saw a rope down one side of the room. All the white people were sitting to the left of the rope and the black people to the right. We had been told during the time we were organizing that the union would make us free men and women. I was astounded when I walked in and saw the rope dividing us as union members. It seemed that our white brothers and sisters wanted to have the benefits of the union yet it took the black workers to sign cards and vote in order for the union to win an election. That day, both white and black members took the floor over the issue of the rope and that was the last time we had a state convention with a rope dividing the audience into black and white. It took a while for us to sit together, but at least the next year the rope was gone.

As I look back, it was the labor movement that started the process of setting me free. It was the labor union that gave me an opportunity to use my skills in organizing. It was the labor union that gave me the chance to learn new skills. And it was the union that helped me to feel that I had at least achieved some measure of control over my own life. It was the labor union that sought to bring dignity for blacks to the work place. I have, for that reason, always felt a great sense of loyalty to the union. There have been times in recent years when the Civil Rights Movement and the union would disagree over politics, especially over what candidates we would support in statewide elections. I stood with the union in every instance.

Voting Rights, Civil Rights

It was through the union that many blacks in Alabama were encouraged to register to vote. At the time I registered to vote, the state of Alabama had passed the Boswell Amendment, which provided that a person, in order to register, could be required to prove his or her "understanding" of the constitution to the satisfaction of the white registrar. This was in fact a new means to keep blacks from voting.

To try to get blacks registered, we set up what we called voting clinics. We would hold these after work, at nights and on weekends. We would take people, one on one, and teach them how to fill out the application that was required by the registrar and we learned to quote portions of the constitution. We held these clinics for all blacks, not just union members. We even organized clinics outside Montgomery to get black participation in voting.

A group of seventeen of us went to the Montgomery County Court House to register on a Saturday morning in 1945. When I finished filling out my form, I went up the registrar and said: "Is there any portion or any part of the Constitution that you would like for me to quote for you?" He looked at me, and very quietly said, "No." I saw that he wrote something on my form, but the next week I got my registration card. Not a single one of the sixteen others was certified to vote that day. This infuriated them, and they went back to the courthouse—some as many as five times—until they were certified. All of them finally were successful, but only because they persisted.

Reliance Manufacturing closed its doors in 1959, which meant that my job was over. At that point my life changed, but in a way that I had never dreamed. When I worked in organizing and holding the voting clinics, I worked with an organization of black leaders in the state that had organized the Alabama Coordinating Association for the purpose of assisting blacks to register and vote. Organized labor had helped this statewide organization. State AFL-CIO leaders along with black organizations put together a fund to hire me full time for a year when Reliance closed. My job was to work to get blacks registered to vote. This gave me an opportunity to work throughout the state. In 1960 I worked in several southern states on black voter registration. Later that year I began working for COPE, the AFL-CIO's Committee on Political Education, where I remained until my retirement in 1987.

There I had an opportunity to work all over the nation in voter registration and in political campaigns. My work was directed toward getting minority and union participation in elections throughout the nation, including presidential elections. The places I traveled, the people I have known and worked with, and the satisfaction I have had in seeing more and more minorities involved in exercising the rights of citizenship have more than rewarded me for those early frustrations and hardships.

The final push for freedom, in terms of my own life story, came in December 1955 when Mrs. Rosa Parks got on the bus in Montgomery for a ride home after working all day. In those days I had no transportation, and when I couldn't get a ride, and if I could afford it, I rode the city bus to or from work. One had to hand money to the driver at the front door, and then go around to the back door to board the bus. Oftentimes, the driver would pull off and leave before a passenger could board from the back of the bus. The drivers treated us like animals. We sometimes would be literally packed in the bus, and if a white person got on, the blacks who were seated were told to stand and let the white person have the seat. There was deep resentment about this treatment among the black citizens of Montgomery. I don't believe there was ever anything that happened to black folks that was worse than the intimidation that we took from the city bus system in Montgomery.

When the bus driver told Mrs. Parks to get up and let a white man have her seat, she refused and remained in her seat when others moved toward the back. Word of Mrs. Parks's subsequent arrest spread quickly through the black community. All the next day at work we heard about her being in jail and that she was soon to have a trial. There was a small meeting that night at the Dexter Avenue Baptist Church, (where the Reverend Martin Luther King was pastor) to discuss what could be done. It was finally decided that we would try to organize a protest movement for one day, and that the black citizens would be asked to walk instead of riding the buses. This first meeting was on a Friday, and it was decided that over the weekend we had to get the word out to the black community to stay off the buses on Monday morning.

On Monday morning, blacks all over town cooperated by not riding the bus. That night after work, I went to the Holt Street Baptist Church, and when I got within two blocks of the church, all I could see were black folks. One couldn't even get to the church, much less inside it. I managed to get close enough to hear Dr. King as he spoke to the crowd. He spoke his heart out, and his voice was like magic to us as he talked about the injustices that we had suffered and told us that we, as a people, must be peaceful and nonviolent.

The eyes of the world centered on Montgomery for the next year. The Montgomery Improvement Association organized car pools and established car and van routes and rented buses where possible. Funds poured in from every corner of the nation to support the blacks in our efforts to ride on public buses with dignity. The labor unions also provided financial support. And we blacks walked and walked and walked. We went from church to church to hold the mass meetings where we would hear Dr. King give us reports, and where we would pray and sing and learn the teachings of nonviolence.

The white community simply did not know how to deal with the black community, especially in view of our commitment to nonviolence. The white folks continually were doing really stupid things like taking the seats out of the public library and closing the city parks and swimming pools. They took the faucets from the water fountains and locked the rest rooms at the airport. They didn't seem to understand that blacks had never been allowed in these places, and to be locked out of where you had never been didn't hurt the black people at all. It simply meant that the white people could no longer use these facilities in the comfort to which they were accustomed.

Everytime things began to settle down, it seems the white folks could be depended upon to do something to stir us all up again. The police, for example, would stop black folks who were driving home late at night (usually from some job waiting tables or working in a bar), and they would make them get out of their car and beat them over the head. A black woman who had come from New York to visit her mother came out of a downtown store, and a Ku Kluxer hit her over the head with a hammer.

On the other hand, there were white people who not only understood our situation and the problems we faced but recognized the damaging effects they had on soceity as a whole and worked very had to correct them. I had the good fortune to be involved with such individuals on numerous occasions, including some when I could have been killed. One of those times was at a meeting of our central labor union in Montgomery during the height of the bus protest. Tempers were short, and while Dr. King was teaching us to be nonviolent, white people had no such leadership. The white churches, the white political leaders, the white educational leaders—none could seem to rise to the occasion to lead in a time of turmoil. At this union meeting, one of my white friends overheard two well-known Ku Kluxers saying, "We'll take care of her tonight," meaning that they were going to take care of me. They called me by a name which left no uncertainty as to whom they had in mind. My friend reported this conversation to the leader of our meeting, a white man named Earl Pippin. As soon as the meeting adjourned, Pipp, as we called him, said to me: "Fannie, I want to see you a few minutes." I waited for him. He mentioned to me something about union business and then said out of the earshot of others: "Come on. I'm taking you home." With that he motioned to Barney Weeks and Dave Norris on the other side of the room, and I walked out of the building and went home among those three white men who were absolutely determined that I would not be harmed. These men continued to display their sensitivity and courage through the years they helped lead the labor movement in Alabama.

The most dramatic event of all during this time period, at least for me personally, was the day the marchers from Selma arrived in Montgomery. I joined the march at seven miles out of the city, and we took the entire family, including the small children. We wanted them to be able someday to tell their own children that they had marched for freedom. There was power in Montgomery that day. As the thousands of marchers, black and white together, arrived at the state capitol, Dr. King spoke to us once again. It was a time of celebration. Although blood had been shed for our cause, the people had triumphed by their peaceful and nonviolent behavior. The spirit of the movement could be felt in the air. We sang the familiar freedom songs as we marched toward the end of a very long journey, a journey that started for me when I was twelve years old.

Conclusion

Allow me to summarize about what meaning there may be in my life story. First, racism has been a pervasive reality in my life. It affected my very physical survival and that of my family. It was an overriding concern for my parents as they tried to raise ten children. Although they were intelligent, hard working, and responsible in every way, my parents lived in a system that kept them down or, as the white folks would say, "in their place." And because they were in that place, there was no way out for them.

Racism determined where I went to school, even if I could get an education. It determined where I would work, and I still had to fight it when I joined the union, which I thought would set me free. Racism kept blacks from voting, and from participating, in our democratic government. Public accommodations, work, recreational facilities, public libraries and museums—all of these were places forbidden to blacks. We couldn't even get a drink of water or use a public bathroom. In effect, blacks were powerless; we had no control over our lives.

Second, those with economic and political power have used racism to keep people divided. There are many white people who lived, and still live, in poverty (more whites than blacks), who were sharecroppers and lived at the very edge of survival. These, however, are the people who were frightened into believing that somehow they were better than blacks. Many of this group made up the mobs and the Ku Klux Klan and White Citizens Councils, and they are the ones who used violence against black citizens. The union gave black and white workers, and poor people, a chance to come together, but the politicians saw to it that this coalition could not grow or flourish. So racism has been used as a tool of special economic interests, and to a large extent this has kept many white families in poverty.

Third, perhaps more than at any other time in history, there was a deficit in white leadership in Alabama during the 1950s and 1960s. This deficit seemed to grow with every event until the federal courts finally established and enforced the law of the land. For a time Federal Judge Frank Johnson was in charge of the state of Alabama. Local and state law enforcement agencies were bankrupt and corrupted; government gave official sanction to breaking the law.

But it was not just our state and local government that had a failure of leadership. When Dr. King was jailed in Birmingham, he wrote his now famous "Letter from the Birmingham Jail" calling on the white ministers of that city to speak out. Not a voice was heard.

On the other hand, in the black community our leaders were teaching us how to be nonviolent, how to cooperate, how to put aside our differences. We had classes that we were encouraged to attend. In fact, I often felt that Dr. King sensed the fact that I have a tendency to strike back. When I get cornered, I have always fought back. Dr. King used to say to me, "Now, Fannie, I want you to be sure to attend the classes on nonviolence." While our ministers talked to us from the pulpit about the strength of nonviolence, in our classes we actually learned how to protect ourselves, what to do when confronted with violence. I must say that it was very helpful to us in keeping our movement going. The white people had no such leadership.

Fourth, I want to emphasize the point that there have always been white people of good will who have helped blacks in many more ways than I can detail. All my life I have known and have interacted with white people who not only have not felt a need to put blacks down but have demonstrated a genuine interest in working with blacks toward common goals. When we lived on the farm, there was a white family nearby that our family respected; we shared food from our gardens and helped each other. The whites, too, were sharecroppers. The white families for whom I was a domestic worker were kind to me, even offered to pay my way to college. At the same time, they treated me like a domestic worker, and I knew that my place was not at the dinner table.

But most of all, when black people were engaged in our struggle for freedom, countless white people from all over the world not only came and marched with us but provided money and other resources that we did not have. They helped enormously to sustain our "stride toward freedom."

Finally, when blacks became free, the whites also experienced a new found freedom. I recall stopping at a service station in Tuscaloosa shortly after the public accommodations law had been passed. I had frequently purchased gasoline there, because I knew that I could use the rest room. On this occasion, I went to the rest room and found it locked. I returned to the front, and before I could even ask, the white owner was getting the key to let me in. He said to me: "You have no idea how glad I am to have the new law. In the past, I had such a hard time keeping the rest room clean for my customers, but now I can lock it and keep it clean for them. The only thing I could do before was just to leave it open all day and night, because I didn't want to ever have to say to a customer that he or she couldn't use my facilities."

But it goes much beyond the freedom to use public facilities. Whites and blacks, particularly in the South, now communicate with each other on a new level. This has to be good for the future of all of us. And in the twenty-five years since The University of Alabama has opened its doors and now has the benefit of having some of our bright black young people, who knows? It just may be that this University, and many others like it, will make up for the deficit in leadership, that from their halls someday we may have a bright black man or woman who will lead our state into a brighter future, a future shared by blacks and whites together.

3

THE SCHOOLHOUSE DOOR

An Institutional Response to Desegregation

E. Culpepper Clark

Events on The University of Alabama campus punctuated two dramatic campaigns in the Civil Rights Movement, the Montgomery Bus Boycott, and the 1963 confrontation in Birmingham, between Martin Luther King Jr., and Eugene "Bull" Connor. Both main events occupied the nation for two full months before the camera's eye switched to Tuscaloosa. From December 1955 through January 1956, a new television generation kept watch as Montgomery's blacks adopted a new approach to protest and a new leader. Then on February 6, following two nights of demonstrations, the campus in Tuscaloosa became a tumultuous scene as White Citizens Councillors, Klansmen, union workers on strike, and students created disturbances that resulted in the suspension and later expulsion of Autherine Lucy, the University's first black student. Seven years later, King brought his direct-action tactics to Birmingham. After continuous demonstrations through April and May, unforgettably marked by Bull Connor's firehoses and police dogs, attention again returned to Tuscaloosa. On June 11, 1963, George Wallace used the entrance to Foster Auditorium to reify his image as the South's most defiant champion of segregation.

If the association with Montgomery and Birmingham events heightened the visibility of what happened in Tuscaloosa, the fact that the University both opened and closed a dramatic phase in the movement for racial justice contributed to the permanence of the unfortunate image. In 1955 The University of Alabama became the first institution ordered to desegregate under the implementation decree of *Brown* v. *Board of Edu-*

40

cation, and, within months, the first institution where court-ordered desegregation was stopped by violence. Eight years later, the confrontation at Foster Auditorium earned Alabama the dubious distinction of being the last state to accomplish desegregation in higher education. Thus, at the beginning, the University took the first shock of violent massive resistance, and at the end, it bore the opprobrium of a nation that had come to view events in the American South as a "moral crisis."

Perspective

We are now seeking to remember, not to erase what happened. Happily twenty-five years have passed, which is about the time it takes historians to rescue events from the journalists and to transform them into the slightly more respectable term, recent history, one that is useful for indicating that our students no longer have any idea what we are talking about. Of more serious moment, these twenty-five years give us a better feel for historical tempo and the relationships between sets of events and time frames so that a chronology begins to emerge. From that vantage, the twenty-year period stretching from 1943 to 1963 seems best for examining the institutional response to desegregation at The University of Alabama. In the first decade, 1943–1953, the University made choices that steered her on to the shoals of massive resistance. There she foundered for another ten years as two major storms broke over her, the last of which, the stand in the schoolhouse door, now makes it not only important but necessary that we engage in this collective act of remembering.

It is easy to take the images of 1956 and 1963 and conclude that all these bad things happened because Birmingham and Montgomery were citadels of segregation in the South's most segregated state (remembering, of course, that Mississippi is *sui generis*) and that the University could not help but reflect all that badness. In this telling, the University becomes a victim of circumstance. However, it is just as easy to construct the opposite case. In the late forties and fifties, Alabama twice elected a populist governor who held the region's most progressive views on racial accommodation. One of the state's senators was a leading New Deal Democrat and the other became Adlai Stevenson's running mate in 1952. Unlike other Southern states, Alabama had a large industrial labor population, and urban boosters continued to debate whether Birmingham or Atlanta would win the race to become the deep South's biggest city. Moreover, the state's black population was well organized and vigorous in pushing for civil rights. In recognition of this vital energy, the NAACP chose Birmingham as the site for its Southeastern Regional Office.

Because the circumstantial evidence can be argued either way, one can choose to lean, for the sake of argument, with those circumstances that could have made things turn out differently. Of course, no scenario can be as probable as what happened. When one looks at the events that led to the schoolhouse door, it seems idle to imagine them otherwise. But absent an alternative reckoning, history's tragic dimension is obscured. From hindsight we have the opportunity to measure choices against options. Unlike Becket facing the second Temptor, we can redeem time, play god for a moment and think what might have been. The starting assumption for this kind of reckoning is that Autherine Lucy, the University's first black student, arrived on campus at the worst possible time. Put another way, had she arrived any time before February 1956, the chances for peaceful desegregation would have improved measurably, and, in turn, there would have been no defiant gesture at the schoolhouse door.

Lucy and her friend Pollie Anne Myers graduated from Miles College in Birmingham in the spring of 1952. That fall they applied for and were denied admission to the University. After exhausting appeals through the University's hierarchy, the attorney for the young women, Arthur Shores, filed suit in federal court on July 3, 1953, ninety years to the day after Pickett's charge at Gettysburg, a small irony that likely went unnoticed. The NAACP Legal Defense Fund, which by that time had joined the case, delayed matters further because Thurgood Marshall wanted to test the right to sue a state agency, a strategy that was statutorily denied in Alabama. This unsuccessful legal disgression cost Lucy and Myers an additional eight months. For the remainder of 1954 and into 1955 both parties to the dispute, but principally the University, allowed the legal process to move at the most deliberate pace. Finally, on July 1, 1955, Judge Harlan Hobart Grooms, for the Northern District of Alabama, ruled that the two women be admitted for the fall term 1955. Further appeals delayed the actual enrollment to February 1, 1956.

Between September 1952 and February 1956, three years and four months passed. In that time the white majority in the South moved from passive to massive resistance. In the last year and a half alone there occurred in succession the *Brown* decision and its implementation decree, the formation of the Citizens' Councils, the murder of Emmett Till, and finally that match in the tinder box, the Montgomery Bus Boycott. To aggravate matters locally, the University's football team, even then a source of state chauvinism, akin to boasting about how many Medal of Honor winners the South had produced, completed the 1955 campaign 0 for 10. The leading passer on the team, a senior named Bart Starr, threw for only 587 yards and the top rusher gained a meagre 164. The opposition scored 255 points, while the once mighty Tide could muster only 48 for the season. For insult, the leading rusher in the SEC that fall was a lad from Auburn named Fob James, (later governor, 1979–83). So early 1956 was not a time like all times: it was quite simply the worst of times.

Separate but Equal

If a measure of leadership is the ability to anticipate change, Raymond Ross Paty served the University well. After receiving his master's degree from Columbia University in 1927, Paty founded the Cumberland Mountain School in Crossville, Tennessee, taught Bible and religion at his undergraduate alma mater, Emory, and became president of Birmingham Southern College in 1938. Paty steered the University through the profound changes occasioned by World War II. Of those changes, none was more profound than the new sense of entitlement among the nation's blacks. As early as 1943, Paty talked with Governor Chauncy Sparks about an appropriate response to the new demands. The conversation took place at Governor Sparks's request and centered on a survey commissioned by the State Department of Education in 1940, titled "A Study of Higher Education for Negroes in Alabama." Edgar W. Knight, a disciple of Howard Odum at the University of North Carolina, directed the survey and reflected his mentor's moderate views on the issue of gradual change in the racial status quo. As the newly inaugurated governor, Sparks planned two speeches on Negro education, one to the legislature and a Founders' Day speech at Tuskegee Institute, and thus he turned to Paty for advice.

Paty read the document and encouraged Sparks to endorse its conclusions. He urged the governor to meet the requirement of equality set forth by the Supreme Court in the 1938 case of Lloyd L. Gaines. In *Missouri ex rel. Gaines* v. *Canada*, the Court declared, "The admissibility of laws separating the races in the enjoyment of privileges afforded by the state rests wholly upon the equality of the privileges which the laws give to the separated groups within the State." Among other things Paty urged that money be spent to upgrade the state's black colleges to a status approximating equality. He even suggested the expansion of selected graduate and professional programs at white universities in order to accommodate blacks, albeit on a segregated basis. (Though the *McLaurin* decision in 1950 forbade the segregation of blacks within an institution, Paty's suggestion is interesting, for it posed the prospect of admitting blacks to the campus, while ostensibly maintaining segregation. Thus blacks would have been physically present when barriers to integration were finally removed. It could have made for a true test of gradualism.)

Paty coached his argument to educate blacks for leadership roles in traditional wisdom. He extolled the plan as a way of assuring that "the point of view and outlook here in the South will be a part of the school environment," and he argued that the needs of the Negroes could be met "more effectively with the educational program in the hands of Southern Negroes." Still, he viewed his program as more than simply reacting to the requirements set forth in *Gaines*. The plan, he thought, "moves in the direction of meeting fully and adequately the needs for education for the Negroes in Alabama to which they are entitled under the State and Federal Constitutions."[1] Paty's memorandum on education for Negroes stands out as the only written statement, before recent times, in which an official of the University committed himself to the principle that blacks were entitled to equal education by virtue of their citizenship. Sparks did not follow Paty's advice completely, though he did spurn demagoguery and called for improved educational opportunities for blacks within segregation.

Unfortunately Paty left at the end of 1946 to become chancellor of the University of Georgia System. Though his plan did not go beyond what many thoughtful Southern whites were willing to accept in 1943, it was nonetheless constructive, especially for an official of the University. Ralph Adams, the Dean of Administration, replaced Paty on an interim basis for the 1947 calendar year, and in 1948, John Moran Gallalee, a humorless mechanical engineer of the old school, began a five-year term.

Both Adams and Gallalee were determined segregationists, and unhappily, it was to them that the first black applicants had to turn. For the most part, the early applications came from soldiers who knew they had won on foreign fields what was denined them at home.

Laws and Customs

One applicant typifies the rest. Writing from Ward Seven East of the Army Regional Hospital in Oakland, California, Nathaniel S. Colley, a 1941 honor graduate of Tuskegee, applied to study law. "I am aware of the fact," he wrote, "that the law in Alabama makes my attendance at the State University (which I help to support) illegal." He added that it was a denial of his constitutional rights "since none of the fictional 'separate-but-equal' facilities in Alabama provide legal training." Moreover, Colley refused to "accept a grant-in-aid for attendance elsewhere," nor did he "plan to attend some makeshift segregated school." Having scored a direct hit with *Gaines* and having anticipated the Court's ruling in *Sweatt*, Colley concluded that "the Federal courts should have the opportunity to pass upon my specific right to attend the University at Tuscaloosa."[2]

To this threat, Adams who in 1946 also served as dean of admissions huffed with a lengthy explanation of why he did not have to be told the implications of the *Gaines* ruling and puffed with a proclamation of his own. "While this may be gratuitous," he told Colley, "I am adding that we at the University of Alabama are convinced that relationships between the races, in this section of the country at least, are not likely to be improved by pressure on behalf of members of the colored race in an effort to gain admission to institutions maintained by the state for members of the white race."[3] Adams's reply to Colley became a form-letter response to all black applicants. Still, the University worried. Dean Hepburn of the Law School wrote a friend in the regents office of the University System of Georgia about the Colley application. "From a strictly legal standpoint," his correspondent replied, "there is no answer to the demand made." Not satisfied, Dean Adams put the question to the president of the state bar. Adams began the inquiry by acquitting himself at some length on his knowledge of the law and then sought to ingratiate himself with an aside: "You and I know, of course, that the negro in the graduate school is just as black as the negro in the freshman class, and I do not believe that we Southerners are going to permit our children to eat and sleep with negroes, which will inevitably follow their admission to our classrooms."[4]

The president of the state bar, a resident of Grove Hill in southwest Alabama, proved to be a more thoughtful man. "Confidentially," he wrote Adams, "I have very serious doubts, after having given further thought to the matter, that the Supreme Court will regard our [state] legislation on the subject as being adequate; I rather think that if this applicant pursues his purpose to conclusion, he may get a court order requiring that he be admitted."[5] Such became the consistent advice of the state's reputable legal community. In 1947, Logan Martin, then president of the bar, appointed a committee at the request of the University to investigate the legal status of segregation. Six years later when Lucy and Myers sought admission, some effort was made to obtain the report, which apparently had been buried. "It is quite possible," wrote John B. Scott, the new president, "that when the situation [Negro applicants in 1947] eased itself the committee did not proceed further with its work." Scott added, "As you know, we have had to fight a rear guard action as to this question. It looks like that for the time being this is a matter for the diplomatic department of the university as our legal position is none too secure."[6]

The University's own very capable counsel, hired after Lucy and Myers brought suit, advised the same. They told the Board of Trustees that, even before *Brown,* institutions of higher education had not been able to maintain segregation under the "separate but equal" doctrine. In unmistakable terms, the lawyers said, ". . . in the institutions of higher learning the court has rendered decrees either ordering the admission or, in the alternative, holding that they could not be denied admission on account of color and, as we are advised, negroes have entered each of the institutions of higher learning where the question has been litigated, without any enforcement decree or extension of time for compliance. We can therefore anticipate such a result at The University of Alabama."[7]

A Window of Opportunity

It is difficult to say how much opportunity existed for token desegregation in the late forties and early fifties. A 1948 student opinion survey, conducted by a graduate student under University auspices and published in the New York *Times,* revealed the following information: a majority

(54 percent) favored abolition of the poll tax; 57 percent opposed the restriction of black suffrage by requiring registrants to interpret sections of the state constitution; 84 percent categorically opposed lynching; 68 percent favored a federal anti-lynching law; and half who expressed an opinion (47 percent) favored the establishment of a fair employment practices commission. Significant minorities favored admission of Negroes to the Medical, Law, and Graduate Schools (38, 35, and 33 percent respectively). Interestingly, exactly half of the students said they would not object to Negroes being admitted to the undergraduate school, although 64 percent of those who held this view favored some form of internal segregation, while 36 percent believed they should be admitted without restriction.[8]

Though not decisive, these numbers do suggest a certain malleability in student attitudes. Morrison Williams, son of Aubrey Williams, one of the state's most prominent liberals, was active in student politics that year and publicly called for the admission of blacks. Two years later in 1950, Sam Harvey of Guntersville, editor of the student newspaper, predicted the eventual admission of blacks and failed to see anything "so terrible" about the prospect. Harvey observed that people rode buses and shopped in stores with them, and he even doubted "if violent proponents of segregation leave the room when a Negro janitor comes in to sweep." "Like it or not," Harvey concluded, "we might as well get ready. They're on the way." The administration observed all this with gimlet-eyed apprehension. The Dean of Students sent President Gallalee a clipping from the Auburn student newspaper in which similar sentiments had been expressed. The dean attached a note saying, "Cold comfort, perhaps, but Auburn too."[9]

Of course student attitudes were but one measure, and arguably not even the most salient, of the environment in which desegregation might have been tried earlier. Still, assertions like those of Morrison Williams and Sam Harvey and of students who occasionally attended interracial meetings sponsored by the Southern Regional Council encouraged Pollie Anne Myers and Autherine Lucy to believe that they might be accepted by the student body, even if not enthusiastically. But the University's elders would have none of it.

The Board Takes Over

When President Gallalee failed in the fall of 1952 to persuade Arthur Shores to drop the Lucy and Myers case, the matter of desegregation eventually wound up in the hands of the Board of Trustees where it remained until 1963. Of all the causes contributing to the University's tragic struggle with desegregation none was more instrumental than the manner in which its Board of Trustees exercised authority. Among its ten appointed members, five determined policy. Their leader was Hill Ferguson, president pro tempore of the board and for over fifty years a tireless promoter of the University. In 1896 he quarterbacked the football team and from 1904 to 1907 served as president of the alumni association. In the latter capacity he raised over half a million dollars for the "Greater University" campaign and laid the cornerstone for Smith Hall, the first of three yellow brick buildings that conspicuously anchor the northern edge of the quadrangle. Ironically, Smith Hall would also be the site of Autherine Lucy's first class. Ferguson, a real estate developer from Birmingham, joined the board in 1919 and by the 1950s was said to "own the board."

His control, however, did not have to be autocratic because he was supported by like-minded men. Gessner McCorvey, Mobile attorney and the state's chief Dixiecrat, grew up on the campus where his father served for over fifty years as professor of history and moral philosophy. Brewer Dixon, Talladega attorney and successor to his father on the board, brought a country lawyer's tenacity to the task of defending the segregationist faith. Bob Steiner, corporate attorney from Montgomery, acted as a lawyer's lawyer for the seven attorneys, one industrialist, one banker, and one developer who constituted the board. Judge Thomas S. Lawson from Greensboro, who sat on the State Supreme Court and who first achieved notice as a prosecutor in the Scottsboro cases, brought a firm judicial temperament to deliberations and an equally firm commitment to the board's obligation to lead the University through its crisis. Ferguson, McCorvey, Dixon, Steiner, and Lawson were born in the nineteenth century and matured in the radical racialist thought that swept the turn-of-the-century South. They dominated a board that was self-perpetuating and jealously guarded its prerogatives to shape policy without political interference and, as it turned out, without much regard for the counsel of its own administration and faculty.

The late spring and summer of 1953 proved an important turning point for the University. In May the board announced Oliver Cromwell Carmichael as the University's next president. In June they decided to take no action on the applications of Lucy and Myers, thereby putting the matter in the hands of the courts. Thus, when Carmichael arrived in the fall of 1953, the University was committed to a legal confrontation with the NAACP, leaving no room for comment or for informal negotiations. This was unfortunate, for in Carmichael the University had acquired the most distinguished educator ever produced by the state. A 1911 graduate of the University, Carmichael became the institution's first Rhodes Scholar and later served as an intelligence officer during World War I. He went on to become president of Alabama College at Montevallo, Chancellor of Vanderbilt University, and at the time of his appointment, president of the Carnegie Foundation for the Advancement of Teaching and chairman of the Board of Trustees for the New York University System, a system which he designed at the request of Governor Thomas E. Dewey. An educational leader with few peers, Carmichael at age sixty-one returned to his alma mater with the prospect of retiring at age seventy.

Carmichael was an Eisenhower-style Republican. When compelled, he declared himself to be a segregationist, but he also knew that those days were numbered. He simply believed and hoped, for his own good and that of society, that the numbers would run beyond his retirement. His sense of gradualism, like Eisenhower's, was counted in generations, not years. Moreover, he took comfort in the board's assurance that the whole affair was in the hands of lawyers, allowing him to concentrate on plans for building a first-rate university. Among other things, he wanted to pioneer in educational television, extension centers, and curricular innovations like American Studies. He also wanted to bring the faculty into the twentieth century in terms of research, self-governance, and academic freedom.

Carmichael and the Board

Carmichael soon learned that desegregation could not, as he hoped, be kept apart from the general business of running The University of Alabama. In both 1954 and 1955 he took steps that could have given him some control over what had become *the* issue and on each occasion was either slapped down by the board or retired from it voluntarily. By far his boldest and best idea was to persuade Eisenhower that a major speech on human rights, if made in the South immediately following the Supreme Court's ruling on the segregation cases, would have a salutary effect.

"The more I have considered it," he wrote in follow-up to a personal conversation with the President, "the more it has seemed to me that the announcement of the Court's decision on segregation might prove a unique occasion and opportunity for a profoundly important statement on human rights. Such a statement made in the South would probably be more effective than if made elsewhere." As a location, he offered the University's spring commencement, provided that the Court reached its decision before May 30th.[10]

Carmichael apparently received sufficiently favorable response from the White House to draft a lengthy memorandum in which he suggested what the President ought to say. While he stressed the hackneyed *tu quoque* arguments about non-Southern transgressions in race relations and appealed for understanding the South's unique situation with respect to proportionate numbers of blacks in the region, Carmichael nonetheless urged the President to come down strongly on the nation's common heritage of human rights and the South's own progress over the past ninety years. Like the Supreme Court a few months later in its famous footnote eleven to *Brown*, he might have added, "see Myrdal *passim*." Carmichael also suggested that Eisenhower emphasize national "idealism" as a beacon to the rest of the world. From that international perspective he urged the President to say: "The recent decision of the Supreme Court was doubtless based upon a consideration of these fundamental facts, of the great stakes involved in our continued efforts to realize the full meaning of the ideals which undergird the American way of life. It has obviously not pleased every segment of the American people, but there is no doubt that the Court was mindful of the profound issues involved and that it sought to achieve what every American hopes and prays for, a step forward in America's effort to strengthen the basis for peace and security in the world."[11]

Carmichael had drafted an apology for a Supreme Court decision not yet written and a brilliant suggestion for presidental leadership. His notion that the President might succeed if his statement of support for the Court were wrapped in the garb of international security was precisely the tack Martin Luther King, Jr., urged on President Kennedy nine years later. One is left to imagine how things might have turned out had Eisenhower taken up Carmichael on his invitation. A Court decree, backed up immediately by a clear signal from the President, and delivered from the very heart of Dixie would have given the forces of desegregation the power of two branches of the federal government rather than one. It also might have saved Carmichael's presidency by confronting the Board of Trustees with a *fait accompli:* a statement urging compliance with the *Brown* decision, uttered by the most powerful man in the free world, and delivered from their campus.

Carmichael in all likelihood told members of the board about his plans to invite the President, but not what he planned for the President to say. In 1954 Carmichael casually remarked to a reporter in Miami, Florida, that he thought desegregation in higher education would go about as smoothly as it had in the armed services. Such a storm broke over that simple assertion that Carmichael declined an invitation from John Temple Graves to defend the remark in the Birmingham *Post-Herald.*[12] Thereafter, members of the board often worried that Carmichael was soft on segregation, and no one worried more than Hill Ferguson. Ferguson provided Carmichael with a maddening stream of advice, much of which was designed to box Carmichael into defending segregation more vigorously. But Ferguson was more than an irritant. In the wake of a particularly nasty incident in which a member of the National States' Rights Party charged a university faculty members with corrupting young people by teaching integration and mongrelization of the races, Ferguson got hold of a James Eastland speech and sent it to Carmichael. Senator Eastland raised questions about liberal foundations and the Supreme Court that Ferguson found persuasive.

Carmichael was reduced to remonstrance by indirection. "To many," he sighed, "it will be a persuasive document. The evidence on which he rests his case leaves the Supreme Court members in really bad company and assumes them to have a pretty low level of intelligence." But as Carmichael must have known, it was not the part of Eastland's speech having to do with the Supreme Court that interested Ferguson—the Court's perfidy was beyond question. What concerned Ferguson was the part about the foundations and particularly the Carnegie Foundation with which Carmichael had been associated. So Carmichael found himself walking gingerly through a minefield planted by Ferguson, trying to separate the Carnegie Endowment for International Peace which had supported Alger Hiss, and the Carnegie Corporation which sponsored Gunnar Myrdal, from the Carnegie Foundation for the Advancement of Teaching which had supported Carmichael.[13] It was a bewildering, if not hopeless task.

Autherine Lucy

The tension between Carmichael and the board spelled disaster in the 1956 crisis. Beginning the last day of January and continuing through the last day of February, a series of events and decisions doomed efforts made by Autherine Lucy and the NAACP on the one hand and the administration of Carmichael on the other. On January 31, under federal court order, the Board of Trustees ordered Dean William F. Adams to admit Autherine Lucy but deny admission to Pollie Anne Meyers (now Hudson) on grounds that "her conduct and marital record" did not meet "the admission standards of the University." (She had conceived out of wedlock.) Autherine Lucy registered on February 1 and attended classes on the third, fourth, and sixth, a Friday, Saturday, and Monday, respectively. Demonstrations on the nights of the third and fourth culminated in a day-long riot on Monday the sixth. That evening the trustees met and voted to suspend Autherine Lucy both for her own safety and that of the faculty and students. The next day Arthur Shores demanded Lucy's reinstatement within forty-eight hours.

Receiving no communication from the University, the NAACP filed suit on February 9 to have Lucy reinstated. Among other things they said that the University "conspired to defy the injunction order" of the Court and "assimilated an air of riot" as a subterfuge to suspend Miss Lucy. While the NAACP lawyers fumed in Birmingham, an air of calm returned to the Tuscaloosa campus, and Carmichael seemed to develop a new sense of resolve. At a faculty meeting on Thursday, February 16, he vowed that the forces of law and order would prevail against the mob. Bob Bird of the New York *Herald Tribune* reported that Carmichael placed his job on the line to insure Lucy's return, a statement that Carmichael later denied.[14] However, Carmichael had determined to take charge so that the University's reputation would not slide further into the sinkhole of massive resistance.

Carmichael underestimated the Board's determination to resist desegregation by all legal means. Meeting in Steiner's office in Montgomery on Saturday and Sunday, the 18th and 19th, members of the executive committee decided to recommend to the Board that Autherine Lucy be expelled permanently because she had libeled members of the board with the February 9 conspiracy charge, an allegation that was broadcast the same day in a press conference. In the meantime Judge Grooms set the hearing

to reinstate Lucy for Feburary 29. At a pre-trial conference on the morning of the twenty-eighth, lawyers for the University told Judge Grooms
that their clients would file an "affirmative defense" against the libelous
conspiracy charge by expelling Lucy. Judge Grooms asked them not to
file the defense of explusion for the hearing that was pending the next
day, because the issue of libel (the February 9 conspiracy charge) arose
subsequent to the February 6 order by the board suspending Lucy and
therefore was not relevant. It also meant that he would not interfere.
Judge Grooms did ask for permission to tell Thurgood Marshall that
afternoon what the University planned, and the lawyers agreed.

The next day, February 29, Marshall opened the hearings in Birmingham by withdrawing the conspiracy charge, saying they had found
no evidence to substantiate the allegation. The hearings then proceeded
for the entire day with the University arguing that Autherine Lucy had
been within "twenty seconds of death on two occasions" during the
Monday riot and that conditions remained too dangerous for her safe
return. The NAACP argued that the University should be held in contempt for failing to provide adequate protection on February 6 and that
officials must guarantee safety in the future or all court orders could be
vitiated by mobs or the threat of mobs. At six o'clock that evening, Judge
Grooms ruled that University officials were not in contempt because they
could not have anticipated the riot but ordered the University to reinstate
Miss Lucy on March 5. Members of the board and university officials left
the courtroom and walked two blocks to the Tutwiler Hotel where,
within the hour, the board voted unanimously to expel Autherine Lucy
permanently.

The events of February 1956 provide strong evidence that the board
was determined to get Lucy at almost any cost. To expel the young
woman for a charge made by her lawyers, especially a charge that was
later withdrawn in open court with a declaration of no proof, smacked of
pretextual motivation. In fact the board's determination was such that
they might as well have conspired with the mob because in the end they
did the mob's bidding. Though the board's action did have its seamier
side, it would be wrong to conclude that the action lay somewhere
beyond reason. First, the board established a policy in June, 1953, to stop
or delay desegregation by all legal means. On February 9, 1956, the
NAACP handed the board legal grounds for delay by charging conspiracy and by broadcasting the charge at a press conference. Attorneys for

the NAACP recognized the charge as a strategic mistake almost as soon as it was issued and since have blamed Constance Baker Motley for the ill-conceived charge. When Judge Grooms told Marshall on February 28 that the University planned to use explusion as an affirmative defense, Marshall knew the case was over. As a defense, expulsion worked because the university had a right to discipline students who undermined its authority by libelling or slandering its officials. In fact, the University expelled the student leader of the riots twelve days later for the same reason. So when Marshall withdrew the conspiracy charge on February 29, he did not expect to stop the expulsion order so much as to lay legal grounds for appeal in federal courts or, less likely, defense in state courts where the law of libel would be adjudicated.

Moreover, it is clear that all parties to the dispute were relieved by the explusion order. The board did not report its final decision to Judge Grooms and subsequently to the NAACP until the next morning, March 1. By ten o'clock that morning Thurgood Marshall, Constance Motley, and Autherine Lucy were on a plane bound for New York. That afternoon, a Thursday, Judge Grooms left for an extended weekend. The timing of these departures indicated that no one seriously expected Lucy to be reinstated the following Monday as ordered by the court, nor did the NAACP simply resign itself to a legal ploy that sealed their fate. They, along with Judge Grooms and university officials, feared for Lucy's safety. It was as if they peered into the abyss of random killings and violence that would mark the next ten years and stepped back. NAACP officials were also looking at a young woman who had placed her life on hold for four years, experienced a traumatic rescue from a howling mob, and who now had other plans for her life. Autherine Lucy would be married in less than two months.

A New Pattern of Resistance

These explanations, however, sanitize a situation that had an uglier side. On the night the board expelled Autherine Lucy they also voted to admit, "should she be qualified in all respects," a black applicant named Ruby Steadman Peters. Peters was a forty-year-old woman who had completed two years of schooling at Alabama State University in Montgomery. She wished to take courses from the University's extension center in Birmingham and to transfer the credits back to Alabama State.

It would have simplified her life greatly. She was even willing to take courses by correspondence or by television in order to avoid interracial contact. It is probable that the board reported to Judge Grooms their willingness to admit her as evidence that in expelling Autherine Lucy they were not seeking to flout his order, but the momentous decision received no other publicity and for an obvious reason. To have published the action would have rallied all the forces of massive resistance which, at least temporarily, had been appeased by the explusion order.

The decision to admit Peters bespoke a board wrestling with its legal obligation. Hill Ferguson cast the only dissenting vote, as he had done on the original court order to admit Autherine Lucy. The next move confirmed a pattern for handling black applicants that began when Ferguson, acting for the board, employed the Bodeker Detective Agency to dig up information on Lucy and Myers. Ferguson now used the same approach to learn about Peters. After gathering sufficient information he asked two men with excellent ties to the black community to persuade Ruby Peters to drop her application. The two were Clarence Allgood, now a federal judge, and James A. Green of the Avondale Federal Savings and Loan Association, which held the mortgage on Peters's home. Green also handled most of the mortgage business for the McCain Realty Company where Peters worked, so he knew her personally. She received their overtures as friendly, but she also knew that she was talking to "the man," or less idiomatically, the white power structure. Under any circumstances, when the deed was done and Peters had withdrawn the application, Ferguson wrote Allgood and Green to say thanks "for the excellent manner in which you have handled these negotiations leading up to this happy conclusion. Please convey our thanks also to our other friends, who assisted you in this undertaking."[15]

Ferguson's personal triumph in the Peters case notwithstanding, most members of the board and university officials believed themselves under a legal, if not moral, obligation to desegregate the University. Most also believed that it would come sooner rather than later. In the spring of 1956, no one yet felt sanguine about repeating the Peters result on a continuing basis. Carmichael even began secret negotiations to obtain the "right" black applicant. The negotiations were not his own idea, but when they developed, he did not turn them aside and apparently saw merit in following through.

The idea belonged to Allan Knight Chalmers, member of the Boston University Theology faculty and chairman of the Committee of 100 to raise money for the NAACP Legal Defense and Educational Fund. His Alabama connections were long-standing. Appointed to chair the Scottsboro Defense Committee in 1935, Chalmers spent the better part of the next decade working with Grover Hall, Sr., of the Montgomery *Advertiser* and other Alabamians to secure the release of the Scottsboro boys. His personal friendship with the Hall family continued into the fifties with Grover Hall, Jr. Chalmers also served as trustee for Talladega College, a small black school forty miles east of Birmingham founded by the Congregational Church with admission open to all races. Chalmers possessed a dynamic personality, uncommonly good looks, and an easy charm. He also possessed patience and optimism, both of which were necessary to continue his role as a diplomat for human rights in Alabama.

On March 3, three days after the explusion of Autherine Lucy, Chalmers came to Carmichael's office. Carmichael liked the proposal for finding the right black applicant, and associates at Talladega College soon recommended Billy Joe Nabors. Nabors, a native of Talladega, came from a large, poor family and attended the local college where he established an exemplary record. With letters of endorsement from the college's president and others, he applied to study law at the University. Carmichael probably signaled the Admissions Office that the Nabor's application was to be treated differently, for even the most adamant segregationists on the board did not know about the application until the Birmingham *News* made brief mention of Nabors on May 15.[16]

Brewer Dixon, the trustee from Talladega, read the newspaper that day and shot off a hot note to the Dean of Admissions. He expressed chagrin at having learned of Nabors through the papers and asked for a copy of his application. When Dixon queried whether Nabors had received the necessary endorsements from practicing attorneys in the county (one of the impediments designed to eliminate black applicants), Dean Adams replied somewhat evasively that Nabors had acquired elsewhere affidavits as to his moral character; whereupon Dixon decided that not enough was being done and launched his own investigation.[17]

Deepening Suspicions

Dixon's anger with the administration unhappily coincided with the release to the Board of Trustees of a document on academic freedom. The document was part of an institutional self-study and did no more than embrace general trends in higher education. Bob Steiner was the first trustee to react sharply. He saw it as part of "a spirit of rebellion" touched off by the "recent Lucy trouble." He charged that some faculty and departments were "more conscious of and ready to assert their freedom to think, teach and say what they please than ever before and to effect a tenure contract or agreement by which they cannot be censured or their utterances and teachings censored, or the members disciplined for such utterances." Judge Lawson saw it as a usurpation of board authority and weighed in with the view that if the faculty were given freedom "to advocate integration at the University in public utterances, we are in for trouble with the people." Brewer Dixon felt that "no one would wish to unduly limit the rights of an individual as to his private ideas and beliefs, but in view of the fact that the state of Alabama has a direct interest in the University and its teachers, I feel that those members of the faculty who have been guilty of teaching and acts which are opposed to the policies of the University Board on this negro question should go. And there is pretty definite feeling throughout the state," he added, "that we have several such members of our faculty."[18]

Carmichael was floored but not speechless. He disabused board members of their fear that the statement on academic freedom had been slipped in on them as an accomplished fact, and he denied angrily any notion that there existed anything amounting to a faculty rebellion. He expressed particular dismay to Steiner "since on two or three occasions in my conversations with you I have tried to make clear that this [rebellious spirit] was not the attitude of the faculty." From the beginning, Carmichael had hoped to keep the issue of desegregation separate from his general plans to build a strong university. Long-range institutional planning was his special talent and now even that was being dragged down by a board consumed by one issue alone. One of the board's steadiest members, Judge Lawson, wrote that he was "unwilling to abrogate to the American Association of University Professors or any other similar group the responsibilities and duties which I understand have been placed by the Constitution of this state on myself and other members of the Board of Trustees of the University."[19]

Resistance Redux

The flap over academic freedom took the heart out of Carmichael and convinced him that he should leave the University as soon as possible.

Allan Knight Chalmers paid a return visit in late July, but this time the mood was changed. Carmichael seemed distracted. He turned frequently to his chief assistant for answers to Chalmers's questions. Even as he talked with the persistent diplomat from Boston, Carmichael knew that Brewer Dixon had turned up enough dirt to sabotage Nabors's application. Among other things, they learned that Nabors had a quick temper and had gotten into a couple of heated arguments in both high school and college. A few weeks later Chalmers, too, came to the reluctant conclusion that Nabors was not good enough (though he was good enough to go on to Howard University where he received his law degree). Just before the end of Nabors's effort, Chalmers wrote the young man comparing his situation with that of Jackie Robinson. "You have something of his fire and I hope you also have some of his intelligence. He knew he had to keep himself under tight rein for all personal things. . . ."[20] Mere mortals would not do.

By late August the University's administration had been moved into lock step with its Board of Trustees. A pattern of resistance to desegregation had been established. The last serious applicant that year, at least serious by University estimates, was investigated thoroughly by the private detective agency. One of the agency's operatives discovered that the young man's mother was a patient of a psychiatrist at University Hospital. This time, without prompting from any member of the board, university officials, with the cooperation of the doctor, persuaded the lad not to go through with his plans for fear that his mother would wind up in the state's asylum for the insane.[21] It was a sad and sorry ending to a decade that began with the prospect of early, if token, desegregation and ended in schemes for thwarting civil rights that were perhaps even more effective (because carried out by men of unquestioned reputation against isolated individuals) than Bull Connor's police or Jim Clark's posse.

Lessons Learned

By late 1956 the University knew that it could dispose of black applicants without much difficulty. The principal reason for such ease was the absence of support groups for the young men and women who wished to apply. After June 1956, the NAACP no longer functioned in Alabama. In the wake of the Lucy episode, the state's attorney general, John Patterson, launched a Communist witch-hunt and subpoenaed the NAACP membership rolls. When the NAACP refused to turn over their lists, Patterson turned to Circuit Judge Walter B. Jones of Montgomery who cited the organization for contempt and imposed a fine of $100,000. Thurgood Marshall and his associates at the Legal Defense Fund refused to reenter the state for fear of walking into a legal quagmire, and the regional office closed its doors in Birmingham. The irrepressible Fred Shuttlesworth set up the Alabama Christian Movement for Human Rights as a replacement for the NAACP, but his leadership was suspect among the old guard. He also took on the more volatile issues of desegregating buses and public schools in Birmingham. Without strong organizational support, no black applicant could succeed against the counter measures adopted by the University, and the Board of Trustees remained steadfast in refusing to admit another black without still another federal court order. Thus, until the Legal Defense Fund reentered the case to support Vivian Malone, James Hood, and others, no single applicant had the means to fight the University. Pigeonholing applicants became a simple matter.

Nor did new leadership within the University change the situation much. Carmichael resigned effective January 1, 1957, and Frank Rose, a charismatic spokesman for the most recent New South, took office a year later. More significantly, the retirement of Hill Ferguson and the death of Bob Steiner, both in 1959, led to the appointments of Ehney Camp and Winton "Red" Blount. Camp and Blount were progressive businessmen who understood that the University had to comply with the law of the land. They played constructive roles in the final drama. But despite new leadership the pace of change did not quicken. While all now agreed that change was inevitable, they still waited for the right time, which of course never came, and as civil rights confrontations heated up in the sixties, there were even more reasons to wait. As they waited, University officials continued to devise new ways to frustrate applicants. For the fall of 1962 and again for the spring of 1963, they closed the processing of applications early in order to avoid consideration of blacks. President Rose wrote to Major W. R. Jones of the Department of Public Safety, and explained, "The closing of the enrollment, as you know, has always been our practice and is one of our legal steps. You know us well enough to know that we don't need any encouragement or advice on closing our registration."[22]

In part Rose was posturing for the new Wallace administration, which had put increasing pressure on the University since the fall elections. Indeed the University no longer had to hire its own detectives (though in certain cases it continued the practice) because the Department of Public Safety had taken over that job—the University simply supplied the names to be investigated. Despite these displays for Wallace, the University prepared for change. Early in 1963 two employees of the Redstone Arsenal in Huntsville asked to study at the Huntsville Center. Their applications renewed old fears that the federal government might cut off funds for the University's burgeoning interest in space-related research. The University also confronted applicants who now had the resources to litigate. Though the NAACP was yet to reorganize in Alabama, the Legal Defense Fund renewed the fight they had won for Autherine Lucy and supported Vivian Malone and James Hood. The two candidates for the Huntsville Center, Dave M. McGlathery and Marvin P. Carroll, hired Charles Morgan, a white Birmingham lawyer. With change imminent, University officials began playing off the Wallace administration with one hand while dealing with the Kennedy administration from the other.

In March, Rose and one of his top assistants, Jefferson Bennett, made several trips to Washington to lay plans for the summer term. In addition, Tuscaloosa civic leaders and University officials consulted with their counterparts at Clemson, Georgia Tech, and Florida State, schools that had desegregated peacefully. In the meantime Winton Blount used his personal connections with the Kennedy administration to orchestrate a letter writing campaign to dissuade Wallace from his pledge to stand in the schoolhouse door. The idea was to have leading businessmen from throughout the state tell Wallace that trouble in Tuscaloosa would hurt the state. Each member of Kennedy's cabinet took about ten names, usually selecting whomever they knew personally before drawing names at random, and then called to enlist their aid. There were 128 business leaders whose names appeared on the list; 108 were contacted, and 80 agreed to call or write Wallace.

The Kennedy administration also kept close tabs on the available security forces. They and the University's administration wished to avoid another Ole Miss at all cost. The federal government was even willing to foot the bill for continued security by coming up with grant money to defray the University's expense. Rose presented a bill for $100,000.[23] Having the federal government pay for compelling a state to honor the rights of its black citizens smacked of an old Southern con game and, no doubt, would have drawn smiles from the courthouse gangs. The Kennedys, however, were not alone in their concern for security. Governor Wallace shared the determination to avoid violence, and while he played political cat and mouse with federal authorities, especially with Robert Kennedy, he used the month leading up to the stand at Foster Auditorium to urge the people of Alabama to stay away from the University. By June 11 the only mystery that remained was the extent to which Wallace would try to block physically the entrance of the two students, a mystery that Wallace maintained to the end for his own political reasons. When on May 16 the federal court once again ordered the University to open its doors, plans began to fall into place rapidly. The University did try one more appeal for delay on grounds that the street demonstrations in Birmingham made it difficult to marshal sufficient police protection in Tuscaloosa. Judge Grooms quickly set aside that objection.

All the planning notwithstanding, fear was as close as heat on that Tuesday in June. The night before, Blount and Jeff Bennett for the University administration talked to the governor and found him noticeably agitated. Each assured the other that they would do everything possible to maintain order, after which Blount and Bennett called Robert Kennedy from a downtown telephone booth to report these assurances. No one, however, could predict what a sniper or other deranged person might do or in fact whether the Klan might ignore Wallace's calls to stay away. As Assistant Attorney General Nicholas Katzenbach approached Wallace at the schoolhouse door, members of the Board of Trustees watched tensely from a building across the way. Trustee emeritus Hill Ferguson had joined them. Tears filled some eyes as the older trustees watched a way of life pass. A few days later Gessner McCorvey spoke for his generation when he remarked that given his views he should have been "born fifty years earlier and thus missed many things that have worried me greatly." Even so, he could take comfort in having made the fight. A year later he agreed with counsel that continued efforts to stop black applicants should be abandoned. Then, as an afterthought, he said, "We have really done our damndest."[24]

When George Wallace left Foster Auditorium for the return trip to Montgomery, trustees, university officials, and Kennedy people celebrated the fact that no blood had been shed. Ironically, that happy outcome owed as much to Wallace as to their efforts. By becoming passion incarnate, the cocky little judge could stand in for those whose anger he stirred. Still, it was a close call. Wallace had played with a rattlesnake, and he knew it. No other political figure knew the Klan better. That night President Kennedy went on television to call the continued deprivation of human rights a "moral issue." A few hours later, after most Americans had turned off their televisions and gone to sleep, a pathetically twisted human being shot Medgar Evers dead. The rattlesnake had struck, albeit in neighboring Mississippi.

For Our Children and Grandchildren

A generation passed between that day in 1943 when President Paty talked about taking the first steps toward gradual desegregation and that day in 1963 when Wallace stood in the schoolhouse door. Of those twenty years, the first ten presented the University with an opportunity to make gradualism work, to adopt policies that might have eased the way toward desegregation, perhaps like that which occurred in the border states. But Paty left for Georgia and was replaced by Adams and Gallalee, two confirmed segregationists. Though consistently advised by legal counsel that segregation could not be maintained lawfully, they adopted a policy of turning aside all black applicants without consideration and by form letter. Then in the last year of Gallalee's administration, two young women applied, backed by the resources of the state NAACP and the national Legal Defense Fund. To frustrate their efforts, the Board of Trustees took control of the case, dug in its heels, and refused to budge until ordered by the courts three and a half years later.

The members of the board might have spared themselves another wrenching experience seven years later but for an invasion of violent men who with their student allies drove Autherine Lucy from campus and made the University look like a haven for goons and thugs. Ironically, the trustees ratified the work of the mob by voting to expel Autherine Lucy permanently. For their efforts, the trustees bought seven more years of segregation and another media-blackened eye as George Wallace used the schoolhouse door to gratify a political promise. During the years of trustee control, the administrations of Carmichael and Rose generally believed that the University's interests would be served best by complying with desegregation, but they lacked the authority to make it happen. Not until Vivian Malone, James Hood, and Dave McGlathery, along with others knocked once again at the door that Autherine Lucy and Pollie Anne Myers had been the first to open, not until then did the University administration and its trustees agree to let them in. Even then it took the power of civil rights lawyers, the federal courts, and the Kennedy administration to help make it happen.

I have talked with people who worked in the University at that time who wanted to make a difference, but who for reasons too numerous to detail here could or would not make it so. They express pain at the memory, and I can understand their pain, for what gives them grief are precisely those compromises that mark our daily lives, only their compromises had to be made in the midst of a drama of huge social significance. Ways of life were changing. People like Gessner McCorvey, born to a corrupt and corrupting system, were being asked to step out of their heritage much as a leopard might be asked to change its spots. At least in the end, the old Dixiecrat voted to yield and did so "because somebody has *got* to 'carry on' and we have *got* to leave behind us the best possible country that we can leave for our children and grandchildren."[25] Perhaps, as Martin Luther King, Jr. so passionately believed, the arc of the universe does bend to justice.

4

FROM FOSTER AUDITORIUM
TO SANDERS AUDITORIUM
The "Southernization" of American Politics

Dan T. Carter

When George Wallace stood in the door at The University of Alabama in June 1963, he was well on his way to being the leading voice for Southern white opposition to desegregation. He reached that "accomplishment" because he was a man of considerable political abilities. However obscured by his personal crudities and his regional accent, Wallace had a powerful intelligence, a remarkably subtle feeling for shifts in political mood, and a political drive and killer instinct that was reflected in his record as a Golden Gloves boxing champion. He understood the defensive psyche of white Southerners as well as any politician in the twentieth century—the sense of grievance, of almost self-pitying sensitivity to "persecution." He shared white Southerners'—particularly *working class* white Southerners'—fear of being looked down upon by all the "respectable" folk, whether those respectable folk were in the big house or in Yankee land. Wallace desperately wanted to be loved, to be admired, to be respected. His many political skills were all yoked to that lust to be loved *and* the angry sense of inferiority and alienation that he shared with white Southerners. It may not have made him a suitable leader for Camelot. But it allowed him to achieve a remarkable rapport with those who shared the feelings, which in turn would make Wallace invulnerable politically in Alabama.

Early Lessons

Some of his success came from the skills and talents honed in two decades of Alabama politics. He had an extraordinary memory for names

64

and faces. His ability to walk into a crowded room and identify individuals—some of whom he had met only briefly eight or ten years earlier—is legendary. Thousands of stump speeches, from county fairs to Kiwanis clubs, had given him an unerring sense of what would "play." He was, in the vocabulary of the students of rhetoric, the perfect "mimetic orator," probing his audiences' deepest fears and passions and articulating those emotions in a language and style they could understand.

He had a perfect laboratory for exploiting emotions in the South of the 1960s. One can see the intensity of white racial feeling in the files on "segregation" and "civil rights" kept by Wallace and other Alabama politicians. Sometimes white Alabamians of the period objected to the Civil Rights Movement, Northern "interference," or the hated Kennedy brothers in the dignified and abstract language of states' rights and constitutional government. Most of it, however, is a terrifying window into a venomous anti-black hatred which seemed to explode in the early 1960s. In the six months following Governor Wallace's stand in the schoolhouse door, for example, the Alabama congressman Armistead Selden received more than one thousand letters—the majority expressing a kind of hysterical rage against, as one writer put it, the "lazy, lying, adulterous [sic], parasitical, nigger communists." And all joined by a kind of bewildered, frustrated anger. One Birmingham businessman said to Selden: "Surely it is plain to see that this Kennedy juggernaut was planned in Moscow and is being carried out by the Coon-Communist Martin Luther King and his followers. What kind of country is this when nothing is being done to stop it?"[1]

The tumultuous journey of the Freedom Riders through the lower South in the spring of 1961 evoked thousands of letters from Southerners to their elected state-house and national officials. While there was a handful of brave souls who condemned the mobs and the criminal dereliction of local and state officials, the vast majority instead expressed satisfaction that (in the words of one Montgomery matron) "they got what they deserved."

Such deep-seated racism had always existed in Southern society, but the heightened level of hysteria of the 1960s stemmed from white segregationists' faltering sense of self-confidence; their awareness that their defense of the racial status quo was losing ground.

That very sense of a region under siege, however, made it impossible for political leaders to espouse "moderation." There were individuals like Congressman Carl Elliott and Senators Lister Hill and John Sparkman who tried to avoid inflaming public opinion. To be "moderate," however, in the climate of political extremisim that gripped Alabama in the 1960s was to court political suicide. As a Texas politician once said, the only things in the middle of the road are "yellow stripes and dead armadillos." It was a lesson the always prescient George Wallace learned in 1958 when he was defeated by John Patterson. It was a lesson encapsulated in the comment which he made sitting outside the Jefferson Davis Hotel the night he was defeated (but would later deny), "John Patterson out-niggered me," he told his friends. But he added with emphasis: "Boys, I'm not going to be out-niggered again."

Given this climate—and George Wallace's ability to mobilize emotions, fears, and anger—his emergence as the leader of Southern resistance is not surprising. Given the performance in the late 1950s and early 1960s of such Southern luminaries as George Bell Timmerman, Strom Thurmond, and Ross Barnett, there was not a great deal of competition. To see the more important question, the real mystery about Wallace's significance, one must think back to the Presidential campaigns from 1964 through 1976.

Presidential Campaigns

In the spring of 1964, less than a year after his stand in the schoolhouse door, Wallace embarked on a national public speaking campaign. On a whim, with less that $700 in cash and no organization he entered the Wisconsin Democratic Primary. Despite the condemnation of the Catholic Church, the entire Protestant religious establishment, the Democratic Party of Wisconsin, and organized labor, he gained nearly 34 percent of the vote. In Indiana with two supporters running much of the campaign out of their filling station he took 30 percent of the vote. In Maryland it was nearly 45 percent and—as Wallace always darkly suggested—"that was with them countin' the votes."

And that, of course, was the first of four campaigns for the presidency. Running as a third party candidate in 1968, he outdistanced Hubert Humphrey in the early polls and remained the choice of 22 to 25 percent of the voters as late as ten days before the election. But Wallace, one may recall, was saddled with the human cannon ball, Curtis Le May, as his running mate. With a multi-million-dollar television blitz, Richard Nixon unleashed his Wallace clone, Spiro Agnew, and embraced a Southern strategy which emphasized conservative racial and social policies. Humphrey's final surge in the Midwest and middle-Atlantic states, led by organized labor, pulled millions of traditionally Democratic voters back into the fold on election eve. Despite this precipitous decline in the last week of the campaign, Wallace carried five Southern states and polled from 8 to 15 percent of the vote in eighteen non-Southern states.

And 1968 was a dress rehearsal for 1972. Running as a Democrat in Florida against a broad field of candidates—Birch Bayh, Hubert Humphrey, George McGovern, Henry Jackson, Edmund Muskie, John Lindsay, Shirley Chisolm, Vance Hartke, Wilbert Mills, and Sam Yorty—Wallace took 42 percent of the votes; no one was even close. (Humphrey got 18 percent.) In Pennsylvania and Indiana, he narrowly lost to Hubert Humphrey who outspent him eight to one and had the frenzied support of organized labor. In the last primaries in Tennessee, North Carolina, Maryland, and Michigan—several of them held just after his shooting—he swept the field. His most stunning victory came in Michigan on the day after he was shot. He won 51 percent of the state's vote to George McGovern's 27 percent and Humphrey's 16 percent. Although he faded badly as news of his physical condition became known, at the time of his near assassination Wallace had polled 3.3 million votes to 2.5 million for Humphrey and 2.1 million for McGovern. Only his lack of political expertise prevented him from blocking McGovern's first-ballot nomination. In the ten primaries he entered, Wallace gained 3.5 million votes, but only 376 delegates; McGovern got 3.8 million votes in fourteen states, but he took nearly 700 delegates to the Miami convention.

In one of the ironies which George Wallace came to savor, he received his final defeat in 1976, of course, at the hands of an even more obscure Southern politician, Jimmy Carter. If he could never cross over into the Promised Land, at least he could—to mix Biblical metaphors—have the satisfaction of having been the John the Baptist of Southern Presidential aspirants.

There was never any likelihood that George Wallace would be nominated by the Democratic Party, or that he would succeed as a third party candidate. From 1964 to 1976, from 55 to 65 percent of the American people said they would *never* vote for Wallace. He did, however, become a major political voice of the sixties and early seventies and he certainly helped to shape the political agenda of the decade.

And that's the mystery. Just how did a small town segregationist politician from Barbour County, Alabama, emerge from regional obscurity in 1963, brush aside the *unanimous* contempt of the American intellectual, political and religious establishment, and establish a political base which would give him the consistent support (if not always the votes) of 15 to 22 percent of the American people during three presidential campaigns?

The first year between his inauguration in 1963 and his presidential campaign in 1964 was particularly critical. During that time he managed to position himself as a defender of Southern racism and, at the same time, to avoid acquiring the kind of explicitly overt racist aroma that surrounded men like Ross Barnett. It was a tumultuous year for Wallace and for the state of Alabama. It began with his fiery January inaugural speech attacking the federal government and promising "segregation now, segregation tomorrow, segregation forever." It was an inauguration speech which seemed to place Wallace side by side with a long tradition of Southern racial demagogues. That year ended with Wallace still breathing defiance, but successfully transcending the traditional restrictions of the Southern racist demagogue; no longer simply the spokesman of white Southerners, but the leader of a national movement for "constitutional government," poised to begin a race for the Democratic nomination for the presidency outside the old Confederacy.

Two Pivotal Events

There were many unexpected twists and turns in 1963, but there are two early moments in the progress of this Alabama pilgrim that seem particularly critical: Governor Wallace's stand in the schoolhouse door and his first major speech outside the South at Harvard University's Sanders Auditorium in November of 1963.

Wallace's performance in Tuscaloosa shows him at his most innovative as the ultimate practitioner of guerrilla politics. On paper, of course, the governor lost the battle. Despite all his promises of resistance to the end, his rhetoric about states' rights and Alabama-styled interposition, Vivian Malone and James Hood were enrolled. But three things stand out in my mind: first, by remaining elusive, by indirectly raising the threat of a repeat of the bloody 1963 confrontation in Oxford, Mississippi, Wallace kept the President and the Attorney General off balance and on the defensive. The transcript of Robert Kennedy's last-minute telephone call on

June 8, pleading with John Kohn and Cecil Jackson for some assurances from the Governor, are particularly revealing in that respect. In retrospect, they are not very flattering to Wallace, but they do show the trump card of threatened violence which he always held up his sleeve. As Burke Marshall later acknowledged, they were unwilling to do anything to put Wallace in a corner lest they have a repetition of the events in Oxford.

Second, by allowing the threat of violence to take center stage, Wallace set the parameters of the debate over his action. The Kennedy administration wanted to make the issue one of constitutionalism: the courts had spoken. It was up to the American people—it was particularly up to elected officials—to obey the orders of the Court. But most Alabamians—and many Americans—were so relieved when that violence was avoided that they tended to overlook the fact that it had all been caused by the fact that the Governor had been willing to play with fire in the first place.

Finally, Wallace already understood a central truth that would elude many of his critics for years: his followers were more interested in rhetoric than reality. As Marshall Frady observed in his biography of Wallace, it has "never been required of Southern popular heroes that they be successful. Indeed, Southerners tend to love their heroes more for their losses."[2]

The second moment came when Wallace boldly took his battle to the Philistines by scheduling his first major "non-Southern" speech at Harvard University's Sanders Auditorium in early November of 1963. The Governor carried a speech written by Grover Hall which was remarkable for its unabashed racism. The speech contained, without self-consciousness, the language of nineteenth-century racism. It gave the usual description of the horrors of Reconstruction, but it was supplemented with a bizarre explanation for the large number of light-skinned blacks in the South. They were the descendants of Yankee soldiers who had occupied the South, he insisted. While they were uppity and assertive, they were more capable and ambitious than the "full-blooded African Negro."

When northern liberals pointed to a handful of capable and talented blacks, declared the Wallace speech, they were always simply describing the mulatto minority whose white blood allowed them to make modest achievements: "When we speak of the Negro in the South, the image in our minds is that . . . of the easy-going, basically happy, unambitious African who constitutes 40 percent of our population. . . ." By age 12, according to Wallace, these full-blooded blacks were two years behind their white counterparts in intellectual development. By eighteen they lagged at least three years, and they would never develop much further.[3]

Such views were entirely consistent with Wallace's private feelings. He had a deep, visceral sense of grievance over the "persecution" the white South had suffered during Reconstruction. And he could be even more lurid in describing the effects of racial amalgamation. He warned a Canadian school teacher the previous month of the dangers of mongrelization, claiming that the "vast majority" of crime in Alabama was committed by blacks who were particularly prone to the most "atrocious acts of [inhumanity] such as rape, assaults and murder."[4]

This Wallace speech was published in the Montgomery *Advertiser* as though it were delivered intact. Bill Jones (who was present in Cambridge) included it without changes in his authorized initial biography of Wallace. But some instinctive antennae within Wallace led him away from this public expression of overt racism. When he delivered the Hall speech, he carefully excluded all the explicit references to black inferiority and concentrated upon the theme of constitutional oppression by a federal executive and judicial dictatorship. The folks back home could still be trusted to handle the raw meat of explicit racism, and Wallace made no public objection to the publication of the Hall speech in Alabama as if it were his own. For Yankees, however, (and later for Southerners as well) the horrors of racial integration had to be described with a series of code phrases which raised the specter of chaos and anarchy, but left it to the audience to imagine the racial context of that chaos and anarchy.

Wallace sensed a shift in national mood and he rode the crest of white backlash into the national limelight. When Lyndon Johnson took office in 1963, only 31 percent of the nation's adults felt that the federal government was pushing integration "too fast." By 1968, that figure had grown to more than 50 percent. From that moment on, white racial fear and hatred of blacks would remain a factor in the Wallace appeal. The governor had already begun to sense that—though there might not be many rednecks at Harvard University—there were an awful lot of Americans deeply concerned about the growing assertiveness of black Americans. Every poll in 1963 and 1964 showed that white backlash was a significant factor in the Wallace appeal outside the region and that appeal would increase in the decade to follow. To cite just one example: Wallace's stunning 1964 primary victory in Michigan (the day after his shooting in Maryland) can be explained primarily in terms of the Richmond, Virginia, federal court decision (later overturned) which called for the consolidation of inner school districts with those of suburban communities. (In that primary, Wallace drew as well in the white-collar suburban districts as in his expected blue-collar strongholds).

The enormous difference between a Wallace and a Ross Barnett was that Wallace—with the unerring instinct of the consummate politician for what will play and what won't—used a rhetoric of constitutionalism and a series of euphemistic code words—notably the emotion laden word "busing"—for his earlier overt racism.

The second thing that Wallace learned at Harvard was (as one of his advisers gleefully confided) just how "dumb those Yankees were." George Wallace learned that he could control and manipulate an audience in the heartland of the enemy as well as in Barbour County. The events from Foster Auditorium to Sanders Auditorium gave Wallace enormous self-confidence in his ability to carve out a national role.

The Range of Wallace Concerns

And he also learned that race was only one of the many emotional issues ripe for manipulation. While his Southern background was a handicap, his Alabama experiences made him particularly skillful at reaching beyond regional constituencies. Alabama, whatever its racist crudities, was not Mississippi. There were by Southern standards a substantial organized labor movement in the state and a vigorous tradition of working-class political activism. For more than one hundred years, yeoman farmers from northern Alabama had waged a political guerrilla war against the reactionary black belt gentry. Few other Southern states had furnished liberal politicans to match Hugo Black, "Big Jim" Folsom, Lister Hill, and John Sparkman. George Wallace was no Strom Thurmond, and his past support of New Deal liberalism (or "progressivism," as he preferred to call it) helped him reach out to blue-collar workers and disenchanted Democrats all over the nation; blue-collar workers who were not only concerned about race, but about unsettling change and a perilous future. The purchasing power of middle income and lower middle income voters rose 40 percent between 1947 and 1966 an average of more than 2 percent per year. But that steady ascension came to a stop between 1966 and 1972 when actual purchasing power went up less than 1½ percent. During these same six years, the federal government transferred approximately $121 billion to individuals living below the poverty line.

Had that amount been retained by individuals in low-middle and middle income brackets it would have added less than three-eighths of one percent in disposable income. But that was not how it was perceived. The slow-down, which had now turned into a decline in purchasing power, was unexpected by a working class accustomed to a rising standard of living. The poor, particularly the black non-working poor, became scapegoats. Each new social crisis of the 1960s and early 1970s was a ripe field waiting to be harvested. The war in Vietnam, for example, would furnish new sources of working class/middle American resentment. It was one of the contributory factors to inflation and the economic decline of the 1960s, but the real importance of the war was first perceived in cultural rather than economic terms. In fact, the war itself was never very popular with Wallace supporters despite the opportunity it offered for a crusade against Godless, atheistic Communism. Their quarrel was with an antiwar protest movement, led by privileged elites (or as Wallace said, "silver-spooned brats") who rejected a whole range of American cultural and religious values of which "patriotism" was at the core.

In some deep psychic fashion, resentment over what was seen as the liberal excesses of the antiwater demonstrators coalesced around a range of loosely connected concerns. Some were overt: the "decline" of the traditional cultural compass of God, Family and Country; a declension reflected in the drug crisis and rising crime rates, legalization of abortion, the rise in out-of-wedlock pregnancies, the increase in divorce rates, the Supreme Court's decision against school prayer, and the proliferation of "obscene" literature and films. And moving always beneath the surface was the fear that blacks were moving beyond their safely encapsulated ghettos into "our" streets, "our" schools, "our" neighborhoods.

Those fears were heightened by the precarious economic and cultural status of many of George Wallace's followers. Many, though certainly not all, the Wallace followers were, in the parlance of the social scientists, "alienated." Much like the Populists, for example, Wallace supporters—North and South—felt psychologically and culturally isolated from the dominant currents of American life in the 1960s. And, like the Populists, they were deeply embittered over the way in which respectable folk sniggered at their lack of cultural sophistication. No Wallace speech was complete without a defensive reference to how he and his supporters were "just as cultured and refined" as those "New York reporters."

All of this would lie in the future, but in the critical nine or ten months following his inauguration, George Wallace performed an extraordinary feat. He had succeeded in transcending his regional limitations. He might remain a racial demagogue to most opinion molders in the country and to the majority of Americans. A substantial minority of alienated Americans, however, had at last found a spokesman who would voice their fears, a man who would cut through the niceties of public debate and speak the unspeakable. One year after his inauguration, George Wallace was posed to unleash a new agenda in American politics. And once he transcended his regional/racial limitations, Wallace was in a position to exploit the fears and emotions of a deeply distempered society.

Molding a National Agenda

He was not alone. As early as 1966 and 1967, Wallace staffers drew upon the computer expertise of the Oklahoma evangelist Billy James Hargis's Christian Anti-Communist Crusade to develop their direct-mail fund-raising program. The portly Tulsa evangelist has long since been overshadowed by the success of Oral Roberts, the Bakkers, Jimmy Swaggert, and Pat Robertson. In the mid-1960s, however, he had 212 radio outlets and 12 television stations, and he was well on his way to becoming the first of the big time Christian broadcasters before being sidetracked by a personal scandal. Overshadowed by this fall from grace is the fact that Hargis was one of the first televangelists to grasp the way in which weekly doses of apocalyptic warnings accompanied by computer-generated "personalized" mailings could help charismatic demagogues tap the pocketbooks of frightened television viewers.

Reporters were often baffled in their efforts to understand how a small-time Alabama politician could mount massive (and expensive) Presidential campaigns. What seems now clear is that a major source of Governor Wallace's campaign kitty was precisely what he claimed: the hundreds of thousands of low- and middle-income Americans who mailed ten and twenty dollar contributions—usually in cash—to the permanent Wallace Campaign headquarters outside Montgomery. What appeared unbelievable to hard-boiled reporters in the 1960s and 1970s now seems commonplace in light of the fund-raising success of today's televangelists. But the connection between Wallace and the religious radical right was more than simply a matter of exchanging fund-raising techniques. Both shared a particularly radical way of viewing the world. For George Wallace—at least in his political rhetoric—had discovered the power of apocalyptic anti-communism.

Most historians have given little credence to the anti-communist rhetoric that dominated every aspect of Wallace's anti–civil rights rhetoric; they have simply regarded it as a cynical attempt to use the cold war hysteria of the period to discredit the Civil Rights Movement. But the Hargis/Wallace linkage is more than simply convenient rhetoric. It foreshadows the computerized, televised politics of the Moral Majority. That in turn is simply a modernized version of a well-established tradition in U.S. society which sees politics not as a conflict between different visions of the common good, but a moral tableau, a struggle between the forces of light and darkness: a religious crusade.

There is, of course, an inherent contradiction between the Wallace who railed against federal interference in one breath and demanded in the next that the government create mechanisms for controlling dissidents or "deviants" as Wallace would have described them, but the particular potency of rhetorical anti-communism lay in its ability—like other religious creeds—to transcend conventional logic.

On one level, of course, George Wallace's listing of villains at each rally was simply political theater; sometimes mildly comic—"These HEW bureaucrats can't park a bicycle straight but they're ready to tell you how to run your schools"; to darkly threatening—"There ain't nothing wrong with Judge Johnson that a good barbed wire enema wouldn't fix." At its most effect, however, there was an underlying apocalyptic tone to Wallace's rhetoric, which had the power to shape his viewers' emotions—their political cosmology. It was in some ways different—and yet in others quite similar—to the nineteenth century Southerners' mythology of the black beast, lurking in the shadows, waiting to destroy "our" white women—"our" culture. In the 1950s and 1960s it was no longer acceptable to talk about the black beast; it was, however quite the thing to talk about anarchists and bestial Communists.

To some degree Wallace was able to substitute a modern version in which political extremism—most vividly expressed in the rhetoric of anti-communism—fulfilled the same emotional and cathartic purposes of earlier rantings about black rapists. It was the "Communist" civil rights activist and their deluded sympathizers who were threatening everything in which decent Americans (not just Southerners) believed: the nation's religion, its culture, its women, its private property, its core sense of identity and security. Dissent against the war in Vietnam reinforced that perspective as new monsters of depravity were added to the pantheon of treason and cultural betrayal. Civil rights activists and antiwar dissenters—"liberals" in the new rhetoric of demonology—were not individuals to be politically outmaneuvered or defeated; they were demons who must be cast into the pit of darkness. Thus, the rhetoric of anti-communism had the power to bridge the gap between racism, apocalyptic religious fanaticism and the secular issues of government economic policy and foreign policy. What George Wallace did was to look out upon the disordered political landscape of the 1960s and give form to a nightmare. On the flickering television screen and in the giant political rallies he offered to frightened and insecure millions a chance to strike back—if only rhetorically—at the enemy. As almost every observer sensed, a Wallace rally was as much a religious exorcism as a political exercise.

Of course it is unfair to blame George Wallace for this anger, just as it is unfair to blame him for the distemper of the 1960s. Hysterical and irrational anti-communism has a long and venerable tradition in American society. The roots of the race riots of the decade, of the self-immolating war in Vietnam do not lie in Montgomery, and it is pointless to blame them on an ambitious politician who exploited cultural unrest.

The events of 1963 were built upon a tortured past and they were a prelude to an equally painful and difficult future. Most Americans are familiar with philosopher George Santayana's well-known quotation, "Those who cannot remember the past are condemned to repeat it." Too often this has been vulgarized into the simple-minded notion that Santayana accepted the existence of cyclical history and (like Thucydides) believed that the past was a reliable roadmap for the future. What he argued instead was that, without historical memory, we are at the mercy of forces we cannot understand, much as "children and barbarians, in whom instinct has learned nothing from experience."[5]

If our memory of these days, like any other recollection of the past, is not a comfortable guide to our future, there are certainly lessons to be learned if we would safeguard a society built upon democratic values. We must always be prepared to challenge the comfortable assumption that the defense of the status quo is patriotism and dissent is subversive (or even treasonable). And we must always be prepared to resist a civic culture in which dissidents and political opponents are reduced to the level of monsters of depravity. That was the path white Southerners followed in the aftermath of the Civil War in their struggle to maintain white supremacy and we are still living with the bitter consequences. In Alabama and elsewhere the creation of a Manichean political university—whether in the context of race or political ideology—strikes at the very foundations of our civil society.

SECTION II

Current Psycho-Socio-Cultural

Assessments of Prejudice and

Discrimination

5

A PSYCHOANALYTIC APPROACH TO THE PROBLEMS OF PREJUDICE, DISCRIMINATION, AND PERSECUTION

Mortimer Ostow, M.D.

Psychoanalysis, which presumes to explain, if not to cure, all deviations of human behavior, has been strangely silent about the phenomenon of prejudice. There have been studies, but they are relatively few in number, and most of them have been concerned with antisemitism, rather than prejudice in general. While some appeared before World War II, most were written—perhaps as expressions of gratitude for survival or of obligation—in response to the Holocaust. One may guess that interest was lost thereafter because the issues identified as relevant were disappointingly few and nonspecific.

Most of the psychoanalytic papers on prejudice phrased their findings in terms of conflict among the psychic agencies, id, ego, and superego, and emphasized residua of conflicts derived from the Oedipal phase of development. As a result, the explanations tended to be thin and stereotyped—and had nothing to say about why prejudice rather than a neurotic symptom evolved. Most authors subscribed to one form or other of the scapegoat theory: anxiety that arose as a result of unresolved conflicts, especially Oedipal conflicts, led to the victimization of others who were endowed with whatever undesirable traits the subject perceived in him or herself or in the Oedipal images that participated in the intrapsychic conflict.

But there are other reasons psychoanalytic therapy has failed to contribute much to the understanding of prejudice. By and large, psychoanalytic therapy does not attract prejudiced individuals. It represents to most people an attitude of openness, humanitarianism, egalitarianism, honesty, and trust, an attitude to which all psychoanalysts aspire if they do not consistently achieve it. Prejudiced people do not usually suffer from any desire to know that they have faults and weaknesses, nor to learn what they might be. Also, psychoanalysts try to purge themselves of prejudicial thoughts, although, as members of a community, they do not always succeed. To the extent that they share the prejudices of their patients, these prejudices do not attract therapeutic attention. They are treated as givens rather than issues that invite concern. Third, even when psychoanalysts do not share prejudices voiced by their patients, they seem to be reluctant to pursue the study of prejudice. Probably without realizing that they are doing so, they ignore it, minimize it, or deal with it perfunctorily, just as, for the most part, we avoid contaminating the analysis with political differences or differences in social outlook. For example, in Austria and Germany today, gentile psychoanalysts do not always easily deal with antisemitism in their patients. Some of the analysts are not entirely free of antisemitism themselves. Others share the problem of many of these patients, of hesitating to sympathize with the victims of antisemitism, when to do so would seem to affirm the guilt of their own parents.

My own thoughts about prejudice are largely derived from the deliberations of a psychoanalytic study group on antisemitism that I have had the privilege to chair for the past six years. The group consists of fifteen psychoanalysts, including both Jews and gentiles, and for several years a black analyst who was interested in the subject. Obviously, in the course of our studies of case histories of antisemitism and of the other primary materials to which we attended, the subject of prejudice in general was discussed. My comments here, to a large extent, derive from these discussions but do not purport to represent them.

Another introductory comment is appropriate at this point. Prejudice is a form of behavior that draws our interest because it is injurious to members of our community and dangerous to the community itself. It belongs, therefore, in the category of ethics. Since psychoanalysts deal with disease, it might be assumed that they see any phenomenon that they study as pathologic. Psychoanalytic studies of art, history, literature, and the products of human creativeness do not, in general, associate them with abnormality. Similarly, I would like to emphasize here that although we study prejudice in patients with one or another mental illness, we do not assume that the phenomenon itself represents psychic pathology. Although in our own patients prejudice frequently does give expression to pathologic behavior, it can, as well, serve to resolve unwholesome discord in individuals whom we would not necessarily label as mentally abnormal. What is immoral or unethical may be abnormal, but it often is not. We must keep our categories distinct.

Because prejudice is also a group phenomenon and psychoanalysis is a tool that studies individual psychology, psychoanalysis is not the ideal approach to the problem. However, what it does have to offer is indeed unique. While in the past psychoanalysts have tried to restrict their studies to individual behavior for which they had source material and a tested method of investigation, both the urgency of the problem and a greater confidence in our ability to extend our methods and to utilize more boldly what we have learned encourages us to attempt to explore interesting and dangerous phenomena that we have hitherto considered out of bounds. Accordingly, I shall devote the first and larger portion of my discussion to prejudice as an individual phenomenon, then present a brief discussion of the mutual influence of the individual and the group in promoting prejudice, and, finally, make a few comments on intergroup relations as an invitation to the further study of this problem by psychoanalysts.

At this point two illustrative case vignettes should be introduced.

Case A

Mr. *A*, a white American of Scottish Presbyterian origin, came for psychoanalytic treatment because of instability so profound and consistent that he had become a drifter, moving from place to place, unable to hold a job or secure an education. He felt shy with young women, but behaved like a tough hoodlum with men.

Early in adolescence he exhibited a need to associate with the more violent fringes of society and to ignore education. He reports having had severe temper tantrums in childhood, but the really uncontrolled behavior began with adolescence when violence of various kinds disrupted his life profoundly. He indulged in gambling, alcohol and drug abuse, and street brawling. He grew up in New York City, the son of an unusually successful father, who had made his fortune in investment banking, and an uninvolved mother. The father achieved his success by virtue of his aggressiveness and his courage and acumen in business, as well as a readiness to challenge, if not to transgress, the limits of the ethical and legal. He had always been a skillful athlete and a vigorous competitor in athletic games.

During what we call latency, that is, the interval between the ages of six and ten, which A attained during the 1930s, at an age when other contemporaries are involved with Superman, he found himself favorably interested in Hitler and the Nazis and espoused a vigorously antisemitic view. As he grew up his obsession with antisemitism continued and he was pleased with what he learned of Nazi persecution. Jews, he said, were slimy, dirty, and not trustworthy. However, he admitted that at one time he had had Jewish girl friends. His view of blacks and other minorities was no more favorable, but his obsession was with Jews and antisemitism. He knew that I was a Jew when he came to see me, but there were no non-Jewish analysts in the neighborhood in which we both lived.

The only sources of childhood distress that we encountered included the powerful and forceful impact of his father, the self-absorption of his mother, and some rivalry with siblings. He recalled childhood dreams of being injured while watching sports events.

His parents were prejudiced against Jews and other minorities, and didn't hesitate to express their prejudice, but it never became the central issue for them that it had for the patient.

My diagnosis was borderline personality disorder, a continuing disturbance of personality characterized by volatility, impulsiveness, self-defeating and self-destructive behavior, and inappropriate and immoderate aggressiveness.

Case B

Mr. B, a black American lawyer, sought psychoanalysis because of problems with aggressiveness and came to a white Jewish psychoanalyst simply because there were no black analysts in the neighborhood. He complained also of anxiety attacks. His irritability and belligerence created difficulties in his relations with colleagues and peers and in his social life, though when properly controlled, it made him a forceful advocate for his clients. In addition, he used alcohol and marijuana freely and had been apprehended for stealing in department stores.

The patient's mother died when he was three, but he soon came under the care of a loving stepmother when his father remarried. His anxiety started early in childhood and he recalls having had nightmares during childhood and adolescence in which he experienced falls from airplanes and crashes. Another possible source of distress during childhood was competitiveness with his stepbrother. Though not especially attractive, reality did not justify his profound conviction of being ugly. He had had Jewish friends in childhood.

B didn't trust whites, even those in the white law firm that employed him, and he provoked attacks by them upon himself. He felt strongly prejudiced against many other minorities, including both dark-skinned blacks and those whose skin was so light that they could pass for white. He participated actively and aggressively in black militant campaigns. But his greatest fury was directed at Jews, whom he considered ambitious, arrogant, exclusive, too intellectual, and too aggressive sexually.

Like *A*, he was shy sexually and confessed to entertaining erotic fantasies about white women.

B's parents were middle class professional people who had made their way successfully in the white world and expressed no prejudices at home.

In the case of *B*, my diagnosis again was borderline personality disorder, though he obviously functioned on a much higher level than *A*. The condition need not necessarily impair creativeness or prevent hard work, but it does cause a problem in the control of aggression.

Study of the Individual

One of the issues emphasized by using the psychoanalytic method is the transference. It is a commonplace of psychoanalysis that during the treatment the patient comes to view the psychoanalyst, at times, as a current version of either or both parents. At times the parents—and therefore the psychoanalyst—will appear in a benign and loving form, and at other times in a hateful and dangerous form.

What is of interest to us is that when the transference turns negative, that is, hostile, the patient, if he or she is of a different racial or ethnic group, may announce that hostility by expressing a prejudicial slur. Prejudicial comments will be expressed on the occasion of negative transference, which sometimes is induced as a defense against positive transference, not only in the case of patients known to have been prejudiced previously, but even among those who could not really be considered prejudiced. *B* made antisemitic comments directed toward me, at times when he found it necessary to deny, in fact to ward off, affectionate feelings for me. What we must infer from this quite common observation is that a recognition of difference has taken place and that differences may well be used when the occasion arises, to express suspicion, fear, or hostility. Merely a recognition of difference creates a potential for prejudice.

Consistent with that observation is its converse, that is, at moments when patients wish to express fondness for and appreciation of the analyst, they may make a favorable ethnic comment. For example, one gentile patient, under such circumstances, would remind me of his helpfulness to Holocaust survivors at the end of World War II.

A related observation deals with the fact that at the beginning of a psychoanalytic treatment many patients are apprehensive, not knowing what the treatment might entail by way of personal pain, and having little basis for trusting the analyst. To overcome this concern, patients might try to establish some area of common interest, including a hint of common ethnic origin, if it is common, or of favorable feeling toward the psychoanalyst's group, or even the expression of similar tastes or interests.

We must conclude that most people are usually aware of differences and similarities and will use them to express positive or negative feelings when an occasion invites such expressions. Prejudice may spring from normal and entirely unexceptional psychodynamic roots.

Psychoanalytic experience teaches us that many neurotic difficulties can be seen as reproductions of the child's Oedipal problems, that is, the inhibitions and anxieties, aggression and guilt that arise as the child finds him or herself in rivalry with one parent for the love of the other and seeks ways to avoid the detachment from one or the other that the rivalry might entail. A persisting tendency to resurrect and then resolve unresolved Oedipal rivalries may seize upon some realistic or imagined rivalry with another individual, and respond to it as though it were the original. Members of other ethnic groups, if they are involved in political, economic, social, or professional rivalries may then be disparaged nominally for their ethnic difference, but actually with the motivation derived from early experience.

For example, a gentile man undertook psychoanalysis because he had been unable to marry. The treatment involved the recovery of disturbing Oedipal memories from childhood, and he finally did fall in love with and became engaged to a young woman. Of course the inhibitions had not been completely resolved, and the patient retained reservations and anxieties. At one point during the engagement, he attended a dance with his fiancée. His neurotic ambivalence created the illusion that it was not he who desired to break the engagement; rather, it seemed to him that a Jewish friend of his was trying to seduce his fiancée away from him, just as it had seemed to him that he had once had to compete with his father for his mother. In his psychoanalytic session the next day, he referred to this friend disparagingly as a Jew.

In treatment, *A* described his view of himself as a vulnerable child who might be physically, and was verbally, abused by his father, and awed by the father's overbearing personality. He did not possess sufficient courage to identify with his father, and certainly not to oppose him. He saw Hitler's persecution of the Jews as the equivalent of his father's imagined threat to him, and he identified with Hitler in both triumph and defeat, projecting his own vulnerability and suspectibility to victimization onto the Jews.

Similar in some ways to Oedipal rivalry and jealousy is the phenomenon of sibling rivalry. Every parent is distressingly familiar with the fact that siblings compete initially, often bitterly, for the love of the parents, and subsequently the rivalry continues with respect to other desiderata, in some cases for a lifetime. The residua of this early rivalry may color and in fact exaggerate and introduce inappropriate acrimony into subsequent rivalries. They can often thereby convert ethnic distinction into ethnic prejudice.

These rivalries are not the only source of persisting anger and bitterness. There are residues of even earlier frustrations that children experience at the hands of their parents. Some children cannot tolerate the loss of the very early feeding experiences at mother's hands, or separation from mother at any point during childhood. Others cannot tolerate the demand that they control bowel and bladder, or defer to parental restriction and forgo infantile pleasures. These conflicts became internalized and continue to strive for resolution with substitute authorities in adult life. In all of these persisting conflicts, the ethnic rival may be portrayed as either the self-indulgent, rebellious child, or as the heartless parent. The self-indulgence may take the form of accusations, for example in the words of *A*, unbridled sexuality, avarice, being "slimy and dirty." As a prohibiting or denying parent, the rival may be accused of harshness and vindictiveness, excessive zeal in the pursuit of justice, immoderate ambition, efforts to obtain control of the community or country or world. He or she is the creditor demanding a "pound of flesh". In the words of *B*, the black lawyer, Jews are "ambitious, arrogant, aggressive, exclusive and excessively intellectual and sexually forward." It seems likely that much of *B*'s anger against rivals, both white and black, derived from fury caused by the experience of abandonment on the occasion of his mother's death when he was three and subsequent rivalry with the stepsibling.

Antisemitic prejudice frequently involved accusing the Jews of physical violence including bloodshed, and of being themselves creatures of "impure blood." With respect to physical violence, its origin and justification in the minds of the antisemite might be associated with the animal sacrifice of the Jewish Bible, the religious practice of circumcision, the story of the prohibited sacrifice of Isaac, and the repeated prohibitions of infanticide. The accusation of the tendency to bloody violence has found expression in the legend of Jewish responsibility for the crucifixion, blood libels, accusations of the violation of the Host, accusations of poisoning the wells, accusations that Jewish physicians poison their patients, and accusations in nineteenth- and twentieth-century Germany, as well as in sixteenth-century Spain, that Jews are of "impure blood." With such calumnies, antisemites have tried to achieve control of their own savagery, that is, their own responses to distress generated internally, or by external conditions, by projecting that savagery out on to the Jews, and then indulging it on the Jews as victims. Blood is the symbol for vicious aggressiveness.

Blood is used as a basis for anti-black prejudice too. Even during World War II, black and white blood for transfusions were segregated. In South Africa, a calculus of dilution of black blood is used to determine degree of segregation in the non-white population, much as it was used to justify racial antisemitism in sixteenth-century Spain and in Nazi Germany.[1]

There is another dynamic that is often encountered in individual psychology that, although not restricted to the phenomenon of prejudice, is nevertheless associated with it. Many children at one time or another wish that they had parents other than their own—that they were members of another family. Some of them even imagine that they were in fact adopted by their present parents. Usually the other family is grander in some way, more desirable than the actual family, more noble, wealthier, more loving. Freud referred to this phenomenon as a "family romance" fantasy. Family romance relates to our subject because the desired family frequently belongs to a social, religious, or economic group that is recognized as different by the actual family. The actual family is prejudiced in favor of or against the desired family that is idealized by the child.

I have found that in many instances of voiced antisemitic comments the individual had on some previous occasion extended him or herself in friendship to a particular Jew, or to Jews in general. I would not have been surprised to encounter that finding from time to time, but its regularity has surprised me. We find it not only among psychoanalytic patients from the Northeastern United States, but fairly generally, including historical figures such as Luther and the Abbe Gregoire, as well as in myths and novels.[2]

The phenomenon is likely to be seen among either of two groups of children. First, children who grow up adventurous and courageous, confident of the love of their parents, free to associate affectionately with strangers, attempt thereby to escape the inhibitions associated with the Oedipus complex. Second, children who seek surrogate parents because their own are found to be unavailable, whether physically or emotionally, may also be attracted to anyone, including strangers. The first group of children frequently give up their flirtation with strangers if they begin to feel guilty about having abandoned their parents, or if some crisis makes them feel obligated to reunite with their parents, or if they feel that they have not been welcomed by their surrogate family. The second group will turn more vigorously against their foreign friends for similar reasons, or simply because of the same emotional instability that induced them to turn toward them in the first place.

I should like to suggest, as a general proposition, that when two groups live in a community side by side, there is a tendency for some of the more adventuresome or accommodating members of each to make contact with and engage the members of the other. This tendency becomes stronger as either group prospers and its members become more confident and courageous. Contrariwise, when circumstances create a feeling of despair or even discouragement and retreat, the centrifugal tendency is replaced by a centripetal one. The centrifugal tendency becomes manifest in personal engagement between individuals in the one group with those of the other. Such engagement finds expression in friendships, business ventures, and common projects, to the accompaniment of an idealization by each group of the other, and increased erotic attraction between the members of the one group and appropriate potential sexual partners among the members of the other. Both A and B engaged, at times, in sexual adventures with Jewish women. What I am saying here is that prejudice has two faces. The recognition of difference can lead to affiliation and fraternization, or to antagonism. When the opportunity exists, we may find an alternation between the xenophilic and xenophobic tendencies, determined in part by the mood of each of the individuals at the boundary between the groups, and by the mood of the two adjacent societies. The phenomenon that I have just described prevails at the borders along which groups communicate with each other. I would guess that the same tendencies may prevail in centers remote from the borders, though attenuated in proportion to their remoteness.

To summarize, studies of the psychodynamics of prejudice disclose that the dynamic bases of prejudice do not differ from the psychodynamics of relations among individuals in general. Prejudice turns out to be only one of the many ways in which conflicts strive to find resolution, whether in the context of normal psychodynamic adjustment or in the context of pathogenic processes.

We find that prejudice and the discriminatory actions that it may entail will be favored by two factors, the degree of aggression liberated by a conflict and the social sanction given to prejudice. The aggression may be elicited by external stress, or it might be liberated in conflict and externalized.

Aggression and Prejudice

While not all aggressive people are prejudiced, when prejudice does exist its intensity and the likelihood that it will be accompanied by discriminatory or even persecutory behavior seem to vary directly with the degree of aggression that the individual is called upon to control. Both *A* and *B* illustrate the relation of prejudice to poorly controlled aggression. When the aggression is adequately controlled, it might find discharge in non-pathologic ways and in prejudicial and discriminatory behavior within limits sanctioned by society. When it is not adequately controlled it might give rise to pathologic behavior and discrimination beyond that sanctioned by the community.

While prejudice can be driven by aggression derived from any kind of conflict, one particularly virulent source of aggression seems explicitly relevant not only to prejudice, but also to discrimination and especially to persecution. That is the fantasy of apocalypse. The classical pattern of apocalypse, as it is found in religious scriptures, anticipates that the world and its contents will be destroyed, but that a worthy remnant of the population will be selected to be saved. They will be reborn into a life of eternal bliss. The apocalyptic pattern appears in the fantasies of schizophrenic patients, and in the dreams of many individuals, especially schizophrenics and patients with borderline personality disorder, as well as manics, depressives, and even many people seemingly without mental disorder. I consider apocalypse a virulent source of aggression because it is my impression that it is invoked as a corrective measure on those occasions when the degree of affective charge or motivational energy threatens to escape from its normal range, to rise either too high or fall too low. In the former instance, a manic or schizophrenic breakdown may ensue; in the latter, a breakdown into inert depression, depressive excitement, or another variant of schizophrenia. In clinical practice, when we encounter this prospect, we can administer corrective medication, which will limit primary or corrective excursions and so either prevent or undo mental illness. Normal individuals who sustain such anomalous oscillations unconsciously apply a moderate and appropriate intrapsychic correction.

The apocalyptic mechanism doesn't create the aggression; it focuses it and finds discharge paths, with the apparent purpose of protecting the subject from his or her own anger, but it does not always succeed in doing so. When the motivational energies rise excessively, the corrective depletion of energies is experienced as a painful blow, a profound loss and threat. In some instances, the pain is so great that the individual automatically withdraws from reality and replaces it with delusional fantasies. That is the mechanism of many cases of psychosis. In such instances, the individual feels attacked or persecuted by an adversary, selected from the real world, from myth, or from fantasy. In other instances, the emphasis is on the effect of these attacks on the individual's self-esteem. The individual becomes aware of various failings, physical, moral, intellectual and social, and puts these self-criticisms into the mouths of other people, whether real or fantasied, and displaces the defects onto others. "It is not I who am homosexual; it is my friend." In other words, as a result of the operation of this corrective mechanism, the affected individual feels pain, which he or she attributes to two sources, an inferred persecutor who attacks the individual, and the individual him or herself whose faults are laid bare. In most instances of individual psychosis, either or both sources are projected onto others who are then seen as dangerous. If the degree of internal misery is great enough, the patient who is impulsive enough may suicide or may murder the individual accused of persecution or the person who bears his or her faults.

Apocalyptic fantasies may be generated also when emotional energies fall too low, either as a result of miscarried inner corrective maneuvers, or as a result of externally imposed humiliation and oppression. In some instances, low energy induces inert depression; in others, it elicits furious, defiant apocalyptic attacks on an enemy, actual or imagined.

Why are these considerations relevant to the subject of prejudice? In most instances of psychosis the targets for these projections are selected from the psychotic person's own group and immediate environment. In some instances, however, psychotic people borrow the prejudices that prevail in their society at the time and select members of a denigrated group as their persecutors, or as the bearers of their defects, or both. The prejudices of psychotic patients would seem to be of little interest to our concern with prejudice in general, because a psychotic almost always operates as an individual and therefore has little power. However, the phenomenon does, in fact, deserve our scrutiny. The psychodynamic mechanism involved, though here associated with gross pathology, seems to apply also to prejudice that occurs in non-clinical situations. Second, a dynamic similar to that of acute psychosis prevails in many individuals over long periods of time. Many individuals who are not psychotic nevertheless experience corrective internal arrests of affective motivation and interpret them as hostile acts imposed by enemies. The phenomenon occurs most explosively and dramatically in the group designated as instances of borderline personality disorder, a condition characterized, as mentioned above, by volatility, exaggerated mood swings, and a tendency to perform self-defeating and self-injurious acts. I do not know whether the apocalyptic dynamic occurs universally, but I should not be surprised to learn that it does. When it occurs, one attempts to externalize both the internal self-defeating agent, and the self that is labeled as faulty and defective.

Non-psychotic individuals do not have the privilege of indulging in personal delusions with respect to specific antagonists, but frequently borrow the prejudices and biases of the community in which they live and adopt the designated enemies of that community as their own enemies. Such individuals require two enemies: one is the person or persons held responsible for feelings of deprivation and emptiness, and the other is the person or persons who, similar to a scapegoat, carry the defects and faults that the individual perceives in him or herself as a result of the operation of the self-limiting and self-critical homeostatic mechanism. Either or both of these influences, the dangerous and the shameful, are attributed to the enemy. As a result, the enemy may be subjected to virtually incompatible accusations. Jews, for example, are accused of mounting a conspiracy to take control of the whole world, whether as international capitalists or international communists, and simultaneously they are denounced as degenerate, as filth, and as sources of contamination and disease to the vulnerable Christians. Blacks, similarly, are accused of endeavoring to rape white women and steal from white men, and simultaneously they are denounced as lazy, ineffectual, and diseased.

A feature of apocalypse that makes it especially dangerous is that, by virtue of its claim that the existing world is being destroyed to be replaced by a new reality, it preempts individual conscience and overcomes moral resistance to savagery. When apocalypse achieves ascendancy in a person's life, prejudice, discrimination, and persecution may assume the role of a determining and irresistible governing force, an imperious idealogy.

To summarize what we have said so far, a psychoanalyst who scrutinizes prejudiced patients finds that the intensity of the prejudice and its tendency to seek discharge in manifest discrimination and virulent persecution can be correlated with the intensity of aggressive energies that seek discharge. The aggressive energies themselves may be generated in response to external stress or injury, especially humiliation. But in many instances they are elicited by the conflicts that complicate and frustrate loving desires and attachments, and in the case of apocalyptic complexes, by the need to contain excessive excursions of the intensity of libidinal energies.

However, we have not dealt with the problem of the choice of the object of prejudice. I mentioned that the psychotic individual designates as an enemy the one or more individuals whom he or she conceives as threatening, usually from among the group of family or other intimates, though occasionally such an individual may select a stranger. People who are not psychotic are not so far removed from reality that they will entertain frank solipsistic delusions, but they will adopt the prejudices of the community to which they belong—a common delusion, which the authority of the group can sanction as real. Note that B found sanction for this anti-white and anti-Jewish attitudes in his community, while A, not finding sanction for his violent fantasies at home, made common cause with a foreign doctrine and its supporters.

The Individual and the Group

When discussion of prejudice comes up in psychoanalytic treatment, and one asks the source of the prejudice, patients invariably discuss prejudices heard from their parents. (One reason for their doing so is that psychoanalysts always try to understand the beginning of a specific form of behavior, perhaps more frequently than justified, inferring that the first experience caused all subsequent experiences. Post hoc propter hoc. My own position about this issue is that the first may indeed be the formative episode, but there is no way to prove that it is not merely the first of a series, rather than their cause in the etiologic sense.) Parents do usually transmit their prejudices to their children. They discuss prejudical attitudes in family conversation. They encourage certain friendships of their children and discourage others. They exhibit discrimination in whom they invite to their homes as their own or their children's guests. Although in their earliest years, children will not dispute their parents' prejudices, because they consider them the givens of the real world, they may evaluate them as they grow into adolescence. Compliant children will observe them. Rebellious children will reject them and adopt opposite attitudes. Independent children try to evaluate them in terms of their own social and political views, and act accordingly. A's parents voiced prejudice against Jews and other minorities, and A identified with them in these prejudices, but made an obsession of them. B's parents did not voice prejudice, but he identified with a community of militant contemporaries.

Although psychodynamics, for all of their dealing with the same basic issues, differ greatly from one individual to another, it is nevertheless striking how closely stereotypes of prejudice, harbored by different people, resemble each other and the mythologic stereotypes promoted by the society in which the various individuals live. Group influence overrides individual differences.

Clearly we will not make much progress in understanding prejudice without examining the mutual relation and influence of the individual and his or her community. Generalizing, we are led to infer that group pressures have to be reckoned among the most powerful sources of prejudicial sentiment and behavior. But we also learn that it is individual psychic need and disposition that determines how individuals respond to group pressure: whether they embrace it as an opportunity to satisfy one or another of their own congruent needs; whether they accept the influence, not because it offers anything directly gratifying to them, but because they must feel completely at one with the community; or whether they disapprove of the group movement and resist its influence out of conviction.

An important aspect of this interrelation struck me with particular force. At the 1985 Congress of the International Psycho-Analytic Association, the first since World War II to be held on German soil, the plenary session dealt with the Nazi phenomenon. One of the presentations focused on a case report of a young woman who was the daughter of an important Nazi official.[3] It was the intent of the author to demonstrate that the patient resembled and might be said to have identified with her father in some behavior traits and in her mourning for the lost Nazi paradise. She exhibited a number of the characteristics of borderline personality disorder: brief attacks of psychosis, sado-masochistic fantasies, self-defeating behavior, and a general bizarre presentation. Some of her fantasies, locutions, and dreams indicated the operation of an apocalyptic mechanism.

As I prepared my discussion of the case,[4] I realized that the patient shared with the Nazi society in which she grew up the apocalyptic fantasy that from cruelty and devastation a rebirth of utopian bliss for the German people would ensue. Her analyst reported that since she was aware that her fantasies were so bizarre, she sought confirmation of them in literature. I soon realized that she sought confirmation also in the myths of the Nazi society. As a result I drew a number of inferences of some interest to our subject. The Nazi phenomenon acted out an apocalyptic scenario: devastation on a global scale in the hope of achieving paradise for themselves. The vicious persecution of Jews, Gypsies, homosexuals, communists, and others effected a partial discharge of the violence that was generated by what was happening in the society, probably humiliation and privation, and that was focused by the apocalyptic fantasy. It is apocalypse that makes the difference between prejudice and persecution.

As events worked themselves out, it became clear that the destruction of these especially singled out enemies preempted enough of the available energy, material, and manpower of Germany to have significantly impeded the war effort. The patient's apocalyptic fantasies and those of the Nazi society were congruent. She looked to the myths of that society to validate her own. I think the same can be said for *A*. His borderline fantasies of unbridled aggression were inappropriate in our society but were sanctioned and validated by the Nazi apocalyptic theory that he embraced. When a socially shared apocalypse is presented by the leaders of a society, it mobilizes and validates the congruent fantasies of many members of that society.

It is obviously not valid to draw extensive inferences from a single case. Not all of the disturbed patients in psychoanalytic treatment in present day Germany and Austria who continue to harbor antisemitic sentiments do so out of identification with the apocalyptic myths of the Nazi regime. Some, out of a sense of obligation to their parents, merely find it difficult to hold them culpable. Yet the following questions suggest themselves for consideration: is it true in general that members of a society are attracted to and adopt those of its myths that match the individual's personal myths? By what process and under what conditions do the myths of individuals become the myths of society and vice versa? Under what circumstances do socially sponsored prejudices become active to the point of becoming persecution, and under what circumstances are they suppressed? This question is based upon the common observation that the intensity of overt sponsorship of prejudice and the degree of its escalation into persecution change from time to time in each society.

With respect to the cultivation of prejudice in groups, observations by colleagues who treat children and adolescents support the following propositions. Starting between ages six and seven, that is, at the time of the decline in the overt manifestations of the Oedipus complex, children tend to organize into cliques and groups. They can then be observed to disparage non-members of their own group as bearers of faults and flaws that they unconsciously perceive in themselves, faults of body, mind, and character. The outsider becomes the object of prejudice. Since group membership, even at such an early age, is based upon perceived similarities, such as a common residence, language, religion, appearance, the resulting prejudice is directed against those who fail to qualify for group membership because they are different.

During adolescence, group formation becomes even more important since the social group serves to support the adolescent taking the first steps to disengage from family and affiliate with the general community. If an adolescent's relation with his or her family is relatively unconflicted, the group that he or she joins at first may resemble in its qualities the family of origin. The choice will be xenophobic. If, on the other hand, an adolescent's relation with his or her family is conflicted, and the disengagement painful, difficult, and ambivalent, the adolescent may seek out for support groups that represent strangers or enemies with respect to the family. The choice will be xenophilic. Therefore the family's prejudices will be preserved in the first case and flaunted in the second. Both *A* and *B*, as adolescents and adults, identified with the central ethnic interests of their respective families, but in their efforts to find sanction and channels for discharge of their own internally generated aggression, identified also with more aggressive groups that were foreign and inimical to their families' basic values.

Who becomes a group leader, the several types of leadership, the relation of the individual member to the leader—these are all subjects that demand study. Under what circumstances does the desire for group unity overcome competitive striving for dominance?

Intergroup Vicissitudes

In our discussion of the relation between the prejudices of the individual and the group we have considered mechanisms whereby the individual and the group could influence each other. How do groups develop and resolve prejudices with respect to each other?

This book itself makes one of the first points that we must acknowledge. Its purpose is to mark and celebrate the remarkable change in our public attitude toward prejudice, the reversal from promoting and encouraging it to deploring it. It would be a mistake to infer, however, that we are on a course of steady improvement, a one-way journey to utopian perfection. In the past, not only has the attitude toward strangers, both specific strangers and strangers in general, fluctuated from time to time, from generation to generation, but the attitude toward prejudice itself has undergone vicissitudes. The golden age of Spanish Jewry was followed by the Inquisition, and the emancipation of the Jews in central Europe was followed a century later by the Holocaust. We, in present day America, have been emerging from a long history of bigotry. Our current attitude, celebrating democratic pluralism, has been shaped partially in reaction against the apocalyptic horrors of the Holocaust and partially by the relative prosperity of the post–World War II American economy.

One cannot assume that this attitude will continue indefinitely. Racist movements continue to appear and to attract adherents. What Adlai Stevenson called "the revolution of rising expectations,"[5] the greater militance of formerly persecuted minorities as they finally achieve emancipation, encourages a stubborn and persistent reactionary element to resist the egalitarian tide. What we consider right and ethical and good changes with our circumstances and finds community sanction in contemporary community consensus.

It would be appropriate to discuss here the response of target populations to prejudice, discrimination, and persecution, to the humiliation that they induce which is even more painful than material deprivation, and the counter-prejudice, fury, and apocalyptic defiance that they generate, particularly at the time of emancipation, as in the case of B. It is difficult to prevent prejudice from engendering reactive prejudice in a persistent vicious cycle, reinforcing boundary fortifications from both sides.

Each of the attitudes of society is reflected and finds support and sanction in the myths of that society. A myth is a story that justifies our beliefs and attitudes. The personal myths that we each devise and treasure rationalize our lives and we credit them. It is in the course of a psychoanalytic therapy or some other revealing experience that we begin to scrutinize them critically and perhaps recognize their mythic quality. Social myths are credited, probably at the time of their origin. Subsequently, when they become irrelevant, they cease exerting a determining influence on the behavior of the group. However, since they continue to serve at least a unifying purpose by attracting common commitment, they are permitted to survive, sometimes in the guise of children's tales, only to be revived as serious presentations of the "truth" when circumstances change and their motivating influence again becomes useful. A most mischievous and deadly legend that justifies and provokes prejudice, discrimination, and persecution is the legend of the responsibility of the Jews for the crucifixion of Jesus. At the time of the writing of the Gospels that record it, it was contrived in order to disparage and condemn the Jewish community that did not accept the new religion. It has subsequently been exploited whenever Christian antisemitism was promoted, and it has been amplified and reinforced by similar myths, such as the various blood libels and conspiracy accusations mentioned above. One antisemitic man recalls vividly coloring a picture of Christ being crucified by the Jews, in a coloring book at Sunday school.

Various practical and material considerations obviously play a role in many situations of prejudice, for example, competition in business, trade or commerce, and the profit from one group's enslaving another. Such motives scarcely require psychologic explanations and probably suffice to explain prejudice persisting over long periods of time in a community. Obviously economic self-interest played a major role in the American practice of slavery and in the devaluation and exploitation of blacks after their emancipation. Yet it would be an error to overlook the psychic mechanisms that exploit these motives in many people, even in the absence of any degree of psychopathology. In the case of B., the real prejudice and discrimination that he did encounter only fed the countervailing racial hostility that was driven by the aggression that arose internally and pervaded and poisoned his whole life.

Frederick Durrenmatt, in his remarkable play *The Visit*, portrayed the corruption of a community, the creation of a murderous prejudice by the promise of large sums of money. Durrenmatt wrote primarily of greed and its rationalization but did not demonstrate how they articulated with more subtle and complex forms of prejudice.

Freud, in his attempt to examine social phenomena from the point of view of psychoanalysis, made the explicit assumption that group behavior resembles individual behavior in the sense that similar mechanisms prevail, and in the sense that historical origins influence subsequent destiny.[6] (I think that assumption should be considered unproven in the absence of clear cut substantiation. However, we are not necessarily inhibited from considering the possible consequences of such assumptions being correct.) For example, can one consider the consistent antipathy of the Church toward the Jews over two millennia, an expression of rivalry, much as two individuals could maintain a lifetime rivalry based upon conflicting interests? If so, would it compare with sibling rivalry, Christianity as the younger sibling that sees itself supplanting its elder as the Church leaders would have it? Or could it more accurately be compared with Oedipal rivalry in which Christianity, the son religion, displaces Judaism, the father religion? These are interesting analogies, and perhaps even homologies. Perhaps how it is regarded by the individual or the group depends upon its sensitivities to the one or to the other fantasy.

A common mechanism is easily visible in many persisting group prejudices. I refer to the need to label the victim of the prejudice as an outsider, a stranger, so that as such, the natural fear of the stranger will be mobilized in order to support the prejudice. It is not that the other is designated an enemy because he is a stranger, but that he is designated as a stranger in order to encourage prejudice. The stigma is a case in point. In the effort to distinguish the enemy from one's own group, attention is drawn to differentiating characteristics. Some are made up in order to create a fictitious but prejudicial image: Jews have horns, tails; Jewish men menstruate. Others are imposed as visible labels: Jews were made to wear distinctive hats in medieval times or yellow badges in the Nazi era. Natural differentiating characteristics are emphasized where they exist, such as skin color, physiognomy, or stature.

The stigma and the various accusations, both those that assert that the stranger is a murderous threat, and those that disparage the stranger as unworthy and subhuman, together constitute the stereotype that is necessary to complement the prejudice. The image of the beast, a favorite stereotype accompanying many prejudices, combines these two elements, power and inhumanity.

These comments are meant to serve as an introduction to a psychodynamic theory of mutual relations among contiguous groups that needs to be created.

Conclusion

Prejudice, by which we mean one person's devaluing another and assigning to him hostile intentions, and its escalation to discrimination and persecution serve to deflect from one individual to his neighbor, and from one community to its neighboring community, the aggressive energies that are triggered by painful internal dynamic operations, or externally imposed frustrations and humiliations. We have discussed prejudice as it occurs in normal life, prejudice generated or encouraged by distressing and sometimes pathogenic internal or external influences, and prejudice as the expression of a pathologic need.

Sanction for the cultivation of prejudice and selection of its targets is provided by the community which is influenced by its current circumstances and by its mythic history.

Prejudice, and its derivatives, will not be permanently overcome so long as the human remains susceptible to psychic pain, so long as human societies reflect the pain of their members, and so long as conscience is hostage to sentiment. Since standards and values and attitudes change continually, it would seem to me that the best hope lies in prohibition of such behavior at times such as these, when prejudice is rejected almost universally, inscribed firmly and permanently in the written constitution of every society, where it might perhaps withstand the seductions and threats of what will certainly be recurrent challenges.

6

SCHOOL DESEGREGATION
Short-Term and Long-Term Effects

Walter G. Stephan

Does segregation of children in public schools solely on the basis of race, even though the physical facilities and other "tangible" factors be equal, deprive children of the minority group of equal educational opportunities? We believe it does . . . [T]o separate Negro school children from others of similar age and qualifications solely because of their race generates a feeling of inferiority as to their status in the community that may affect their hearts and minds in a way unlikely ever to be undone . . . We conclude that in the field of public education the doctrine "separate but equal" has no place. Separate educational facilities are inherently unequal.

With these words in the 1954 *Brown* Supreme Court decision, Chief Justice Earl Warren set in motion the train of events that led to George Wallace's stand in the schoolhouse door. Whatever else that stand was— and most accounts of his behavior suggest that there were many items on his agenda, including fulfilling a campaign promise, standing up for states' rights, and playing to a national political audience—it was a stand against desegregation.

We can get a sense of Wallace's attitudes toward desegregation from his tape-recorded conversations with Robert Kennedy on April 26, 1963, six weeks before the event. Wallace said that he thought it was wrong for the courts to "force upon the people that which they don't want, . . . I will never submit myself voluntarily to any integration of any school system in Alabama . . . there is no time in my judgment when we will be ready for it—in my lifetime, at least." He also said, "You just can't have any peace in Alabama with an integrated school system." Later in this conversation he added, "We people feel that eventually this whole effort is going to bring a breakdown [in peace and goodwill] between the races." At the end of their conversation he made his feelings known in clear and simple terms, "I think integration is bad. I don't think it is good . . . I just don't believe in educational mixing . . . It creates disorder."[1] In a campaign brochure he had written that integration is "foreign to our way of life and disruptive of the peace and tranquility of our citizens."

It is reasonable to ask who was right here, Chief Justice Warren or Governor Wallace. Did desegregation bring about the benefits anticipated by the Chief Justice, or did it bring about the racial chaos anticipated by the Governor? The social science evidence that has accumulated in the twenty-five years since Wallace's stand can help to answer this question. But before pursuing this question in detail, it would be useful to describe exactly what the social scientists who participated in the *Brown* case expected desegregation to accomplish, because their thinking underlay the reasoning behind the Chief Justice's unanimously supported opinion. A status report on the state of desegregation in this country will then be presented, along with an evaluation of the social scientists' predictions concerning the short-term effects of desegregation using the available social science studies. After this, the chapter will review the long-term effects of desegregation and will discuss briefly the techniques that have been developed to improve race relations in the schools. It will end by summarizing the accumulated evidence from the perspective of opponents and supporters of desegregation.

The Social Scientists' Predictions

Two important elements of the social scientists' argument in the *Brown* case are well captured in the opinion of Judge Huxman in the original *Brown* case in Kansas before the case was appealed to the Supreme Court. In his opinion he wrote, "Segregation of White and colored children in the public schools has a detrimental effect upon the colored children. The impact is greater when it has the sanction of law; for the policy of separating the races is usually interpreted as denoting the inferiority of the Negro group. A sense of inferiority affects the motivation of the child to learn. Segregation with the sanction of law, therefore, has the tendency to retard the educational and mental development of Negro children and to deprive them of the benefits they would receive in a ra-cial[ly] integrated school system."[2]

Judge Huxman had accepted the social scientists' arguments that seg-regation causes feelings of inferiority among black children and that it reduces their achievement levels. The third element of the social scien-tist's argument was that segregation fostered negative race relations be-cause it supported whites' beliefs that they were superior and it caused blacks to resent their inferior treatment. The social scientists' thought these three elements, feelings of inferiority among blacks, low achieve-ment by blacks, and negative race relations were interrelated in a vicious circle.

The vicious circle started with the fact that white prejudice was respon-sible for creating segregation. This segregation then led to low self-esteem and low achievement among black students. The low self-esteem and low achievement, combined with resentment over segregation and the inade-quate facilities provided to them, fed black prejudice against whites. And black prejudice and hostility toward whites was then used by whites to justify their prejudices and the policy of segregation, thus completing the circle. It was expected that desegregation would break this vicious circle. Specifically, it was expected that desegregation would lead to increases in black achievement, increases in black self-esteem, and more favorable relations between the races.

Wallace's argument speaks most directly to the third prediction. He believed that desegregation would lead to a deterioration of relations between the races. Similarily, as recently as the late 1970s, white parents in Los Angeles expected desegregation to increase discipline problems, risk the safety of students, and increase racial tensions, and they did not expect it to improve minority or white education or reduce prejudice.[3] All three predictions will be evaluated using the available social science evidence, with an emphasis on race relations.

Effects of Desegregation

This review depends heavily on studies that have attempted to quan-tify the effects of desegregation on achievement, self-esteem, and race-relations. These studies can be combined to create a view that is greater than can be achieved by any single observer—although denying the validity of each individual's experience is not intended or desired. At its best, social science yields a relatively objective view of the overall picture. However, in interpreting these findings one must bear in mind their limitations. The meaning of these studies depends on the measures that were used, the care and skill with which these measures were administered, the contexts in which they were obtained, the samples that were obtained, the region of the county in which the studies were conducted, the types of desegregation plans that were examined, the age of the students, the racial composition of the communities, the amount of opposition to desegregation in these communities, and such things as whether adequate control groups were used. The most complete picture possible will be drawn, noting the specific limitations applying to the studies as they are presented.

The State of School Desegregation

After the 1954 Supreme Court decision in *Brown,* desegregation moved at a virtual snail's pace for the next decade. Indeed, at the end of this decade the Supreme Court caustically commented, "There has been entirely too much deliberation and not enough speed."[4] There were some acrimonious confrontations between the federal government and local school districts and state governments, most notably in Little Rock, Mississippi, and of course at The University of Alabama. Still, by 1964 only 1 percent of black school children were attending desegregated schools. School districts in the South attempted a wide variety of evasion and delaying tactics to avoid desegregation. However, with the passage of the Civil Rights Bill in 1964, the federal government had a weapon it could effectively use to force some compliance with the law—namely the power of the purse. The Civil Rights Bill empowered the federal government to cut off federal funds to school districts that were not in compliance with the Supreme Court's order.

Through the use of this statute, desegregation took place at a rapid rate during the second decade after *Brown.* Nearly all of the desegregation that has occurred in this country happened during the decade between 1964 and 1974. By 1972, 44 percent of black children in the South were attending schools that were majority white, while in the North 29 percent of black children were attending such schools.[5] These increases in desegregation came at some cost to black teachers and administrators, a substantial number of whom lost their jobs when segregated black schools were closed, although blacks in more recent years seem to have made up for these losses.[6] Also, as desegregation plans began to be implemented a disproportionate number of black students were suspended or expelled from school in some school districts.[7]

In the third decade after school desegregation began, a few highly visible desegregation cases were prosecuted, in Boston for instance, but typically only one or two new school districts initiated desegregation each fall.[8] However, this new desegregation was nearly balanced by the resegregation of a substantial number of school districts due to changing demographic patterns, in particular the suburbanization of whites and the higher birth rate of minority groups.

The most recent statistics on desegregation were presented in a report in 1987 by the U.S. Commission on Civil Rights.[9] This report indicates that in 1980, 70 percent of black students were attending school with some whites (at schools more than 5 percent white), although many of these schools were not racially balanced. In contrast, almost exactly the same percentage of whites (69 percent) had little or no exposure to blacks (attended schools that were less than 5 percent black). As in the previous decade, the South was more integrated than the North, with the West falling in between (52, 31, and 44 percent, respectively, of black students attending racially balanced schools).

These relationships were reversed at the college level where the South was the most segregated region of the country.[10] As a case in point, in the mid-1980's the Justice Department re-opened a case in which they claim Alabama's colleges and universities are still segregated.[11] The segregation of America's colleges is likely to increase in the future due to declines in black enrollment. Between 1976 and 1986 the percentage of black high school graduates enrolling in college dropped by 5 percent.[12] The number of black doctorates is down 27 percent in the last decade.[13] Also, a recent court ruling will make it more difficult to put pressure on state university systems to desegregate.[14] This ruling may have the effect of eliminating the funding to traditional black colleges.[15]

The latest figures continue to indicate that the introduction of desegregation causes some white flight, but it occurs primarily when desegregation plans requiring the reassignment of substantial numbers of white students (and which are not community wide) are implemented in large, majority black, urban school districts that are surrounded by suburbs.[16] White flight typically tapers off after the first year or so.[17]

Surprisingly, private school attendance did not increase in the country as a whole in the decade from 1970 to 1980.[18] However, there was an increase in the South. A good example of this increase occurred in some of the rural counties of Alabama such as Greene, Lowndes, Macon, and Sumter where the creation of private schools for whites helped maintain a dual school system—a public system for blacks and a private system for whites.[19] In the South many rural school districts are nearly as segregated now as they were before the *Brown* decision.

In the future, desegregation seems headed for further declines. One reason is that resegregation poses a major problem in many large urban school districts.[20] A second reason is that for the most part, the federal government is not pursuing new desegregation cases. And some cities, such as Cleveland and Los Angeles, are attempting to have their desegregation plans reversed. In addition, the Supreme Court seems likely to continue to narrow the scope of desegregation remedies in future desegregation cases.[21]

Should desegregation be allowed to fade into the sunset as a social policy? An examination of the data, beginning with the short-term effects of desegregation, can be used to answer that question.

Short-Term Effects

One direct short-term effect of desegregation has nothing to do with the social scientists' predictions and it concerns the physical plants of schools for blacks and whites. Faced with desegregation, many school districts moved quickly to equalize the facilities provided to blacks and whites within their districts.[22] Even when actual desegregation plans were delayed through opposition, most Southern school districts improved the physical plants at the schools attended by blacks. Given the deplorable state of many of these schools before *Brown*, this was not a trivial consequence of desegregation. However, most attention has been devoted to the effects of desegregation on achievement, self-esteem, and race-relations.

School achievement, as measured by national standardized tests, furnishes a crucial index of how much the students in our schools have learned. We use it to measure the progress of individuals, to compare schools within systems, and to compare districts, states, and regions. It also has important practical implications for tracking within schools and for admission to colleges and universities. Does desegregation improve black achievement? This question has been extensively investigated because many school districts routinely administer achievement tests to their students. There are several ways of looking at the results of these studies. One way is simply to count up the number of studies finding improvements and compare this to the number of studies finding no effects or decreases.

A review of these studies found that desegregation improved black achievement in 25 percent of the cases and decreased black achievement in 4 percent of the cases.[23] Other reviews have produced similar conclusions[24]—that is, that desegregation sometimes increases black achievement and rarely decreases it.

In an attempt to do a more refined analysis, the National Institute of Education brought together a group of experts in 1983 to examine these studies. They chose to examine only the best designed studies (as noted already, few districts were desegregated after this date so these data are reasonably current). They broke down the achievement test scores into those on the reading and math sections of these tests. The results indicated that, during the first year, desegregation leads to small increases in reading achievement but has no effect on math achievement.[25] The magnitude of the size of the effect for reading achievement would amount to an increase of 5 percent on a standardized test. This effect, if it were maintained in successive years, would eliminate the gap in reading achievement between blacks and whites in about seven years. However, these studies were almost exclusively concerned with the first year of desegregation so it is not known whether the gap in reading achievement continues to close after the first year. Thus, these studies suggest that desegregation leads to small improvements in black reading achievement.

One of the shortcomings of these studies is that they furnished very little information on the characteristics of the desegregation programs that do improve achievement. For example, it is not clear from these studies which types of desegregation plans—freedom of choice, magnet schools, voluntary transfer programs, neighborhood attendance zones, rezoning, pairing or clustering—have the most positive effects. Similarly, desegregation often, but not always, means that blacks are in better physical facilities, receive instruction from more experienced teachers, have better curricula, and are attending schools with white students whose social class background differs from theirs. Do these aspects of desegregation have an impact on the outcome? We simply do not know. One of the few characteristics that does appear to be associated with achievement effects is age. Younger black children appear to experience the greatest gains.[26] It should be noted that there are no studies in which it has been found that desegregation has negative effects on white achievement.[27]

Self-esteem may be thought of as a distillation of our relationship to ourselves. It is the springboard for personal initiative and without it life holds little joy. Does desegregation increase black self-esteem? In a word—no. A review of these studies showed that, during the first year of desegregation, black self-esteem increased in only 4 percent of the cases, there were no changes in 71 percent of the cases, and desegregation decreased self-esteem in the remaining 25 percent of the cases.[28]

Before concluding that desegregation did not lead to the expected increases in black self-esteem, one should recognize that the argument that desegregation would increase the self-esteem of black schoolchildren was based on a false premise. It was believed that black children in segregated schools had lower self-esteem than white children—due to being segregated. Four decades of research on self-esteem indicate that blacks do not have lower self-esteem than whites in segregated or integrated schools.[29] The reason apparently is that the self-esteem of black children, like the self-esteem of white children, is based on the evaluations of significant people in their lives, not on the evaluations of their group by other groups.[30] If segregation did not cause blacks to have lower self-esteem than whites, then there is little reason to believe that desegregation would increase black self-esteem. Thus, while desegregation rarely increased black self-esteem, there appears to be little reason that it should have.

Prejudice is a punishment we inflict on those who differ from us. We make our enemies suffer the burden of our hatred. And hatred, when sown, usually reaps a harvest of hatred. Does desegregation improve race relations? Here the answer is decidedly mixed. A review of the evidence indicates that for blacks desegregation reduced their prejudices toward whites in more cases than it increased them (38 percent vs. 24 percent).[31]

However, for whites, the results were just the opposite. Desegregation increased their prejudices toward blacks in three times as many cases (48 percent) as it decreased them (16 percent).

One effect that desegregation does not have is that it does not lead to increases in opposition to desegregation among white parents.[32] In several of the communities studied, attitudes toward desegregation among parents became more positive as a result of desegregation.[33] It should be noted also that rarely did desegregation result in the kind of chaos that Wallace apparently anticipated. There were protests that resulted in some violence in a few cities, but the violence subsided quickly in nearly all cases.[34] Desegregation has become an accepted aspect of education in most of the communities in which it has been instituted. Some people may not like it, but it has not been associated with continued disruption in these communities. Within desegregated schools, interracial aggression also has not been found to increase, contrary to what Wallace and others may have anticipated.[35]

This is, of course, a relatively narrow view of the effects of desegregation on race relations because it deals primarily with the experiences of school children and their parents during the first year or so of desegregation. The effects of desegregation on race relations will be assessed further when the long-term effects of desegregation are discussed.

But before discussing the long-term effects of desegregation, some reasons should be mentioned for us to be very cautious about drawing strong conclusions from the studies of the short-term effects of desegregation. First, the initial year of desegregation is perhaps the most aytpical school year the students in these school systems will ever experience. It isn't just that they are now attending desegregated schools; desegregation is often accompanied by community opposition, anxiety on the part of students and parents, and changes in curriculum and teaching staffs. In addition, the measures used in these studies vary considerably and many are of unknown validity. The sample sizes in some of the studies were quite small and the samples in other studies may not have been representative. Also, many of these studies employed weak designs: they used cross-sectional rather than longitudinal designs with control groups of segregated students.

Thus the conclusions that in the short-term desegregation leads to small improvements in black reading achievement, rarely improves black self-esteem, and has mixed effects on race relations must be regarded as tentative at best.

Long-Term Effects

Until recently it was impossible to study the long-term effects of desegregation because there simply were not enough students who had graduated from desegregated schools. However, in the 1980s numerous studies have been done that examine the effects of attending desegregated schools on college attendance, occupational choice and achievement, and voluntary interracial contact.

Although the studies are not entirely in agreement, in general it has been found that blacks who attended desegregated high schools are more likely to finish high school, attend college, earn higher GPAs while in college, and they are less likely to drop out of college than blacks who attended segregated high schools.[36] The increase in attendance rates appears to occur primarily in the North. In the South, blacks who attended desegregated high schools are more likely to attend traditionally white universities than blacks who attended segregated high schools.[37] Also, it has been found that the more extensive the students' experience with desegregation the more likely they are to attend traditionally white universities.[38] These studies suggest that desegregation increases black educational achievement and increases blacks' willingness to interact with whites in educational settings.

The studies on occupational status suggest that desegregation may lead to some improvements in the earnings of blacks.[39] The results of attending desegregated colleges present a similar picture. The better studies indicate that attending desegregated colleges enables blacks to get better jobs than attending segregated colleges.[40]

It is clearly the case that blacks are now represented in a much wider variety of occupations than they were thirty-five years ago,[41] and it appears that desegregation played a role in this process.[42] Several studies have provided information on how this process may occur. Blacks from desegregated schools are more likely than those from segregated schools to choose nontraditional college majors in fields such as science and technology.[43] Also, blacks from desegregated backgrounds believe that a greater range of occupational opportunities is available to them than do blacks from segregated backgrounds.[44] Eventually, these processes may lead black students from desegregated schools to land more non-traditional and better paying jobs than blacks from segregated schools. Another finding showing how blacks from desegregated shools may ultimately fare better in the marketplace is that employers say they would assign better jobs to blacks from desegregated (suburban) schools than to blacks from segregated (central city) schools (even though they are identical in other respects).[45]

In the realm of work, the best established finding is that blacks who have attended desegregated schools are more likely to work in integrated environments as adults than blacks who have attended segregated schools.[46] These desegregated blacks also have more favorable evaluations of their white co-workers and bosses than blacks from segregated backgrounds.[47] Moreover, they form more cross-race friendships.[48] One study found that for whites also, those who attended desegregated schools were more likely to work in integrated settings.[49]

Both blacks and whites who have attended desegregated schools are more likely to live in integrated neighborhoods as adults and to send their children to desegregated schools than blacks or whites who attended segregated schools.[50] These and other studies suggest that desegregation leads to greater integration in housing, particularly when the desegregation plans are community-wide plans which cannot easily be avoided by moving to the suburbs.[51] Since segregation in housing is still pervasive, the effects of desegregation on integration in housing shows that desegregation can counter an otherwise very powerful trend.

In sum, the studies on the long-term effects of desegregation show that it increases educational and occupational attainment among blacks and leads to greater integration in colleges and universities, in the workplace, and in housing. In assessing these results it should be kept in mind that the sizes of the effects in these studies were generally relatively small (although they were typically statistically significant). The number of studies is still not large and the findings, while generally consistent across studies, do show some variability. Although the sample sizes in some studies were small, a number of these studies employed national samples and were considerably more comprehensive than the studies of the short-term effects. Finally, it should be kept in mind that only general trends are being considered here, which means that in some school districts these positive effects were not found, and many individuals did not experience any of the benefits these studies indicate desegregation can have.

Long-Term Indirect Effects

In addition to the direct short- and long-term effects, desegregation has also had a number of indirect effects on race relations in our society. While it is possible to quantify most of the direct short- and long-term effects of desegregation, it is not possible to do this with the indirect effects of desegregation. However, such effects cannot be ignored in a comprehensive assessment of desegregation.

One indirect effect was largely symbolic. The *Brown* decision was the spark that ignited the Civil Rights Movement. In this respect the effects of *Brown* were ramified throughout the social system. George Wallace viewed desegregation as a threat to a way of life, and in this he was almost certainly correct. Desegregation marked the beginning of the end of an era in U.S. race relations. *Brown* was particularly important as a lesson in how the courts could be used as a tool to forge social change from a reluctant society. This lesson was learned by many other minority groups, including Hispanic and Asian Americans as well as the handicapped and the elderly to mention just a few, and it was applied to areas of American life other than the schools.[52]

Likewise, there have been vast changes in the racial attitudes of whites in the post-*Brown* era. Racial tolerance is now the norm. Tolerance does not mean liking or even respect, and it is often accompanied by a reluctance to interact with members of the other group, by anxiety, and by reservations about the other group.[53] Attitudes toward desegregation have paralleled these positive changes in racial attitudes.[54] The principle of providing equal educational opportunity through school desegregation is widely accepted in this country, although the majority of whites do not favor one of the most effective techniques of achieving it—busing.[55]

A few words about busing are in order at this point. Most busing, 93 percent, is not done for purposes of desegregation.[56] Busing for desegregation is not a major expenditure for most school districts, averaging 2 percent of the budget. Busing is not unsafe. In fact, it is safer than walking to school.[57] And the vast majority of people who have experienced it (85 percent) find it to be satisfactory.[58]

Attitudes toward desegregation are largely positive and rarely negative. For instance, in one recent survey only 4 percent of whites and 6 percent of blacks said they believe that blacks do worse in racially mixed schools than they do in segregated schools.[59] A particularly interesting statistic comes from a study done at The University of Alabama that covers the period from 1963 to 1982.[60] In 1963, 56 percent of white students at the University said they would be willing to attend class with blacks. In 1982 the figure was 97 percent. Desegregation itself almost certainly played some role in the changes in whites' attitudes, but it is not possible to specify this role precisely.[61]

Contact Hypothesis

Now that a picture of the effects of desegregation has been derived from the social science data it is appropriate to analyze the causes of these effects, relying once again on the social scientists' predictions. Recall that the social scientists expected improvements in achievement, self-esteem, and race relations. Were the social scientists wrong? Perhaps, if only short-term effects are considered. They apparently misjudged how negative the circumstances would be when desegregation was ultimately implemented.

The prediction concerning race relations can be used to illustrate this point. The social scientists' thinking in the *Brown* case was based on what has come to be known as the contact hypothesis. Several versions were available at the time of the *Brown* decision.[62] One statement of this hypothesis comes directly from the *Amicus Curiae* brief written by four social scientists for the *Brown* trial. The relevant portion stated

> Under certain conditions desegregation . . . has been observed to lead to the emergence of more favorable attitudes and friendlier relations between the races . . . There is less likelihood of unfriendly relations when change is simultaneously introduced in all units of a social organization . . . The available evidence suggests the importance of consistent and firm enforcement of the new policy by those in authority . . . It indicates also the importance of such factors as: the absence of competition . . . the possibility of contacts which permit individuals to learn about one another as individu-

als; and the possibility of equivalence of positions and functions among the participants . . . These conditions can generally be satisfied in . . . public schools.[63]

One does not have to think long or hard about how often these conditions were fulfilled in the typical desegregation plan to understand why the social scientists' predictions fell short of the mark. Desegregation was often introduced piecemeal, by reluctant authorities, in schools where competition was characteristic, where cliques, tracking, and other factors that foster within-school segregation prevented individualized contact, and where equal status contacts between blacks and whites were the exception, rather than the rule.

Later research on the contact hypothesis has only added to the number of conditions that are thought to be needed for interracial contact to improve race relations.[64] A recent review of this voluminous literature found over twenty different situational factors that have been shown to contribute to improved relations between groups. In addition to those factors that have already been mentioned, it includes such factors as working in small groups, having balanced ratios of members of the two groups, having the groups succeed, and providing a degree of structure for the interaction. Again, few of these factors are present in the typical desegregated school. Perhaps we should be surprised that the outcomes of desegregation were not more negative than they were.

A digression may be in order at this point to illustrate how difficult it is to improve race relations in the schools by discussing what is required to modify a critical component of race relations—racial stereotypes. For stereotypes to change, the members of the other group must first behave in ways that clearly contradict the stereotype. This behavior should occur frequently in a variety of low-stress settings (where group membership is obvious). The behaviors should be performed by a number of different group members who are perceived as responsible for their counter-stereotypical behavior, but who are otherwise typical members of their group.[65]

To take but one example of how difficult it is to change a negative stereotype in desegregated schools, consider the stereotype that blacks are intellectually inferior to whites. In most desegregated schools there are social class disparities between blacks and whites that lead whites to be better prepared academically than blacks, particularly if the whites have been attending superior schools prior to desegregation. Thus, there may not be a high frequency of superior academic performances by a large number of different blacks. In addition, if the blacks who do excel academically are not given personal credit for their superior academic performances or if they are viewed as exceptions to the rule, the negative stereotype will stand unchallenged. This is not to argue that desegregation cannot reduce racial stereotyping or prejudice, but rather that desegregation as it usually occurs is not likely to lead to reductions in stereotyping or prejudice. In most cases desegregation simply fails to meet the conditions necessary for change to occur.

In contrast to the short-term effects of desegregation, the long-term effects on race-relations are largely positive. How can desegregation have so few short-term positive effects yet have so many positive effects in the long run?

We do not have a complete answer to this question, but the following processes appear to play a role. First, experience with desegregation in the schools may lead blacks in adulthood to be more willing to interact with whites in universities, on the job, and in their neighborhoods. Desegregation may provide blacks with knowledge of the norms, behaviors, and values of whites that lead them to be more skilled in interacting with whites. Second, attending desegregated schools creates interpersonal networks that open up access to higher paying jobs in integrated settings.[66] Third, attending desegregated schools leads blacks to believe that greater occupational opportunities are available to them, which may lead them to apply for jobs that students from segregated schools do not even attempt to get.

Improving Intergroup Relations in the Schools

Given that desegregation does not generally improve race-relations in the short-term, are there techniques that can be used to improve race relations in desegregated schools? Since the mid-seventies a great deal of research has been devoted to developing such techniques. These techniques often draw on the contact hypothesis. Two general types of programs have been found to be successful.

The first type is based on the idea that prejudice is founded in ignorance. Ignorance causes prejudice because it creates a fear of members of the other group, because the other group is assumed to differ from one's own group in important ways, and because the information void created by ignorance is filled in with negative stereotypes and myths about the other group. The techniques designed to overcome ignorance are usually aimed primarily at white students and attempt to educate them concerning the history and nature of black culture. [An evaluation of the literature on these techniques indicates that most programs (69 percent) are successful.] The most effective programs employ multiple materials and media, such as movies, books, lectures, and field trips.[67] The differences between the two groups in norms, values, and attitudes are presented in ways that respect the cultures of both groups.[68] Myths about differences that do not exist are countered and the diversity of the members of both groups is highlighted. In addition, the similarities between the groups are stressed, as is their common humanity. The most successful techniques actively involve the participants and last for several months, usually for an hour or more a day.[69]

The second type of technique is more directly tied to the contact hypothesis. It is based on the idea that cooperative, equal status, individualized contact that is supported by authority figures will improve race relations.[70] The typical technique involves having children work together in small interethnic groups. They are usually assigned ordinary schoolwork, but they are required to cooperate in learning the material. For instance, in one technique the students divide up the material to be learned and each student is responsible for teaching his or her portion of the material to the other students.[71] The work groups meet together for an hour or more every day. In some of these cooperative techniques the students are graded on how well they do individually, while in others the students' grades depend on the success of the group. Not only do these techniques improve race relations, but they have also been found to lead to increases in self-esteem and minority achievement, precisely the three factors involved in the predictions made by the social scientists in *Brown*.

Conclusion

Before summarizing what the social science studies do tell us about the effects of desegregation, some of the things they do not tell us should be mentioned. They tell us very little about the effects of desegregation on political participation, or on adult social adjustment problems like crime, suicide, and the use of welfare, or on indices of assimilation such as inter-marriage. They provide little information on the integration of teachers, administrators, or school boards. They do not provide much information on the effects of desegregation on other minorities. Also, we know little about what types of desegregation plans are most effective.

Because the evaluation of any public policy should include an assess-ment of the costs and benefits of that policy, the summary of these studies should include an evaluation of the costs of desegregation as they might be perceived by blacks and whites opposed to it as well as those who support it.

Blacks opposed to desegregation would note the negative short-term effects it has had. There were increases in the prejudices of white students more often than not. No improvements in math achievement occurred, and self-esteem dropped in a quarter of the cases studied. A substantial number of black teachers and administrators lost their jobs during the initial phases of desegregation. A disproportionate number of black stu-dents were suspended or expelled in some school districts. Many segre-gated black neighborhood schools were closed. And blacks more often than not bore the burden of busing.

Whites opposed to desegregation might see the following costs. Deseg-regation contributed to the end of a segregated way of life. However, it might be proposed that these changes would have occurred whether or not school desegregation had been implemented. George Wallace tried to stem the tide of integration by standing against desegregation, but the movement to end segregation would have continued, even if the effort to desegregate the schools had failed. Whites opposed to desegregation would disapprove of the fact that many white neighborhood schools are now desegregated. Considerably greater numbers of white students are riding buses to school than would have been the case if the schools had remained segregated. White flight occurred in a considerable number of metropolitan areas (those with suburbs to which whites could flee), al-though most of these school systems would eventually have become ma-jority black anyway, as a result of ongoing demographic changes in the population. Interracial contact increased in the workplace and blacks seem headed toward better jobs as a result of desegregation and these trends, too, might meet with the disapproval of the more strident segre-gationists.

Both black and white opponents might agree that money was spent on busing and other facets of desegregation that might have been spent in better ways had desegregation not occurred, although they probably would not agree on what these "better ways" are.

The benefits of desegregation would probably be evaluated in a similar manner by blacks and whites. Although opposition to busing is still widespread among whites, desegregation was accepted within a relatively short period of time in the great majority of the communities in which it was implemented. Desegregation did not increase violence in the schools. Busing as a tool to desegregate did not jeopardize children's safety. White flight generally lasted for only a short time after desegregation was implemented and did not occur at all in many cities.

Desegregation led to small improvements in black reading achievement, at no cost to white achievement. The short-term negative effects on prejudice were offset by an almost equivalent number of cases in which prejudice was decreased, and we now have the tools to counteract prejudice in the schools. Desegregation has led more blacks to attend college and they have done better in college. These blacks sought out a wider range of majors and jobs. Blacks from desegregated backgrounds successfully used the contacts they made to get better jobs than those obtained by blacks from segregated backgrounds. Employers apparently value desegregation, for they recommend students from desegregated backgrounds for better jobs. Blacks and whites who experienced desegregation were more willing to interact with each other in neighborhood and work settings than blacks and whites who had not. The blacks also had more favorable attitudes toward their white co-workers and made more white friends as a result of desegregation (there were no data on whites for these factors).

Desegregation increased residential integration in some cities (those with community-wide plans) and probably has contributed to the more positive racial attitudes that now exist in our society. Desegregation did play a role in the movement to create greater social justice in our society.

At the time of Wallace's stand in the schoolhouse door segregation was one of the most important links in the chains of oppression that maintained blacks in an unequal status. Twenty-five years later blacks and whites are still separate and unequal. The gap has narrowed, but it has not been closed. Desegregation has contributed to narrowing the gap and has brought us closer to being the kind of society many Americans want to live in, one in which the different racial and ethnic groups in our society have a mutual respect for one another that enables them to live and work together productively.

It may be appropriate to end with a paraphrase of the quote which introduced this chapter. Does desegregation of children in public schools on the basis of race improve the educational opportunities of minority children? The evidence suggests it does. To integrate minority and majority children generates a feeling of equality as to their status in the community that may affect their attitudes and behavior in a way unlikely ever to be undone. In the field of public education the doctrine of equal opportunity has a special place—for desegregated facilities can indeed provide equal opportunities.

7

CHANGES IN THE EXPRESSION AND ASSESSMENT OF RACIAL PREJUDICE

John F. Dovidio
Samuel L. Gaertner

This chapter focuses on white America's racial attitudes—what they have been, what they currently are, and what they seem to be becoming. In the first section, we review surveys and nationwide polls that illustrate how racial attitudes have changed across time. These data essentially demonstrate that, at least in what they say, white Americans are gradually becoming less prejudiced and more egalitarian. Despite these overall trends, there are, however, indications of the persistence of negative feelings toward blacks and other minorities, which are today expressed in more subtle, indirect, and rationalizable ways. In the second section we propose that survey methods generally exaggerate racial tolerance because the old-fashioned and direct form of racism is being replaced by more modern and indirect forms that are more difficult to detect. Next, we examine the nature of contemporary racial attitudes and present three related perspectives describing modern racism: aversive racism, functional racism, and modern/symbolic racism. Because of the complexity of modern forms of racism, more elaborate and sensitive measures are required to detect racial prejudice among people who genuinely believe that they are racially tolerant and who incorrectly regard themselves as part of the solution to racial injustice. In the third section, we review some current measures of racial prejudice. Finally, despite the subtlety of their expression, we argue that these new forms of racism are as insidious as the traditional form and have consequences for minorities that are anything but subtle.

Trends in Racial Attitudes: Toward Egalitarianism

The United States was founded on principles of social equality; the premise that "all men [sic] are created equal" was a guiding principle for our nation. Currently, white Americans, more than ever before, are rejecting negative characterizations of blacks and are endorsing the ideal of equal opportunity for all people. For example, adjective checklist studies, in which respondents are asked to select traits that are most typical of particular racial and ethnic categories, indicate that negative stereotypes of blacks are consistently fading.[1] As Table 7.1 indicates, in 1988, in contrast to earlier years, only small proportions of whites described blacks in strongly negative terms. In addition, white respondents more frequently selected positive characteristics, such as "loyal to family."

Several nationwide polls have also demonstrated that whites are increasingly rejecting negative characterizations of blacks.[2] National Opinion Research Center (NORC) surveys from 1942 to 1968 revealed that increasing proportions of whites responded affirmatively to the question, "Do you think Negroes are as intelligent as white people—that is, can they learn things just as well if they are given the same education and training?" The percentages answering "yes" steadily increased from 1942 (47 percent yes) to 1944 (48 percent yes) to 1946 (57 percent yes) to 1956 (80 percent yes). In each of the succeeding years 1963, 1964, 1966, and 1968, about 80 percent of white respondents answered "yes" to this question. A more recent series of Gallup Polls[3] has shown that from 1963 to 1978 there were substantial declines in the percentages of white respondents agreeing to the statements "blacks tend to have less ambition than whites" (from 66 percent to 49 percent), "blacks have less native intelligence than whites" (from 39 percent to 25 percent), and "blacks are inferior to whites" (from 31 percent to 15 percent).

Furthermore, although there is a general tendency for people to consider personal factors within the afflicted to be more important than external, structural factors in accounting for poverty,[4] the majority of white Americans do *not* currently blame blacks for their disadvantaged economic situation. In 1972, only 31 percent of whites agreed that

Table 7.1. Changes in Racial Stereotypes across Time: Percentage of Subjects Selecting Traits[1]

Percent of Subjects Selecting a Trait to Describe White Americans in 1933, 1951, 1967, 1982, and 1988

	1933	1951	1967	1982	1988
Industrious	48	30	23	21	13
Intelligent	47	32	20	10	6
Materialistic	33	37	67	65	41
Ambitious	33	21	42	35	35
Progressive	27	5	17	9	10
Pleasure Loving	26	27	28	45	32
Alert	23	7	7	2	1
Efficient	21	9	15	8	5
Aggressive	20	8	15	11	27
Straightforward	19	—	9	7	8
Practical	19	—	12	14	10
Sportsmanlike	19	—	9	6	4
Individualistic	—	26	15	14	24
Conventional	—	—	17	20	8
Scientific	—	—	15	4	3
Ostentatious	—	—	15	6	6
Conservative	—	—	15	15	22
Stubborn	—	—	—	20	8
Tradition Loving	—	—	—	19	22
Loyal to Family	—	—	—	—	20
Nationalistic	—	—	—	—	24
Boastful	—	—	—	—	13
Ignorant	—	—	—	—	10

Percent of Subjects Selecting a Trait to Describe Black Americans (Formerly "Negroes") in 1933, 1951, 1967, 1982, and 1988

	1933	1951	1967	1982	1988
Superstitious	84	41	13	6	2
Lazy	75	31	26	13	6
Happy-go-lucky	38	17	27	15	4
Ignorant	38	24	11	10	6
Musical	26	33	47	29	13
Ostentatious	26	11	25	5	0
Very Religious	24	17	8	23	20
Stupid	22	10	4	1	1
Physically Dirty	17	—	3	0	1
Naive	14	—	4	4	2
Slovenly	13	—	5	2	1
Unreliable	12	—	6	2	1
Pleasure Loving	—	19	26	20	14
Sensitive	—	—	17	13	15
Gregarious	—	—	17	4	6
Talkative	—	—	14	5	5
Imitative	—	—	13	9	4
Aggressive	—	—	—	19	16
Materialistic	—	—	—	16	10
Loyal to Family	—	—	—	39	49
Arrogant	—	—	—	14	7
Ambitious	—	—	—	13	23
Tradition Loving	—	—	—	13	22
Individualistic	—	—	—	—	24
Passionate	—	—	—	—	14
Nationalistic	—	—	—	—	13
Straightforward	—	—	—	—	12

Note. From Karlins, Coffman, and Walters, 1969.

[1] It should be noted that because of changing cultural labels the term "Black Americans" was used in place of "Negroes" and the term "White Americans" was used instead of "Americans." Thus, the specific stimulus (label)-response (trait) connection is different in 1982 from that in the previous adjective checklist studies. It was assumed, however, that the concept (racial category)-trait connection would be fundamentally similar.

"blacks come from a less able race and this explains why blacks are not as well off as whites."[5] In 1988, only 29 percent of whites reported feeling that the reason "poor blacks have not been able to rise out of poverty . . . [is] mainly the fault of blacks themselves."[6] Thus, a number of questionnaires, surveys, and polls converge on the same result: white people are less likely than ever before to say disparaging things about blacks.

Increases in racial consciousness and changes in racial stereotyping have also occurred in the mass media. These changes, no doubt, are an important link in the circle of causality toward a more tolerant America. Blacks, for example, appear more frequently in magazine advertisements. In 1949–1950, about ½ percent of magazine advertisements portrayed blacks; in 1967–1968, 2 percent depicted blacks; but, by 1982, 9 percent of magazine advertisements included blacks.[7] How blacks are portrayed has also changed. In 1950, blacks were presented in subordinate role relationships with whites 62 percent of the time, whereas, in 1980, 89 percent of the advertisements showing blacks and whites together depicted equal-status interactions.

Blacks have also made significant gains in television portrayals over the past twenty-five years. In one of the earliest studies of minority representation in programming and advertising, Plotkin reported that blacks appeared on television only once every two-and-a-half hours.[8] Almost always, blacks were seen in a position of subordinate status to whites. Since that time, however, black presence in television commercials has systematically increased. In 1967, 4 percent of television commercials portrayed blacks, whereas in 1978, slightly less than 20 percent depicted blacks.[9] On prime-time television, by 1978, 59 percent of the dramas and 52 percent of the situation comedies had black characters.[10] In addition to the general increase in television exposure for blacks over the past three decades, how blacks are portrayed also seems to be changing. Liebert, Sprafkin, and Davidson observed that "the formal social-occupational status of blacks has also been elevated since the early days of television. While they used to be cast as servants and entertainers, blacks in the late 1960s and early 1970s were presented as 'regulators' of society in positions such as teachers and law enforcers."[11] In 1984, Bill Cosby's situation comedy, which portrayed him as a caring obstetrician and family man married to an attorney and which did not make race an integral part of the storyline, earned the highest viewer ratings of all prime-time programs. In general, then, mass media portrayals of blacks have become more frequent and positive and seem to be enthusiastically accepted.

In addition to characterizing the personal qualities of blacks more positively, white acceptance of equal opportunities for blacks is at an unprecedented high. In nationwide polls, for example, white respondents have increasingly expressed support for the assertion that blacks "should have as good a chance as white people to get a job."[12] The percentage of whites agreeing with this statement has risen from 45 percent in 1944 to 49 percent in 1946 to 85 percent in 1963 to 89 percent in 1966. In 1972, virtually all of the whites surveyed (97 percent) supported this view. In terms of attitudes toward integration (see Figure 7.1), pro-integration sentiments among whites concerning bringing a black person home for

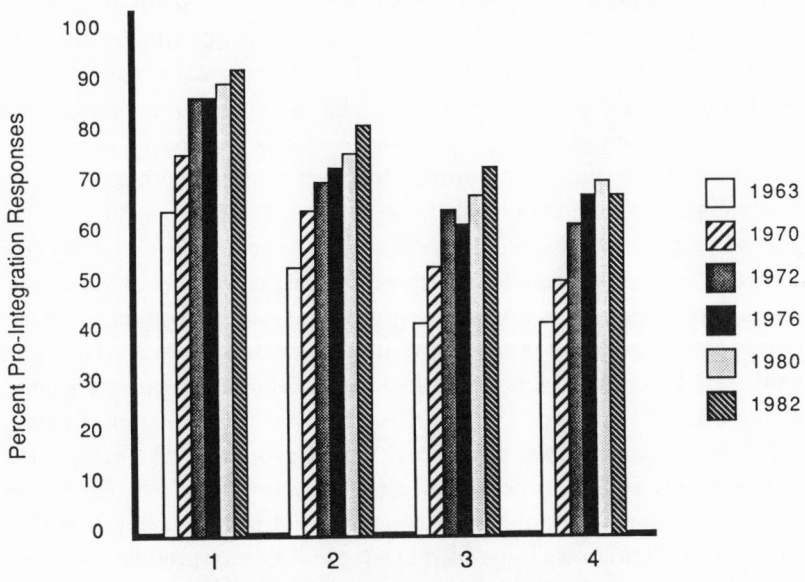

1. Do you think white students and black students should go to the same schools or different schools?

2. How strongly would you object if a member of your family wanted to bring a black friend home for dinner?

3. White people have a right to keep blacks out of their neighborhoods if they want to, and blacks should respect that right.

4. Do you think that there should be laws against marriages between blacks and whites?

Figure 7.1. Percentages of pro-integration responses to questions on racial attitudes that were administered to a nationwide sample of white respondents in 1963, 1970, 1972, 1976, 1980, and 1982. (Adapted from Taylor, Sheatsley, & Greeley, 1978, and Schuman, Steeh, & Bobo, 1985.)

dinner, allowing blacks into the neighborhood, and permitting interracial marriage have become generally stronger across time.[13]

Furthermore, since 1942, both Southerners and Northerners have shown a dramatic shift in their stances toward school integration. In 1942, 2 percent of Southerners agreed that blacks and whites should go to the same schools, whereas in 1970, 45 percent of Southerners supported integrated schools. In 1942, 40 percent of the Northerners believed that blacks and whites should go to the same schools; by 1970, 83 percent of the Northerners expressed this view. By 1972, over 80 percent of all whites surveyed expressed the belief that blacks and whites should go to the same schools (see Figure 7.1). Moreover, by 1980, over 90 percent of white Northerners and 75 percent of white Southerners came to support school integration.[14] In 1982, 90 percent of all white respondents to an NORC poll said that they believed that white students and black students should go to the same schools. Thus, white Southerners are rapidly closing the gap with white Northerners in terms of support for school integration. In addition, clear majorities of both groups currently express pro-integration beliefs on this issue.

Pro-integration and egalitarian sentiments appear to be on the rise for a variety of other personal and professional issues, as well. Despite historical opposition to residential segregation, more whites in 1988 reported that they would prefer to live in a neighborhood "mixed half and half" with blacks and whites than in a neighborhood with mostly whites, 46 percent vs. 33 percent.[15] Kluegel and Smith reported that most whites (76 percent) agreed that "affirmative action programs that help blacks and other minorities to get ahead should be supported."[16] Finally, in terms of political leadership, the percentage of people saying that they would *not* vote for a well-qualified black candidate for president declined from 54 percent in 1958 to 16 percent in 1984.[17] Thus, on the basis of these survey data, whites in the United States are becoming more accepting of blacks personally, professionally, and politically.

In summary, across a variety of surveys concerning personal characterizations and social and political issues, approximately 80 percent of white Americans consistently respond in a nonprejudiced and egalitarian manner. Only a minority of whites, 20 percent, seem to exhibit the old-fashioned, direct, and traditional form of racial prejudice. We believe, however, that racial bias is not confined to this 20 percent of the white population but may also characterize the attitudes of many of the people who appear racially tolerant using traditional survey methods. Thus, in the remainder of this chapter, we do *not* focus on the 20 percent of the white population who express racial prejudice in the traditional way. We do not deny that the traditional form of racism continues to have a negative impact on the quality of life for blacks—it does.[18] The dynamics of the traditional form of racism, however, have been well-researched[19] and are discussed in detail in Ostow's chapter in this volume. In terms of our emphasis, we believe that, because old-fashioned racism has evolved into more subtle and indirect forms, survey and traditional self-report techniques underestimate the degree of prejudice among white Americans. Therefore, we focus on modern forms of racism that may reflect, in part, the current racial attitudes of a large portion of the 80 percent of the white population—the vast majority of whites—who say that they are not prejudiced, who may believe that they are not prejudiced, but who nonetheless may be exhibiting subtle types of racial bias because they cannot completely escape cultural and cognitive forces.

Indications of Ambivalence

Despite the impressive range of data that show that the racial attitudes of white Americans are generally positive, accepting, and supportive concerning blacks, there are, nevertheless, indications of lingering negative feelings, ambivalence, and subtle bias. With respect to racial stereotyping questionnaires (as with other self-report measures), there is evidence that respondents often systematically alter their answers to appear more egalitarian than they actually are. Thus, what may have changed across time in the adjective checklist studies is what people regard as socially desirable rather than racial attitudes per se. In support of this hypothesis, Sigall and Page found that white subjects who believed that their truthfulness was being monitored through their physiological responses gave more negative evaluations of blacks and more positive evaluations of whites than did control subjects who believed that they were not being physiologically monitored.[20] Furthermore, even these social desirability pressures have not been sufficient to eliminate the gap between the favorability between black and white stereotypes in the adjective checklist studies. As Table 1 illustrates, although black stereotypes have become less negative across time, white stereotypes remain more positive.

Nationwide polls also indicate that personal acceptance of blacks is far from complete. Relatively high proportions of respondents continue to show racial biases on items involving some degree of intimacy between blacks and whites. A Harris poll in 1978 revealed that only 35 percent of whites favored full integration (another 42 percent favored integration in some areas). In 1981, 31 percent of whites surveyed preferred not to have blacks as neighbors;[21] in 1988, one-third of white respondents preferred to live in "a neighborhood with mostly whites."[22] Although in 1982 the majority (66 percent) of whites opposed laws prohibiting interracial marriage, in 1983, the majority of whites (60 percent) personally did *not* approve of interracial marriage. In addition, despite the consistent trend toward acceptance of egalitarian principles across time, feelings toward blacks, as measured by the cold-warm 100-point thermometer scale of the Institute for Social Reserach (ISR), has remained remarkably stable. Whites' thermometer ratings of blacks was sixty in 1964, sixty-three in 1974, and sixty-one in 1982. Incidentally, between 1965 and 1979, Gallup polls indicated that whites became more accepting of the Ku Klux Klan. In 1965, 3.5 percent of the respondents evaluated it favorably, 7.5 percent mildly negatively, and 88.9 percent very negatively. In 1979, 9.8 percent rated it positively, 15.4 percent mildly negatively, and only 74.8 percent very negatively.

In terms of mass media portrayals, critics have argued that despite the apparent gains for blacks there is still substantial evidence of tokenism. Colfax and Sternberg reported that a large proportion of blacks who appeared in print advertisements were token blacks, appearing with five to one thousand white people, or were children interacting with a white teacher, counselor, or superior.[23] Even into the 1980s, white authority figures were frequently shown helping poor blacks or supervising black children. Greenberg and Mazingo observed that much of the increased presence of blacks in television advertisements between 1967 and 1973 could be accounted for by increases in the number of blacks in background or walk-on roles rather than in major parts;[24] Weigel et al. noted that in 1978 although blacks appeared in over 50 percent of the prime-time drama and comedy shows, black appearances accounted for only 8.3 percent of the total human appearance time.[25] Furthermore, qualitative analysis has revealed that blacks on television receive more negative consequences for their behaviors than do whites[26] and generally are "neither forceful or powerful."[27] In addition, Weigel and colleagues found that interracial interaction was underrepresented, occupying only 2 percent of human appearance time, and when it did occur, relationships between blacks and whites, compared to relationships involving only whites, "were less multifaceted and evinced less intimacy, less shared decision making, and fewer romantic implications."[28]

Even though there is widespread acceptance of the *principles* of integration, equal opportunity, and affirmative action, there remains substantial white resistance to the *implementation* of policies designed to insure racial equality. For example, in 1982, 88 percent of the respondents to an ISR survey agreed with the principle that blacks have the right to choose to live in white neighborhoods, but in 1983, only 46 percent of the respondents to an NORC poll supported open housing laws that would guarantee blacks this right. Although, as previously discussed, 90 percent of whites feel that white and black students should go to the same schools, only 25 percent in 1978 believed that the government should intervene to ensure school integration, and in 1983, only 21 percent of respondents favored busing[29] (also see Stephan's chapter in this volume). In terms of the implementation of affirmative action, approximately 80 percent of whites oppose giving *preference* to a black worker over a white worker of equal ability.[30] In 1988, only 14 percent of whites felt that "because of past discrimination . . . qualified blacks [should] receive preferential treatment over equally qualified whites in such matters as getting into college or getting jobs."[31] Overall, 35 percent of whites view preferential treatment for blacks as fair, but only 10 percent support it.[32]

In the next section, we consider, from a psychological perspective, the fundamental nature of contemporary racial attitudes. As the survey literature suggests, although egalitarianism is a dominant cultural value, whites' racial attitudes are neither uniformly favorable nor totally negative, but rather are complex and ambivalent.[33]

Psychological Processes Underlying Contemporary Racial Attitudes

Researchers currently involved in the psychological study of racial prejudice generally agree that prejudice, discrimination, and racism are not necessarily a reflection of psychopathological processes (as the work on the authoritarian personality by Adorno, Frenkel-Brunswik, Levinson, and Sanford hypothesized;[34] see also Ostow's chapter in this volume). Instead, the prevalent belief is that biases related to *normal* human functioning can predispose a person to develop racial prejudice. Several reviews of the psychological literature indicate that cognitive, motivational, and socio-cultural factors that characterize the functioning of normal human beings contribute to the formation and maintenance of racial bias.[35]

A list of some of the basic psychological processes that can support racial prejudice appears in Table 7.2. Cognitive factors concern how people process information. Hamilton and Trolier, for example, reviewed how the simple and arbitrary categorization of people into groups produces ingroup favoritism[36] (see also Brewer[37]). In particular, the mere categorization of people into distinct groups is sufficient to arouse intergroup bias. That is, even without actual contact, members of each group generally have more favorable regard for members within their own group than they have for members of other groups. Greater belief similarity to the self is also attributed to ingroup members,[38] and belief similarity is a powerful determinant of interpersonal attraction.[39] In addition, people are more likely to be helpful and cooperative and to exercise greater personal restraint in their use of limited common resources when they are interacting with ingroup members than with others.[40] Moreover, with specific regard to race, physical characteristics can play a role in the types of impressions that are formed. The colors white and black in our culture, as in virtually all cultures, have very different connotations: white is considered good and active, whereas black is considered bad and evil.[41] In literature, the white knight is good, and the black knight is evil. Even in terms of food, *angel's* food cake is white, whereas *devil's* food is black.

The motivational factors presented in Table 2 involve the satisfaction of basic needs. At the individual level, for example, needs for self-esteem can promote the derogation of outgroups in order to improve one's subjective well-being.[42] At the societal level, economic competition that threatens to alter the traditionally subordinate status of blacks relative to whites fosters discrimination of whites against blacks.[43] Given that traditional social structures have bestowed privileges onto whites, practices that threaten deprivation of that advantaged status, particularly when they involve preferential treatment of blacks, may produce negative reac-

Table 7.2.   Some Factors Contributing to Prejudice

Cognitive

Inherent associations with the colors "black" and "white" (Williams et al., 1971)

Effects of categorization into ingroup and outgroup (Brewer, 1979)

Assumed belief similarity (Rokeach & Mezei, 1966)

Illusory correlation (Hamilton & Gifford, 1976)

Stimulus salience, distinctiveness, and defensive attribution (Taylor, 1981)

Motivational

Needs for self-esteem and status (Allport, 1954)

Downward comparison (Wills, 1981)

Social identity theory (Tajfel & Turner, 1979)

Internal colonization (Hechter, 1975)

Socio-cultural

Cultural stereotypes (Karlins et al., 1969)

Mass media portrayals (Weigel et al., 1980)

Institutional racism (Feagin & Feagin, 1978)

Historical and contemporary differences in prestige, social power, and standard of living.

tions even among people who in principle support ameliorative programs such as affirmative action.

Social and cultural factors can also contribute to whites' negative feelings toward blacks (see Table 7.2). The socio-cultural approach focuses on the transmission of cultural values through normal socialization. Prejudice is a tradition in the United States. For example, the negative stereotype of blacks in 1933 had not entirely faded in 1988 (see Table 1). From a sociological perspective, the structure of society tends to perpetuate prejudice and discrimination. Specifically, the institutional racism framework proposes that beliefs about relative status and power become embedded in social roles and norms.[44] These beliefs, in turn, help to maintain the social, educational, political, and economic advantages that whites have over blacks.

While we have identified cognitive, motivational, and socio-cultural factors that can contribute to the formation and maintenance of prejudice, the list we have presented is by no means exhaustive. Thus, it is likely that the most normal and well-intentioned persons are susceptible to prejudice, in part because they are normal, rely on cognitive processes that simplify, and bias the manner in which information is handled in a complex world, and are socialized into mainstream American values and traditions with historical racist roots.

Nevertheless, in a nation founded on the principle that "all men [sic] are created equal," there are strong forces that promote racial equality. Norms of fairness and equality have had great social, political, and moral impact on the history of the United States. The prevalence of these egalitarian norms has been clearly demonstrated in experimental[45] and survey[46] research. It should be noted, however, that whereas the forces that support prejudice often involve fundamental psychological processes, the factors promoting egalitarianism often involve higher order, more complex, and abstract social, moral, and religious principles.

Because prejudice is rooted in normal human functioning and related to mainstream socialization, we interpret the rather strong and consistent decreases in expressed negative racial attitudes with great caution (see Pettigrew & Martin,[47] and Pettigrew's chapter in this volume). Rather than viewing these changes as straightforward decreases in prejudice, we believe that these apparent decreases in overt negative attitudes may reflect, to a great extent, a change to a more subtle and indirect form of racism that does not directly challenge abstract principles of egalitarianism. In the next section, we discuss three conceptions of modern racism. Specifically, in one subsection, which draws primarily on our own empirical work, we present the aversive racism perspective. In subsequent subsections, we present overviews of Jackman's functional theory of racial attitudes[48] and symbolic/modern racism theory.[49] It should be noted that, while we believe that the prevalence of the old-fashioned red-necked form of racism may have declined since the 1930s, we also recognize that the old-fashioned form of racism continues to be a significant force in the United States. Indeed, not all racists are ambivalent or subtle.

Aversive Racism

We conceive of aversive racism[50] as an adaptation resulting from an assimilation of an egalitarian value system with (1) impressions derived from human cognitive mechanisms that contribute to the development of stereotypes and prejudice, and (2) feelings and beliefs derived from historical and contemporary cultural racist contexts. The aversive racist perspective assumes that cognitive and motivational biases and socialization into the historically racist culture of the United States with its contemporary legacy lead most white Americans to develop negative feelings toward blacks and beliefs about relative superiority to blacks. Because of traditional cultural values, however, most whites also have convictions concerning fairness, justice, and racial equality. The existence of both almost unavoidable racial biases and the desire to be egalitarian forms the basis of an ambivalence that aversive racists experience.

The focus of our research has not been on who is biased—we assume that most people, because they are normal, have developed some racial biases; nor do we focus on why prejudice exists—the work of many others has identified a number of processes that can underlie prejudice (see Table 7.2). Instead, our focus is on systematically identifying the situational conditions that will prime the egalitarian portion of an aversive racist's attitude and reveal the contexts in which the negative feelings will be manifested.

In general, we propose that, because aversive racists consciously recognize and endorse egalitarian values and ideals, they will *not* discriminate against blacks in situations in which norms prescribing appropriate behavior are clear and unambiguous (see Figure 7.2). Wrongdoing, which would directly threaten the egalitarian self-image, would be obvious in these situations. We further propose that, when the normative structure within the situation is weak, ambiguous, or conflicting, or if a person can justify or rationalize a negative response on the basis of some factor other than race, negative feelings toward blacks will be manifested (see Figure 7.2). Here, blacks may be treated unfavorably or in a manner that disadvantages them, yet whites can be spared the recognition that they behaved inappropriately. Thus, an aversive racist can discriminate against blacks without challenging his or her egalitarian self-image. Indeed, across a

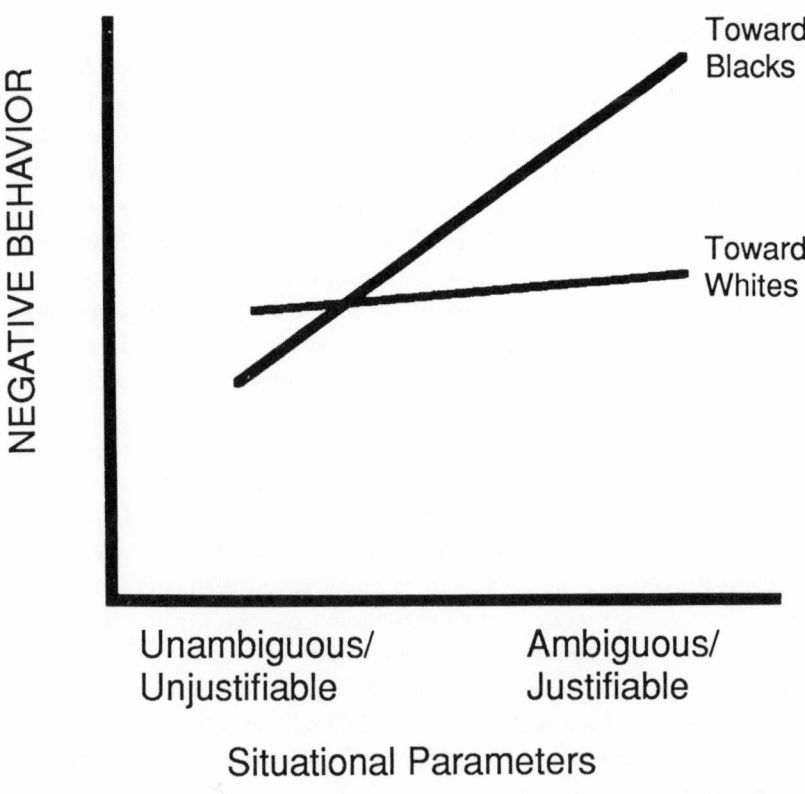

Figure 7.2. Predictions of the aversive racism framework concerning racial bias as a function of whether the norms for appropriate behavior are unambiguous or ambiguous and whether a negative response is justifiable or unjustifiable on the basis of a non-race-related factor.

number of paradigms, we have found consistent support for this framework.[51]

In one test of this perspective, we investigated whether white subjects would help black or white victims in emergency situations depending upon the clarity of norms regarding intervention.[52] In this experiment, college women were led to believe that they were participating in an extrasensory perception (ESP) study in which they would try to receive telepathic messages from a sender who was located in a nearby cubicle and whom they heard through an intercom system. The race of the sender, who would later become the victim of the emergency, was manipulated by her dialect and also by the picture on her college identification card, which was exchanged with the subject at the beginning of the session. Half of the participants in the experiment were informed that they would be the only receiver, whereas the others were told that there would be two others (also white female undergraduates) in nearby rooms.

The presence of other bystanders was introduced in this study to provide a non-race-related factor that could allow a bystander to justify or rationalize a failure to intervene. In Darley and Latane's classic experiment, it was discovered that the mere belief that other bystanders are capable of helping affects the likelihood that a bystander will intervene.[53] When a person is the only bystander, all of the responsibility for helping is focused on this one person. Under these conditions, the probability of this bystander helping is quite high. As the number of bystanders is increased, though, each bystander becomes more likely to believe that one of the other bystanders will intervene or already has intervened, and each bystander's share of the responsibility for helping is decreased. Consequently, the likelihood that each person will intervene is reduced. In our study, after several ESP trials, the sender interrupted the procedure and explained that a stack of chairs piled up to the ceiling of her cubicle looked as if they were about to fall. In a few moments the emergency occurred. The sound of chairs crashing to the floor was accompanied by the victim's screams: "They're falling on me!"

We predicted that the belief that other bystanders are present would have a greater inhibiting effect on the subject's response when the emergency involved a black victim than when it involved a white victim. Failure to help a black person in this situation could be justified or rationalized by the belief that the vicitim is being helped by someone else. Bystanders believing themselves to be the sole witness, however, were not expected to discriminate against black victims relative to white victims because, under these conditions, a failure to help a black victim could readily be attributed to bigoted intent.

The results for both high and low prejudice-scoring subjects conformed to our predictions. Bystanders who thought that they were the only witness helped black victims somewhat more often than they helped white victims (94 percent vs. 81 percent). Subjects aware of the presence of others, however, helped black victims much less frequently than they helped white victims (38 percent vs. 75 percent)—about half as often in this potentially life-threatening situation. Thus, the opportunity to diffuse responsibility for intervening, an apparently nonracial factor, had greater salience and potency when the victim was black than when the victim was white, and this process had significant negative consequences for black victims.

In addition to predicting the way white people behave toward blacks, we believe that the aversive racism framework has direct implications for the conceptualization of the nature of contemporary racial attitudes. In general, because current racial attitudes may be more subtle than traditional forms, conventional methods of assessing these attitudes may not be sufficiently sensitive. For example, when we asked subjects to evaluate black and white people on the ubiquitous 6- or 7-point scale (for example, good——bad) we found no differences in evaluative ratings of blacks and whites. A biased response ("bad") is obvious, and subjects consistently rated others, both black and white, on the positive end (averaging about 2). However, when we varied the measurement instrument slightly by placing positive and negative characteristics in separate scales (e.g., good: 1 = "not at all" to 7 = "extremely"; bad: 1 = "not at all" to 7 = "extremely"), we found that bias does exist—but in a subtle form. When the ratings of blacks and whites on the negative scales are examined, no racial bias appeared: blacks were *not* rated more negatively than whites. The ratings on the positive scales, however, did reveal a significant difference. (Results reported as significant in this chapter meet the .05 level of significance.) Whereas, blacks were not rated more negatively than whites, whites *were* evaluated more positively than blacks. Similarly, Gaertner and McLaughlin's Study 3 replaced the conventional positive to negative scales (e.g., Ambitious—Unambitious) with negative-negative scales (e.g., Unambitious—Lazy) and positive-positive scales (e.g., Ambitious—Not Lazy).[54] Discrimination did not occur on the negative-negative scales but did appear on the positive-positive scales.

For example, blacks were not rated as being lazier than whites, but whites were evaluated as being more ambitious than blacks. Thus, we have convergent self-report data that indicate that white people do not characterize blacks more negatively than whites—a response that could readily be interpreted as racial prejudice—but that white people systematically characterize whites more positively than blacks. Note that this phenomenon is not the old-fashioned bias reflecting open and unqualified negative feelings and beliefs about black inferiority. Nevertheless, although more subtle and less overtly negative, it is still racial bias.

Convergent evidence for bias that does not implicate negative traits comes from another study in which white Colgate students were asked to evaluate on negative-positive 6-point scales (e.g., bad——good) first the "typical white Colgate student" or the "typical black Colgate student." Then, subjects were asked to evaluate themselves on the same scales. The results indicated that if only the ratings of the typical black or white student were examined, no bias was revealed (which replicates our previous null findings with negative-positive scales). The ratings were all quite positive. However, when other- and self-ratings were compared, bias became evident. Specifically, our white subjects evaluated themselves somewhat more positively than the typical white Colgate student, a general egoistic bias. The egoistic bias, though, is significantly stronger among white subjects who had just evaluated (quite positively) the typical black Colgate student. These results suggest that although blacks may be rated quite positively on an absolute dimension, on a relative dimension subjects seem systematically to evaluate whites more positively than blacks.

Clearly, self-report is susceptible to evaluative concerns and impression management motivations.[55] Consequently, we have followed up these self-report studies with a series of reaction time experiments that may provide more social desirability-free measures. In one study,[56] a lexical decision task was used.[57] Subjects were presented simultaneously with two strings of letters and were asked to decide (yes or no) if both strings were words. Meyer and Schvaneveldt reported that highly associated words (e.g., doctor, nurse) produce faster reaction times than do unassociated words (nurse, apple).[58] Gaertner and McLaughlin paired the words "blacks" and "whites" with positive and negative attributes.[59] In a second reaction time experiment, a priming paradigm was used.[60] Rosch found that "priming" by first presenting the name of a category, such as "fruit," facilitates decisions about typical instances (e.g., "orange") more than atypical instances (e.g., "prune"). In our study, subjects were first presented with the primes of "black" and "white," representing the racial groups. These primes were then followed by positive and negative characteristics. The subject's task was to decide if the characteristic could ever describe the primed social category.

The results of our two reaction time studies were consistent (see Figure 7.3). Faster reaction times are assumed to reflect greater association. In both studies, negative characteristics were not more associated with blacks than with whites; in both experiments, positive characteristics were more associated with whites than with blacks. As in our self-report studies, bias exists but is expressed in a subtle, indirect form.

Although we believe that the reaction time methods we used in our lexical decision and priming studies help to avoid contamination from the gross impression management strategies commonly associated with self-report measures, our procedures do not preclude the influence of some fundamental controlled, or conscious, processes (see Messick & Mackie).[61] That is, the mere knowledge that our studies involved judgments of blacks may have primed the conscious, egalitarian aspects of our subjects' racial attitudes and reduced bias, particularly for negative attributes. Consequently, in another study, we adopted a method used by Bargh and Pietromonaco[62] for studying *unconscious* processes.

Briefly, subjects were presented with instructions similar to the instructions used in our prevous priming study. They were told that they would see a string of letters, *P*s or *H*s, on the left or right side of a computer screen. When they saw *P*s, they were asked to think of a typical person; when they saw *H*s, they were instructed to think of a typical house. Subjects were then presented with various characteristics, including the positive and negative traits used in the earlier priming study, and asked to decide if each trait could ever describe the designated category (i.e., person or house). What subjects were not informed about was that the word "black" or "white" was presented subliminally for a fraction (less than a tenth) of a second before the *P*s (representing the person category). Thus, the purpose of this study was to determine how the unconscious associations with black and white persons corresponded to the conscious attributions.

The results for positive characteristics were the same: Subjects responded to positive characteristics more quickly following the white

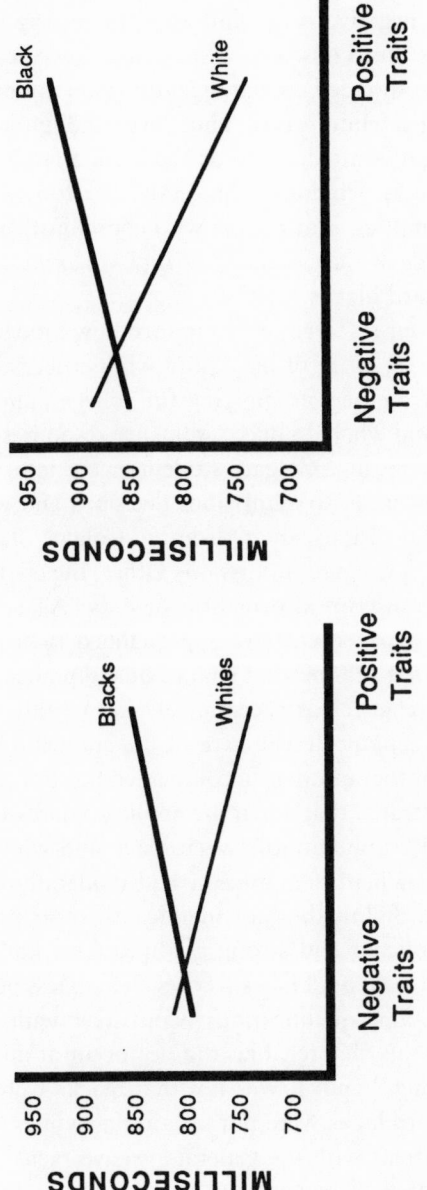

Figure 7.3. Results of lexical decision task and priming reaction time studies.

subliminal prime than following the black subliminal prime. Even unconsciously, positive characteristics were associated more with whites than with blacks. For the negative traits, however, there was a discrepancy between unconscious and conscious responding. Specifically, negative characteristics were responded to significantly faster following a black prime than following a white prime. Thus, even though at a conscious level whites reject negative attributions of blacks, at an unconscious level they do have negative associations. This study therefore provides direct support for our assumption that people who consciously and genuinely embrace egalitarian ideals may, *outside of their awareness*, still harbor negative feelings toward blacks.

In the next part of our research, we examined how modern biases pertaining to the racial *categories* of black and white affect responses to a *particular* black or white person applying for college admission.[63] The questions were how and when do biases influence responses to black and white applicants. Specifically, Colgate students were informed that the study involved student input to admissions decisions and were asked to evaluate, on several dimensions, an applicant to Colgate. Based on information provided by the Colgate Admissions Office, the credentials of the applicant, based on transcript information such as SAT scores, rank in class, and activities, were varied: strongly qualified (which admissions officers reported merited a 90 percent chance of acceptance), moderately qualified (50 percent chance for acceptance), and weakly qualified (10 percent chance for acceptance). The race of the applicant was manipulated by varying a photograph that accompanied the transcript.

The results demonstrated that when the applicant had weak qualifications there was no discrimination between black and white applicants: both were rated low. When the applicant had moderate qualifications, whites were evaluated slightly, but not significantly more positively than blacks. When the applicant had strong qualifications, both blacks and whites were evaluated well, but blacks were evaluated less positively than whites who had the same qualifications. Consistent with the previous research presented in this chapter, bias did not occur at all levels; it occurred only at the "high" end. It was not that blacks were worse than whites, it was just that blacks were not as good as whites.

Furthermore, consistent with the general aversive racism framework, ambiguity was a significant mediator of bias. In this study, we had the individual items that contributed to the overall evaluative score scaled according to how directly they related to the information presented in the applicant's transcript. More bias was revealed the less directly related the item was to the transcript information. In addition to the ambiguity due to subjective evaluation criteria, the difficulty of a decision process provides another source of ambiguity. When candidates' credentials are extremely poor, their suitability for a particular position can be clearly and easily determined: they can be decisively rejected. As candidates' credentials approach the stated criteria, however, the decision regarding suitability becomes more difficult and ambiguous, a situation in which aversive racism theory would expect higher levels of discrimination. While these candidates may be regarded as generally suitable for the position, their degree of appropriateness is more difficult to judge compared to when the credentials are clearly weak. Consistent with this explanation, more discrimination against blacks was evidenced in our study as the applicant became more qualified for admission.

To examine how the aversive racism framework can aid in understanding resistance to programs, such as affirmative action, that are designed to ensure fair treatment to blacks, we conducted another study.[64] Although common protests by whites regarding affirmative action seem to express mainly the concern that *qualified* whites will be disadvantaged relative to *less qualified* blacks such as in the 1989 Supreme Court decision, *Regents of University of California* v. *Bakke*,[65] it is possible that the reversal of the traditional role relationship, in which whites occupied positions of superior status, represents the primary threat to whites. Thus, the purpose of this study was to investigate the possibility that the generally articulated issue of relative competence is a rationalization in which a nonracial factor, competence, is used by whites to object to affirmative action programs that increase the likelihood that they will be subordinated to blacks.

In our study, white male undergraduates were introduced to a black or white male confederate who was presented as either the subject's supervisor or subordinate. In addition, the confederate was described as being higher or lower than the subject in an intellectual ability that was relevant to the dyad's task. The dependent measure was an incidental helping task, picking up pencils that the confederate "accidentally" knocked to the floor. This situation provided subjects with an opportunity to offer assistance which was not absolutely necessary but which could connote affiliative and friendly feelings.

Overall, subjects helped black partners more than white partners. The effect of race, however, was moderated by status and ability. Specifically, the results indicated that relative status, rather than relative ability was the primary determinant of helping behavior toward blacks. Black supervisors were helped less than black subordinates (58 percent vs. 83 percent), whereas white supervisors were helped somewhat more than white subordinates (54 percent vs. 41 percent). Relative ability, in contrast, did not affect prosocial behavior toward blacks. Collapsing across status, high and low ability blacks were helped equally often (70 percent each), whereas high ability white partners were helped more frequently than were low ability white partners (67 percent vs. 29 percent). Thus ability, not status, was instrumental in determining helping toward whites, but status, not ability, was the major factor influencing prosocial behavior toward blacks. Given that there were no significant effects involving subjects' self-reports of prejudice, it seems that even well-intentioned whites will respond negatively to a black supervisor compared to a black subordinate, *regardless* of apparent qualifications.

How could people in this experiment rationalize not responding positively to competent blacks? Subjects' post-experimental evaluations of their partners revealed that their behaviors may have been mediated by perceptions of *relative* intelligence (competence). Although subjects' ratings indicated that they accepted high-ability white partners as being somewhat more intelligent than themselves, the ratings revealed that subjects described even high-ability black partners as significantly less intelligent than themselves. It therefore appears that although whites may accept that a black person is intelligent on an absolute dimension, similar to what we found in our self-report study that implicitly involved an interracial comparison, white subjects are reluctant to accept an authority's single statement that a black person is higher or equal in intelligence compared to themselves. Perhaps repeated and specific evidence is required before whites will accept that a black person is superior in intellectual ability. If subjects believed that black partners were relatively less intelligent than themselves, irrespective of their introduced ability, it is not surprising that their prosocial behavior was unaffected by the competence of black partners.

It is important to note that our research on aversive racism has produced results that are consistent with other frameworks of modern racism. We discuss two of these other approaches, Jackman's functional racism theory and symbolic/modern racism theory, in the next two subsections.

Functional Theory of Modern Racism

Jackman presented a functional, Marxist perspective that hypothesizes that the racial attitudes of the dominant group, whites, function, often non-consciously, to maintain the group's advantaged status.[66] In particular, Jackman and Muha argued that "dominant social groups routinely develop ideologies that legitimize and justify the status quo, and the well-educated members of these dominant groups are the most sophisticated practitioners of their group's ideology."[67] In interpreting the survey data, Jackman made a distinction between "general" and "applied" measures of racial tolerance and suggested that the divergent trends for responses to principle and implementation items reflected "superficial racial tolerance." General measures involved endorsement of abstract values, whereas applied measures relating to implementation of affirmative action policies involved a genuine commitment to integration. Thus, Jackman interpreted the positive relationship between education level and support for integration in principle as a reflection of the recognition and acceptance of popular, egalitarian ideals. She viewed the lack of correlation between education and support for the implementation of integration policies as an indication that more-educated people do not actually have a greater commitment to that position when real-life issues are at stake.[68]

Drawing on Campbell's threshold or hurdle model of attitudes,[69] whites appear egalitarian when there is little personal cost involved (a low hurdle) but resist situations and policies that can have actual negative personal consequences (high hurdles) (see also Crosby, Bromley, & Saxe[70]). As Kluegel and Smith concluded, white Americans oppose affirmative action policy "on the grounds of the threat they perceive it presents to a stratification system they believe benefits themselves personally or American society more generally."[71]

Symbolic/Modern Racism

Another approach that hypothesizes that a subtle form of racism underlies resistance to affirmative action is symbolic racism[72] or modern racism[73] theory. According to symbolic racism theory, negative feelings toward blacks that whites acquire early in life persist into adulthood but are expressed indirectly and symbolically, in terms of opposition to busing or resistance to preferential treatment, rather than directly or overtly, as in support for segregation. McConahay distinguished modern racism, a concept related to symbolic racism, from old-fashioned racism, which involves traditional stereotypic beliefs about black intelligence, industry, and honesty; support for segregation; and acceptance of open discrimination.[74] The basic tenets of modern racism are that racism is bad, discrimination is a thing of the past, blacks are making unfair demands, and blacks are currently receiving more attention than they deserve. McConahay further proposed that because modern racism involves the rejection of traditional racist beliefs and the displacement of anti-black feelings onto more abstract social and political issues, modern racists, live aversive racists, are relatively unaware of their racist feelings.

Individual differences in symbolic and modern racism correlate with a variety of policy-related actions. These behaviors include voting for a white versus a black mayoral candidate,[75] opposing busing,[76] and making simulated hiring decisions.[77] In addition, Jacobson, using 1978 Harris Poll data, found that symbolic racism was a stronger predictor of resistance to affirmative action than either self-interest or old-fashioned racism.[78]

Although both the aversive racism perspective and the symbolic/modern racism approach propose that contemporary forms of racism are more indirect and subtle than traditional form, these approaches developed with emphases on two different types of people. They therefore make different assumptions about the underlying causes. In particular, our perspective on aversive racism originated from how liberals behaved in interracial situations.[79] The symbolic/modern racism approach developed from work on conservatives. McConahay and Hough proposed that "symbolic racism rests upon anti-black socialization and conservative political and value socialization."[80] Therefore, at least as initially formulated, symbolic racism represented subtle prejudice originating from the political right, whereas aversive racism reflected a type of racial bias of people who endorse the ideology of the political left.

Rather than viewing the aversive racism perspective, Jackman's functional framework, and the symbolic/modern racism framework as competing models of racial attitudes, we see these as contemporary approaches. Each approach identifies and emphasizes various factors that, in concert, contribute to contemporary racism. In addition, despite differences in assumptions and explanatory constructs there is substantial common ground. For instance, these approaches all converge on Kluegel and Smith's conclusion that "opposition to equal opportunity programs stems from the threat these programs present to an economic order that is believed to be just in principle and to work well in fact."[81] Thus, although racist traditions may have initially produced social inequalities, many whites, truly believing that they are non-prejudiced and non-discriminating, may presently be participating in the continued restriction of opportunities for blacks and other minorities by opposing programs that threaten their own advantaged status. The issue of how to assess contemporary racial attitudes validly is considered in the next section.

Assessing Modern Racial Attitudes

The measurement of prejudice has been the focus of inquiry in psychology for over sixty years. As Harding and colleagues noted in 1969, "The tradition begins with Watson's monograph, *The Measurement of Fair-Mindedness* (1925)."[82] The concept of stereotypes was introduced by Lippmann,[83] and Katz and Braly[84] popularized the adjective checklist technique of stereotype measurement. In tracing the history of *ethnic* prejudice, Harding and colleagues wrote:[85]

> It was not until the 1930's that American social psychologists really became sensitized to discrimination as a social problem and began looking at ethnic attitudes in terms of the extent to which they embodied a failure of justice. The first investigator to develop an attitude scale from this general point of view seems to have been Minard (1931). . . . Meanwhile, several psychologists had realized that high rejection rates on the Bogardus social-distance scale necessarily implied both a failure of adherence to the norm of justice (in the sense of the American Creed) and a failure of human-heartedness. Murphy and Likert[86] were the first to sum up the number of social relationships to which an individual would willingly admit members of a variety of ethnic groups and to use this score as a measure of "tolerance for nations and races." . . . The authors of *The Authoritarian Personality* (Adorno et al.[87]) reject the term "prejudice" in favor of something they call "ethnocentrism," but . . . we would unhesitatingly describe the California E scale as a measure of ethnic prejudice. . . . A questionnaire intended to measure a special kind of failure of human-heartedness was constructed by Schuman and Harding.[88]

As we have pointed out previously, not all racism is subtle; the old-fashioned form of racism still persists. As a consequence, many traditional prejudice scales continue to predict racial discrimination. Weigel and Howes, for example, demonstrated that a subset of items from the Multifactor Racial Attitude Inventory (MRAI)[89] predicted racially oriented voting behavior in 1984.[90] The full MRAI is comprised of twelve content-defined factors: Integration-Segregation Policy, Gradualism in Desegregation, Private Rights versus Minority Rights, Local Autonomy versus Federal Authority in Desegregation, Black Inferiority, Acceptance of Superior Status Relationships, Acceptance in Close Personal Relationships, Derogatory Beliefs, Ease in Interracial Contacts, Approaches to Racial Equality, Interracial Marriage, and White Reactions to Black Militance. In addition, in a second study[91] Weigel and Howes replicated earlier findings showing correlations between the personality dimension of authoritarianism[92] and prejudice toward various groups, specifically blacks, homosexuals, and the elderly. Thus, the existence of modern forms of racism has not entirely overshadowed the persistent influence of the old-fashioned, red-necked form.

In terms of modern forms of racism, aversive racism, functional racism, and symbolic/modern racism theories all hypothesize that contemporary racial bias is complex and subtle, and is often an elusive phenomenon. The aversive racism framework, in particular, proposes that when people are made self-conscious in interracial situations, they will generally respond in a racially tolerant manner. Therefore, with respect to self-report measures of prejudice, we have previously argued that "given the high salience of race and racially symbolic issues on questionnaires designed to measure prejudice, as well as aversive racists' vigilance and sensitivity to these issues, effective questionnaire measures of aversive racism, in our opinion, would be difficult if not impossible to develop."[93]

Despite our pessimisim, other researchers have developed promising measures of more modern forms of racism. Attitude scale development, for example, has been an integral part of research on symbolic and modern racism. McConahay observed: "The theory draws on some well-established findings in the social learning theory of attitudes[94] and racial socialization,[95] but it emerged as a result of a practical problem. How do we measure racial attitudes in the general public when the issues, the climate and the structure of public opinion has changed? . . . Thus, the

theory has developed simultaneously with the instrument used to opera-
tionalize aspects of the theory."[96] A comparison of a recent version of
the Modern Racism Scale to old-fashioned racism items appears in Table
7.3.

According to McConahay, the Old Fashioned Racism is reactive and
the Modern Racism Scale is relatively non-reactive.[97] He proposes that
the wording of the Modern Racism Scale is more likely to permit negative
responses than does the Old Fashioned Racism Scale because a prejudiced answer in each case can be explained by a non-race-related attribution or ideology. More detailed discussion of the reliability of Symbolic
Racism and Modern Racism scales can be found in Sears and Allen and
in McConahay.[98] Despite some criticism of the approach,[99] the weight
of evidence indicates that symbolic and modern racism are significant
predictors of race-related political behaviors over and above old-fashioned racism and self-interest.[100]

The assumption of white ambivalence is directly embodied in a method
for assessing modern racism that has been developed recently by Irving
Katz and his associates.[101] In particular, these researchers proposed that
the racial attitudes of whites are currently complex and differentiated,
characterized by both positive and negative feelings. This ambivalence,
they hypothesized, is rooted in the conflict between the two core American values of communalism (involving humanitarian-egalitarian pre-
cepts) and individualism (relating to the Protestant work ethic). Within
this framework, Katz and Hass developed two scales to measure, largely
independently, problack and antiblack sentiments. Examples of items
from the Problack Scale are: "It's surprising that Black people do as well
as they do, considering all the obstacles they face," and "Sometimes
Black job seekers should be given special consideration in hiring."
Among the items in the Antiblack Scale are "Blacks don't seem to use
opportunities to own and operate little shops and businesses," and "The
root cause of the most of the social and economic ills of blacks is the
weakness and instability of the Black family."[102] Because these scales
have only recently been developed, the validity of this assessment method
has yet to be demonstrated. Nevertheless, research by Katz and his associates has demonstrated the important role that ambivalence plays in
producing extreme reactions to minority group members;[103] these scales
promise to provide a method for directly measuring the conflicting attitudes.

Table 7.3. Factor Loadings for Modern and Old-Fashioned Racism Items in 1976 Louisville Sample after Maximum Likelihood Extraction and Oblimin Rotation.

	Factor loadings[a]	
	Factor 1	Factor 2
Modern racism items		
Over the past few years, blacks have gotten more economically than they deserve. (Strongly Agree = 5)	.808	
Over the past few years, the government and news media have shown more respect for blacks than they deserve. (Strongly Agree = 5)	.800	
It is easy to understand the anger of black people in America. (Strongly Disagree = 5)	.553	
How many black people in Louisville and Jefferson County do you think miss out on jobs or promotions because of racial discrimination—many, some, only a few or none? (None = 4)	.398	
Blacks are getting too demanding in their push for equal rights. (Strongly Agree = 5)	.338	.220
How many black people in Louisville and Jefferson County do you think miss out on good housing because white owners won't rent or sell to them—many, some, only a few, or none? (None = 4)	.302	.118
Old-fashioned racism items		
If a black family with about the same income and education as you, moved next door, would you mind it a lot, a little, or not at all? (A lot = 4)		.695
How strongly would you object if a member of your family had friendship with a black—strongly, somewhat, slightly or not at all? (Strongly Object = 4)		.686
How do you feel about the open housing law in Louisville/Jefferson County which allows more racial integration of neighborhoods? Do you strongly favor, somewhat favor, somewhat oppose or strongly oppose this law? (Strongly Oppose = 5)	.111	.569
Generally speaking, do you favor full racial integration, integration in some areas of life, or full separation of the races? (Full Separation = 3)	.131	.539
In principle, do you think it is a good idea or a bad idea for children to go to schools that have about the same proportion of blacks and whites as generally exists in the Louisville/Jefferson County area? (Bad Idea = 3)	.173	.381
Generally, do you feel blacks are smarter, not as smart or about as smart as whites? (Not As Smart = 3)	.161	.300
Percent of variance	35.3	10.4
Correlation between factors	.68	
Sample N	879	

[a] Standardized regression coefficients for item and factor from the pattern matrix. Loadings less than .100 are not shown.
Note. From McConahay, 1986.

Conclusion

In summary, the consistent decline in whites' expressed negative stereotypes of blacks and feelings toward blacks and whites' increased acceptance of blacks socially and politically are sources of optimism for the future of race relations in the United States. What should not be overlooked, however, is that racism still exists and, in a variety of direct and indirect ways, has an important negative impact on the quality of life of blacks and other minorities. Approximately 20 percent of white Americans still adhere to the tenets of old-fashioned racism. Personally, they consider blacks to be less intelligent than whites and to be generally inferior; politically, they reject principles of integration and equal opportunity. And 20 percent of white America is a significant social force.

In addition, we believe that modern, subtle forms of racism characterize the racial attitudes of a sizable portion of the 80 percent of the whites who consistently reject old-fashioned racism and appear racially tolerant on surveys and polls. For these people, negative feelings may be expressed in ways that are rationalizable or justifiable on the basis of factors or issues that are ostensibly non-race-related. Because of its complexity and subtlety, modern racism is an elusive phenomenon that is difficult to detect and assess. The causal role of modern racism that can be determined in controlled laboratory settings generally cannot be conclusively proven in a single instance under more naturalistic conditions. Typically an event has many causes—racism being but one—and hence multiple justifications and explanations. In addition, because modern racists are guarded concerning threats to their egalitarian images, the assessment of modern racism requires techniques with the sensitivity, complexity, and subtlety that approximate those qualities of the phenomenon itself.

Because modern racism is more subtle than the traditional kind, it does not mean it is less insidious and less debilitating to its victim. First, as Jackman and Muha suggest, it may typify the racial attitudes of well-educated people.[104] It is from this pool of candidates that the leaders of society come. Second, people who exhibit more subtle, modern forms of prejudice may, during periods of anger or stress, regress to more primitive, old-fashioned forms of racism, often with violent consequences.[105] Third, traditional attitude change strategies for eliminating prejudice, for example, emphasizing the immorality of bias, are not effective with modern racists. Modern racists, who do not recognize their own prejudices, would be among the first to agree with these points, but with little consequence on their own behavior. Their sympathy for blacks, their support in principle for programs designed to ameliorate the consequences of racism, and their failure to recognize the negative portions of their racial attitudes convince them that they are part of the solution to racism and certainly not part of the problem.

Nevertheless, there are also several reasons to be optimistic about future race relations. At the societal level, formal legislation, outcome-based policies, and ameliorative programs (such as affirmative action) can be effective in shaping society.[106] Indeed, the civil rights legislation of the 1960s was a critical factor in moving white America from blatant, overt racism to more modern, covert forms. Thus, future legislation aimed specifically at modern forms of racism may be as effective at eliminating subtle racial biases. At the intergroup level, the recent surge in research on social categorization and ingroup-outgroup bias has focused psychology's attention on theoretical issues that are important for understanding and eliminating prejudice.[107]

At the individual level, because most whites genuinely embrace egalitarian ideals, awareness of subtle forms of prejudice may motivate change. Research has demonstrated, for example, that when people who endorse egalitarian values are confronted with the possibility that they may be prejudiced, they often respond more favorably to blacks than to whites.[108] In addition, in applied settings, the implementation of affirmative action programs has been facilitated by awareness training, which was designed "to put participants in touch with the ways their behaviors reflected their attitudes and to illustrate there was often a significant inconsistency in what they were saying and what they were doing."[109] As McConahay noted, there is reason for "optimism about the long-range future so long as the norm that 'nice people can't be racists and racists can't be nice people' establishes a climate for creative ambivalence."[110] Perhaps the racial tolerance that is prominent in America's consciousness today may tomorrow become part of America's unconscious.

SECTION III
Strategies for Change

8

MAKING A STAND FOR CHANGE

A Strategy for Empowering Individuals

Rhoda E. Johnson

My purpose in this chapter is to suggest a functional, practical strategy for empowering individuals to eliminate prejudice and discrimination from our social interactions. As I attempt to synthesize, build upon, and extend the previous chapters, I recognize that questions must be raised concerning which voices have not been heard, perspectives that have not been represented in this book. For example, the voices of Alabama's African-American community are not adequately represented here. Thus, any discussion that I undertake will of necessity not include all the voices I would like. Other conferences and other books will be necessary to present these other views.

As I outline a strategy to allow others to discover their voices, I am ever mindful that I walked right through the door which had been cracked by the courageous efforts of others. I, fortunately, was old enough to know what had been accomplished by Vivian Malone Jones, James Hood, and others. I felt what it was like to be forced to ride in the back of the bus.

As a child of five I had cried to go to Birmingham's Kiddieland Amusement Park. I remember the hurt in my uncle's eyes as he tried to explain why I could not go. I can recall an even deeper hurt when my uncle later took me to the separate, but definitely unequal, Kiddieland for blacks. It seemed that everything was done to make it as unattractive as possible. All of the worn and, perhaps, dangerous equipment from the other park had been brought out and placed in a dusty hot field. I remember the feelings of anger I had there. I also remember being stuck in the air for an hour on the Ferris wheel. I thought it must be my punishment for being there. We never went back.

My Kiddieland experience left me with a sense of powerlessness. I now knew what it felt like to settle for less than one deserved. I didn't like the feeling, but what could I do? It seemed that to fight what I then perceived as an unjust world would necessitate my giving up the perceptions of myself as a good law abiding person. At some level my feelings must be representative of those of the average African-American in the high drama of racial unrest which had swept the South during the 1950s and 1960s.

The 1963 Civil Rights Movement of Birmingham seemed very far from my hometown, Bessemer, Alabama, only thirteen miles away. In the summer of 1965 I learned that at some point in our lives even the average person could be called to make a stand. My chance came in the form of a court case filed by the United States Justice Department.

I had just graduated from high school and was leisurely sitting on my front porch when a young, male, Euro-American introduced himself and indicated that he wanted to interview me about my school. After I had spent perhaps an hour talking in detail about the inadequacies of my school building (we, in fact, had highly competent and dedicated teachers), he told me I would have to testify about this in court. I remember my heart sank into my feet. After some discussion with my grandmother I consented to go. I, along with another classmate, Marguerese McCall, was ready to be grilled. I remember my grandmother saying that it was our duty to go because this man represented the federal government.

The court case, however, turned out to be very different from what I had expected. On arriving I came face to face with the superintendent of the Bessemer School System, who had just the other day given me a diploma and proclaimed how good a student I was. I immediately recognized from his face that I was lucky to have already received that diploma. Then I took the witness stand and after my testimony for the Justice Department, the cross examination consisted, to my surprise, of one major question: "Who is your mother?" The ominous question, I knew instinctively, was meant to intimidate me. I recall asking the judge if I had to answer and somehow I knew, when he said yes, that he was being fair.

My mother was a teacher in Georgia who had completed her education at the age of thirty-five and had not been able to get a job in the Birmingham or Bessemer school systems. We had, however, always maintained fond hopes that she would eventually be able to work near home. In a split second I realized my actions had seriously jeopardized that dream. But along with that feeling came another emotion—a powerful surge of energy. I said to myself: "Well, so be it."

From that point on, the opposing attorneys could have given me the third degree. It was liberating; I felt "free" for the first time in my life. I had taken a stand and I could feel the freedom that it brought. The connections between my intimidation at a personal level and the intimidation at a societal level were finally clear. Years later, I came to recognize this experience in the accounts of others. Fannie Allen Neal has recounted similar responses in her earlier chapter.

The recounting of events such as these from the past is important in the process of reclaiming the history of our struggles. Others need to know of these experiences. Rothenberg has shown that, "The greatest secret kept by many traditional history texts was that women and people of color and working people created the wealth and culture of this country."[1] During the last twenty years or so, many new approaches to the study of history (e.g., women's history, African-American history, and labor history) have been developed to confront traditional interpretations of events. These new approaches have also validated the experiences of the "average citizen."

My research involves understanding and documenting the process by which the "average" person obtains a sense of empowerment and then has the ability to channel it for change. The major hypothesis is that empowerment is gained from knowledge of the ways in which our struggles at a societal level interplay with our personal efforts to fight injustice. The documentation of these struggles is, in my opinion, very important to the process of assisting others to gain empowerment.

The epilogue to my experience in the court room was that the Justice Department personnel packed up their bags and went back to Washington, D.C., I went back home to Bessemer, the case was lost and then appealed, and, eventually, my high school was closed. I learned a hard lesson—how very important that school and those teachers had been to the community and to me. Change, even sometimes for the better, can be extremely painful. An acknowledgement of the problems that any change can make often diffuses some of the fear, and thus some of the resistance. It is also important for me to note that, in 1983, my mother retired from the Georgia School System after twenty years of service.

The Intersection of Race, Gender, and Class

The desegregation of one of Alabama's major academic institutions forced its citizens and those of the country and the world at large to confront the uncomfortable realities that our society was not just or democratic. In order to deal with racism certain sacred images had to be challenged. At an anecdotal level, the South had always tried to justify its treatment of residents who had been classified as "black, colored, or negro, poor, and/or female." Now here on television for all to see were symbols (e.g., the stand in the door, the bombings, the dogs, fire hoses, and the violence) of the devastating personal and social domination Euro-Americans exercised over African-Americans in the South.

When African-Americans started challenging the system, other disadvantaged groups were faced with the inconsistencies in status which could arise if the challenges were successful. Many in the mob which forced Autherine Lucy to leave The University of Alabama's campus in 1956 probably would not have been admitted to the campus because of income and/or background factors. Frank Rose, President of the University during the 1963 enrollment of James A. Hood and Vivian J. Malone, recalled how years earlier as a Mississippi high school graduate he had been denied admission to the University because he was too poor to pay the University's tuition and had no access to financial assistance.

The fact that the position of women and the poor had in many ways been comparable to that of African-Americans was unknown to most of those protesting the desegregation of The University of Alabama. The idea of an African-American male and female being admitted to an institution, perceived as beyond poor Euro-American males' own aspirations, must have shaken the foundation of their beliefs. Of course, African-Americans, regardless of economic status, could not be allowed into the University because poor Euro-Americans had accepted the fact that they themselves could not go.

It soon becomes very clear that, while this book is concerned with issues of race, the stand in the school house door represents more than simply a racial issue. There is an entangled reality of class and gender mixed in the pot. As Rothenberg put it, "being born a woman, a person of color, or both, in addition to being poor, makes it far more likely that an individual will have less education, inferior health care, a lower standard of living, and a diminished set of aspirations compared with those who are born white, wealthy, and male."[2]

When Rothenberg asks how this differentiation of opportunity happened, we are inevitably forced to turn to history for answers. Legal documents, for example, have been used to trace the gradual and systematic restriction of the rights of individuals on the basis of race, class, and gender. The readings of our legal history show that from the very beginning "the laws and institutions of the United States were designed to create and maintain the privileges of wealthy white males." Rothenberg argues that discrimination was no accident. "It has a long and deliberate history. Understanding this history is essential if we are to create a more just and democratic society."[3]

Aldon Morris's scholarly work on the origins of the modern Civil Rights Movement suggests that the organizers of the movement had a sense of the history of that oppression. The political protests of the 1960s forced the society to look at the disparities between what was said and what was actually done. These organized efforts produced two major impacts, as identified by Morris: First, it altered the system of domination. Schools and public accommodations, such as the University of Alabama, were desegregated; the political and economic arenas were opened; and "imperative acts of deference to white supremacy" were to a large extent eliminated. Second, the movement "altered and expanded American politics by providing other oppressed groups with organizational and tactical models, allowing them to enter directly into the political arena through the politics of protest."[4]

If we view the contents of the chapters of this book as representative of the progress which has been made over the last twenty-five years, we are struck by both how effective the politics of protest can be and how ineffective they can be if they occur in isolation of appropriate follow-up and follow-through. We simply do not have the same network of organized effort in place to deal with the more illusive forms of oppression of modern times. The systematic and overt acts of domination have been diminished, but their effects from long ago are still with us.

Wilson, in the controversial book, *The Declining Significance of Race*,[5] and his later work, *The Truly Disadvantaged*,[6] attempted to show that there are two categories of African-Americans—one that has taken advantage of equality of opportunity and another that is a truly disadvantaged group. The Civil Rights Movement seems to have done less for minorities who are truly disadvantaged. In fact, their plight sometimes seems worse. The implication is that more is needed to bring poor African-Americans into the mainstream of the society than just changing the laws to make them race-neutral. Wilson argues that the class issue is now the major factor in the lives of the disadvantaged. Kline and associates found similar results when they studied the impact of the Voting Rights Act of 1965. The conclusion of this preliminary report suggests that empowerment, defined as exercising the right to vote, had not yet led to meaningful policy changes or an increased standard of living for the majority of the African-American residents of the Alabama Black Belt.[7]

Such findings are controversial because the obvious conclusion is that even political power can't change the plight of African-Americans. In the award-winning study of the Civil Rights Movement in Tuskegee, Alabama, Norrell concluded that political power had not brought about the hoped for economic development because "(b)y the time blacks gained political power, local government, already weak in Alabama had lost most of its remaining authority." The power was now at the state and federal levels which were much less likely to be impacted by the voting power of African-Americans.[8] What is seldom discussed at a societal level anymore is that the legal abuse of African-Americans was also accompanied by economic, psychological, sexual, and physical abuse. If we are going to have meaningful change, strategies must address more than just voting rights. This does not negate the fact that this abuse was the major issue of concern and allowed the other abuses to take place legally.

Whereas the efforts to eliminate the legal oppression of African-Americans have led to a decline in and acceptance of overt forms of racism in our society, the empirical evidence, especially that presented by John Dovidio and his colleagues,[9] supports the notion that this reduction does not mean that our society has become more egalitarian. What the research does suggest is that more subtle forms of racism may have replaced the overt legal forms.

There appears to be a rise in "well-intentioned" majority group members who exhibit what Gaertner and Dovidio term "aversive racism."[10] These individuals seem to have negative feelings (usually unconscious) about African-Americans or other minorities which conflict with a "conscience" that tries to separate these feelings from the individual's "non-prejudiced self-image." This research implies that under ambiguous circumstances these individuals can blame negative reactions to African-Americans on factors other than racism.

The reduction of overt forms of racism has made it easier to focus attention away from oppression. Ella Baker was one of the major civil rights leaders who recognized a need to develop strategies to deal with the more subtle forms of oppression.[11] It was never enough, she often said, to just concentrate on legal oppression. As Paulo Freire's work with the Brazilian oppressed predicts,[12] strategies for change must not focus primarily on the oppressive situations of the minority group but rather on that part of the oppressor which is within each of them. We only know the oppressor's ways. Audre Lorde spoke about this complex problem in a paper at a similar conference: "For we have, built into all of us, old blueprints of expectation and response, old structures of oppression, and these must be altered at the same time as we alter the living conditions which are a result of those structures. For the master's tools will never dismantle the master's house."[13]

We must seek to convince key policy makers and administrators that there is a need to review our society's efforts to be more egalitarian. The belief that society is no longer responsible for an individual's condition must be challenged. Our society seems less and less willing to want to deal with the realities of oppression; one result of this reluctance is the increasing difficulty found in identifying racism, classism, and sexism as factors in the poverty of a disproportionately large number of African-Americans. Often the successes of some of the oppressed are used as examples of what could be achieved if one just worked hard enough. The notion that societal level change can be accomplished just by the hard work of individuals must also be challenged. If the history of struggle tells us anything it is that the struggle must be organized.

A Strategy for Change

Any efforts to make this a more egalitarian and just society must 1) identify what the concept "oppression" really represents to our society; 2) confront the perception that oppression is no longer an issue; 3) deal with a lack of knowledge about how groups were legally disenfranchised by race, class, and gender; and 4) empower individuals to assist in the elimination of racism, classism, sexism, and other forms of domination. These efforts must be organized and institutionalized. One way I have addressed these issues is to develop a training model which incorporates these components.

A basic assumption behind much of the work that I do to help empower others to effect change is that those in power depend on the tacit approval of others to stay there. The control of information about the past and current events is the key to maintaining power. At a time when overt forms of racism by the majority of Euro-Americans appear to be on the decline, several distinct groups seem willing to break the silence on the issues of overt racism. One group is the community leadership training group often sponsored by the local Chambers of Commerce. These groups are nationwide and consist of local leaders and potential leaders in the community. These leadership groups are very amenable to have training in this area, especially if leaders must interact with diverse groups who have evidenced power in the community. Usually these leadership meetings are the only places where such interaction is possible. Churches, neighborhoods, and community schools often do not provide racial and class interaction. The job setting, given its hierarchical nature, is usually not as appropriate. The city leadership phenomena are growing, and they provide an opportunity for real change. Another group consists of organizations that espouse an egalitarian philosophy, for example the Girl Scouts. There has been an attempt by such organizations to bring actual practices of the organization into congruence with their goals and philosophy.

Communities involved in conflict, where one group does not have sufficient power to realize its objectives, also seek out help to deal with problems. Often these communities are willing to consider issues of racism because they have no other choice. In the past, the models for progress have come from the federal government. Today they will probably come from the local level with communities assisting in the design of training that best fits their needs.

Last, it is my belief that the training should have both content and process. That is, the training sequence should include both information about oppression and material which helps break through previous conditioning about oppression. The hope is that by going through this process the level of awareness will be such that the content will be more readily comprehended.

Over the years my work in the development of empowerment training had forced me to start incorporating concepts of race, class, and gender. I was discouraged to find that there was very little in the literature that adequately addressed all three issues. I had been experimenting with various approaches when I was contacted to work with a leadership group in a small Alabama community. This community, located in a historically poor, predominantly black county with pockets of white populations, had been for some time experiencing conflicts which could be directly related to race and class. Since a female was one of the persons instrumental in attempting to make changes in the interaction patterns in the community, gender was also a factor. The members of the group wanted to address their problems and improve their working relationships with one another, although they knew neither how to begin nor how to overcome the barriers they perceived had long been separating them in their daily activities.

The model I applied to assist these individuals in making change in their community involves two phases. The first phase centers on assisting those participating in the community leadership program to develop a sense of empowerment while the second phase consists of joint goal setting.

The process I used incorporated what I consider the best from Katz's *White Awareness*,[14] the NOW *Guidelines for Feminist Consciousness-Raising*,[15] and the theoretical framework outlines by the Federation of Child Care Centers (FOCAL) in "Racial Scripting and Social Change."[16] To begin to accomplish the group's goals, we had to deal with reluctance to bring forth issues of oppression, to confront the defensiveness that persisted about the past. One way to diffuse this defensiveness is to allow majority group individuals to identify with victimization, that is, to identify themselves as victims. There is usually a tendency to fight such a characterization. I found in my previous work with various groups that acknowledging that individuals who are rich, males, and/or Euro-Americans also have a rough time does indeed lead to reductions in the tendency to be defensive about the feelings of prejudice that they possess. We give permission to everyone to step back, recollect, and be a victim, to recount for themselves, and to share with the group if they so desired, the times they felt oppressed. Then we move on.

The community leadership-development workshop included a ten-step process moving from an increased awareness about racial, sexual, and class oppression to a commitment to try to eliminate oppression, starting with race, then moving on to gender, and class. The steps in the process moved from understanding oppression in its various forms to understanding personal feelings about that oppression.

The first phase consists of three essential components, which related to and are outlined in greater detail by Sara Evans in *Personal Politics*:

1. providing individuals with safe spaces to express feelings of oppression, both from the oppressor and oppressed points of view;
2. providing role models of people who have broken away from patterns of racism, sexism, and classism; and
3. explaining the vision of what the future could be like and presenting an ideology that can explain the sources of oppression and justify change.[17]

The objectives of the first steps are directed toward helping participants begin to understand prejudice and to develop together a functional definition of prejudice. We begin by first distributing definitions of prejudice and discrimination, for example, using such sources as the 1974 edition of the *Encyclopedia of Sociology*.[18] Prejudice is defined therein as a feeling, opinion, or attitude, usually unfavorable or hostile, directed toward a person or group. Discrimination is seen as the differential treatment of groups of people on the basis of perceived distinctions, such as race, class, and gender. These definitions are discussed, and participants then form their own working definitions. Participants are also allowed to validate their own experiences of being the victims of prejudice and discrimination. Uniformly, prejudice and discrimination are rejected by all participants, black, white, male, female. This effect corresponds with that derived in other, similar situations: no one has ever indicated that they liked being seen in an unfavorable manner or being discriminated against.

Then participants discuss definitions of racism. Because most members of such groups have no idea of what racism entails, despite living in a socio-economic environment that entails significant racist elements, the objectives of this step of the process are to identify the key elements of racism, discover how racism functions in our society, and begin to pinpoint the different kinds and levels of racism. It is often enlightening when participants see that prejudice and discrimination can become monumental problems when oppressors have the ability to make their feelings, beliefs, and behaviors the law of the land. That, in effect, racism combines discrimination and prejudice with power.

Next, participants create their own racist society (patterned on the design by Harris, Bidol & Kirchbaum[19]), and then discuss how their hypothetical society compares to the one they perceive to exist around them. Illustrations from the history of oppression in this country are appropriate and incorporated here as well for they constitute appropriate points of comparison. Every attempt is made to keep people from feeling defensive or guilty. We consistently try to keep this part of the training program at the societal rather than the personal level. We have found it is also helpful at this point to stress the notion that, although African-Americans can prejudge and discriminate, they cannot be racist because they do not have the societal power to oppress. Participants of Euro-American background are then forced to see this situation as their problem. Katz reminds us that "minorities have been placed in the position of teaching white people."[20] Katz's work suggests that it is more effective if whites teach themselves. This process can be facilitated if both an African- and a Euro-American serve as moderators for the sessions.

When individuals are comfortable with the issues and concepts they confront at this level, we then can move to the individual level. We now work toward achieving clarity in the group's individual and collective thinking and in its discussions. Individual participants are now better able to clarify further the elements of racism and to clarify the difference between racism and prejudice. These efforts at clarification are important, both for individual consciousness raising and for expanding the foundation needed for subsequent steps of the process.

In the steps that follow, we examine the connection between ideology and behavior. Participants must face the fears they have when they confront their non-expressed wants and needs. The Federation of Child Care Centers' work with similar groups suggests that participants will not be able to realize their explicitly stated goals to eliminate racism unless they first deal with their discounted non-expressed beliefs and values.

These non-expressed values and beliefs are often interrelated with the ideology of their culture and their society. Participants assume that this ideology has always existed and is firmly rooted as part of a higher natural order. It can be an enlightening experience when they discover that their personal ideology may relate back to the works of a single author with perhaps no more credentials than they possess. For example, many are suprised to discover that the idea of race as the basis for a classification of people first appeared in a 1684 essay published anonymously by a French traveler and physician, Francois Bernier.[21]

In addition to recognizing how deeply rooted racism is in our social systems and how powerful language is in maintaining cultural racism, participants at this step of the process are also helped to become aware of the racist attitudes they presently accept or have previously accepted. Having previously achieved understandings at the societal level, and having opened discussions of issues and concepts focused on the individual level permits participants to volunteer their thoughts and feelings and to begin to establish a true dialogue with one another here. Sensitive moderation of the group, aimed at eliciting attitudes that generally have been maintained for some time but not articulated, can cause participants to identify commonalties in their seemingly idiosyncratic experiences, begin to explore the myths that support and perpetuate some of their attitudes, and therefore begin to understand how and why these attitudes are racist in character and effect.

Such revelations help guide participants through the process that leads from curiosity, to identification with other people and the issues, to anger about the barriers to change, and to consolidation in which participants recognize the ways in which they have collaborated in their own victimization and accepted society's assumptions. Their energy can now be focused into goals and activities to effect change. There is a sense of solidarity with the group. A sense of empowerment can also result as the participants move from the collective identity of the consolidation stage to examine their individual potential. Personal responsibility is a key element here that needs to be highlighted and reinforced.

In the last step of this phase of the process participants establish their own commitment to make change. They do so by generating ideas about actions they can take to deal effectively with racism. These ideas can range from committing to ask friends and relatives not to tell racist jokes in front of them to outlining ordinances or legislation that could be passed to ensure all citizens participate equally in specific community initiatives. Last, when they reconvene at subsequent meetings, they assess how successful they were in actually meeting their goals to combat racism.

The leadership group which just completed the process was very successful and identified the core group to move to Phase 2. It is during Phase 2 that the goals and objectives are outlined which might be necessary to move toward a truly egalitarian community. Participants must confront the contradictions that exist within the society and culture and the contradictions that exist within themselves. Often it is here that a network of persons interested in social change can be formed. It is also here that the first serious threats to a new image of self and empowerment might be experienced. Participants find that among the new conflicts they experience are the perceptions others have of them as being "radical" in their communities. The dual purposes of this phase are to strengthen the support network for the core group, and thus reinforce the members' individual and collective commitments to change, and to help them expand and bring others into the process of being community change agents.

Since starting Phase 2 the leadership group has been confronted by powerful forces in the community who see the type of change being advocated as threatening. One member has lost a political contest in the community, but the group seems to be still committed to continuing Phase 2. Taking one's stand against injustice in public is often a crucial act for individuals of both minority and majority groups. The history of our experience aptly demonstrates that, once a stand is taken, the process of change hasn't been completed but has just begun and will require continuing effort and commitment. As the activist group Sweet Honey in the Rock has pointed out in a song in honor of Ella Baker, "We who believe in freedom cannot rest until it comes."

Summary

I have tried to show that one of the unforeseen effects of the oppression we faced twenty-five years ago was the fostering of the empowerment of courageous individuals. These individuals were able to understand in some real way the nature of oppression and its impact on their lives and the lives of their communities. They sacrificed and committed themselves to do what was necessary to make a change in the system of domination in our society. In doing so they inspired others to make similar types of commitments.

For many diverse reasons, the oppression of today seems not to generate the same commitment and sacrifice. In part it is a more illusive form of oppression which seems to intersect race, gender, and class. The inability of those feeling the oppression to coalesce to fight this form of domination has made it easier for it to survive and to grow. Old wounds from previous battles for equality have left those who are oppressed suspicious of not only the oppressors, but others who are oppressed as well.

It is now the obligation of those who see the need for change to assist in the empowerment of others. This empowerment must use a more structured and organized approach. It must unite the oppressor and oppressed. Today it may be necessary to create the strength necessary to make change through consciousness-raising and support groups. These efforts are in the tradition of the politics of protest that never received the publicity of the sit-ins or demonstrations but were nevertheless important for change.

9

ADVANCING RACIAL JUSTICE

Past Lessons for Future Use

Thomas F. Pettigrew

The South and the nation have still miles to travel before they have fully shed their burden of racial injustice. A generation is insufficient time to overcome the legacy of two centuries of slavery and another century of state-enforced racial segregation. Yet the event we observe, the Wallace stand, helped to begin to free us all—not the least of which was The University of Alabama itself.

To plan for all that remains to be done to achieve true racial justice in the United States, we must reexamine the lessons for the 1960s for future use. Such a glance back does not require an expectation of a future period similar to that of the 1960s. The next period of significant racial change, whenever it comes, will probably be strikingly different from the Civil Rights Movement of a generation ago; and it will have to face more subtle, "second-generation" problems of racial injustice. This is only to suggest that particular past lessons can provide a useful perspective on the changing future.

Many of the valuable lessons of the past are suggested by the apparent anomalies in racial change over the past generation, anomalies marked by the fact that these years have witnessed greater racial change in the South than in other regions of the country. To be sure, the South has further to go to achieve racial justice. Yet, even allowing for that fact, ironies abound. Five examples suffice.

1. Two southern Presidents over these years pressed for racial change in contrast to three other Presidents who attempted to turn back the racial clock.

2. The racial attitudes of white Southerners have improved more than any other group of white Americans.[1] White racial views in the South are still not the equivalent of the attitudes of other white Americans. But the regional gap in traditional racist thinking and in resistance to desegregated institutions has rapidly narrowed since the 1960s. New, more subtle forms of racism and discrimination have partly replaced these forms, as we shall see; but this is a national, not simply Southern phenomenon.

3. A far higher percentage of black children attend desegregated public schools in the South than in any other region.[2] Despite the determined resistance of all-white private schools and the enormity of the educational segregation that remains in the South, no other region approaches the degree of school desegregation that has been achieved. Moreover, black achievement gains during the 1970s were greatest in the South.[3] Though not generally known, black academic achievement has risen throughout the nation over the past two decades, particularly in the South. Though the causes cannot be cleanly decomposed, data from the National Assessment of Educational Progress show that between 1970 and 1980 "the gap between average academic performance of white and black schoolchildren narrowed appreciably. The effects are visible for all levels of ability, for all regions, and for all types of community."[4] And the gains appear to be of particular note in the South,[5] where the greatest amount of school desegregation and other social changes took place during the 1970s. Jones concludes: "We may not safely conclude from the evidence that achievement gains across cohorts of black students are due simply to school desegregation or simply to social programs initiated in the 1960s . . . However, the results do present a major challenge to commentators who judge that these programs failed."[6] His point received support from some widening of black-white differences in reading achievement scores for inner city and rural blacks between 1980 and 1984—years of rising inner city school segregation and significant Reagan Administration cutbacks in social programs.[7]

4. The South now annually receives a significant net immigration of black citizens for the first time in American history.[8] For the past twenty years, what has throughout our history been a net outflow of black Southerners has reversed into a net inflow to the South. Most of those black citizens are literally coming home. Often with consider-

able training, they typically return to their home areas from a large non-Southern city.

5. Finally, there is the rise of a black Southerner as the first serious black contender for the presidency. The 1988 Jesse Jackson candidacy was, of course, national in scope and rooted in solid black support—a black electoral power that was itself a creation of the past generation and was greatest in the South. But its significance for white Americans, and for white Southerners in particular, cannot be overlooked.

What Fueled These Changes?

The key lesson to be learned from this recent past becomes clear when we ask—What fueled these changes? Obviously, they did not result from any initial attitude changes of white Southerners themselves. The old saw insisted that social change can come only when attitudes are first altered to favor the social change. Nothing in our national history has so dramatically demonstrated the falsity of this proposition than the South's desegregation process.

As Governor Wallace made clear in his futile gesture to bar black Alabamians from their state university, these changes were imposed on an unwilling white South. They were wrought by black protest followed by federal court and legislative action. The vital point is that these changes were structural; they fundamentally altered the region's basic institutions. In providing for black inclusion, these structural changes began the slow, too-long-delayed task of lifting the South's racist burden from the shoulders of all its citizens. From a social psychological perspective, these institutional alternations began, slowly, to reshape the behavior of Southerners which in turn began to reshape both black and white racial thinking.

The Underlying Social Psychological Processes

Four interrelated social psychological processes underline this top-down sequence of institutional change that leads to behavior change that, in turn, finally results in the attitude change being proposed:

(1) The perception of the inevitability of institutional change is critical.

(2) Behavior change typically leads to attitude change more than the other way around.

(3) Intergroup contact under optimal conditions can reduce intergroup conflict and improve intergroup attitudes.

(4) Even in the absence of intergroup interracial contact, the disconfirmation of intergroup fears can reduce both prejudice and discrimination.

Each of these processes should be considered briefly.

(1) The perception of inevitability, with or without approval, is a vital ingredient in the acceptance of social change generally. The importance of inevitability has been clearly demonstrated in the racial change process of the past two generations. In May 1954, when the U.S. Supreme Court ruled racial segregation of public schools to be "inherently unequal," there was a widespread sense of the inevitability of sweeping racial change. The highest court in the nation had spoken unanimously; a major breech in the wall of segregation had been made; and even the angry and threatened white South believed resistance was futile. It was not until the next year, 1955, when the Supreme Court retreated in its implementation order to a vague "all deliberate speed" formula—and as native Southerners we know we move with speed that is all-too-deliberate— that the White Citizens' Councils began to form, Southern politicians became openly defiant, and white resistance to racial change throughout the South hardened. In short, the High Court's tentative implementation order weakened the sense of inevitability and thereby invited white resistance, an invitation too many southern officials readily accepted. This heightened resistance caused deep wounds in the South which are still healing. And it delayed the school desegregation process about a dozen years, for the region's school desegregation did not take hold until the Federal Courts finally lost patience between 1968 and 1972 with the white South's all-too-deliberate speed.[9]

One interpretation of the regressive 1980s is that the Reagan Administration eroded the sense of inevitability of continued racial progress. When a presidential candidate begins his Southern campaign with a "states' rights" speech in Philadelphia, Mississippi, near the lynching site of three civil rights workers, and when U.S. Justice Department lawyers appear repeatedly in racial cases only to defend segregation and discrimination, one should not be surprised when a new national wave of racist incidents erupts. Although it has not managed to turn back the racial clock completely, this Administration influenced the general perspective on racial change in the nation for eight years.

(2) Behavior change leads to attitude change.[10] This is one of the most solidly established principles in social psychology. Note that it is the exact reverse of the popular conception that attitudes must first be altered before new behavior is adopted. Social psychology does not deny the possibility of the attitude to behavior sequence. But a half century of work shows vividly that behavior change is far more often the percursor of attitude change. The leading explanation is that human beings are consistency seekers; we shift our thinking in time to be psychologically, not particularly logically, consistent with the behavior we have already exhibited. This process is enhanced when our new behavior is public and positively rewarded. Public, reinforced acts commit us before significant others, and further our need to have our behavior and attitudes appear consistent.

(3) The most studied process of changing racial attitudes has involved intergroup contact. My teacher, the late Gordon Allport, outlined "the contact hypothesis" in his volume, *The Nature of Prejudice*. He pointed out that the naïve belief that mere contact between groups will improve intergroup attitudes is clearly wrong. What matters are the conditions of the contact. On the basis of the then-available research, he advanced four conditions that predict positive effects from intergroup contact: equal status of the groups in the situation, common goals, interdependence of the groups in achieving the goals, and authority sanction for the contact.[11] Recent research has suggested further factors, and there are problems with the theoretical structure of the contact hypothesis.[12] Yet Allport's basic factors have proven useful in evaluating interracial institutions. When these institutions are merely desegregated, blacks and whites have contact under less than optimal conditions; hence, few positive intergroup effects should be expected. In institutions where Allport's conditions are at least approached—integrated institutions—positive intergroup outcomes are predicted.

Note that Allport's optimal conditions seldom existed between black and white Southerners until recent years. Note, too, that integration is often claimed by its critics to have "failed" when positive interracial attitude and behavior changes do not result at once from such interracial institutions as public schools.[13] Yet from this social psychological perspective, integration cannot be said to have failed when it has yet to be tried in the institution. Such claims of failure are based on the old misconception that any interracial contact, no matter how hostile its conditions, should be expected to improve interracial attitudes. Negative results of interracial institutions indicate that the conditions of black-white contact in the institution need to be altered, not that integration has failed.

(4) Interracial contact is by no means the only, or even the major, process by which American racial attitudes and behavior have been reshaped in recent decades. Another important process involves the disconfirmation of racial fears and expectations. Perhaps the only positive aspect of the many racial fears and expectations that have historically bedeviled America is that their very extremity makes it easier for them to be disconfirmed. Put another way, the grossly exaggerated nature of most racial fears makes it more likely that they will be found baseless.

There is growing evidence that this generally overlooked process is important. For example, one study of white attitudes toward interracial housing in Connecticut suburbs found sharp improvement after black families overcame discrimination and moved into the neighborhood.[14] Yet the greater acceptance of interracial housing did not require extensive, or even any, interracial contact. Rather, the significant shifts in opinion were related to the disconfirmation of their racial fears. Even these well-educated white suburbanites had believed much of the racist thinking that has permeated American thinking for centuries. Many of them had believed that the housing values of the area would come tumbling down when black families moved in; and that their new black neighbors would not maintain their property. When these and similar fears did not happen, white views of interracial living altered without the necessity of face-to-face contact.

Black Americans, too, have their racial fears that need to be disconfirmed. But if mere desegregation exists, without Allport's optimal conditions, black fears are more likely to be confirmed. With their worst fears validated, black insistence on and use of racial change may understandably decline. This possibility is an insight of recent racist resistance: make certain that the interracial conditions that operate in newly desegregated institutions are far less than optimal with blacks themselves bearing the full burden for the change (such as having black children do all the busing for desegregated schools); then, as blacks understandably cool to the change, claim that the desegregation "failed" and black people themselves do not want the change.

Initiating the Sequence with Institutional Change

To specify these underlying social psychological processes—the perception of inevitability, the precedence of behavioral change, the optimal conditions for intergroup contact, and the disconfirmation of racial fears—begs the question, of course, of how the institutional alterations are begun in the first place in order to trigger the institution-behavior-attitude change sequence. Examples from Northern Ireland to South Africa show that this sequence is not automatic. Attitudes can be causally important; they can bolster resistance initially so that the necessary institutional change is never successfully accomplished.

But there are important reasons that over the past three decades this sequence took place in the South more than elsewhere in the nation. First, the white South lacked sufficient political power in the nation as a whole to maintain white supremacy. Black Southerners were able, albeit with great difficulty, to mobilize national against state power. This is a key structural difference with the plight of South Africa, where the oppressed non-whites must appeal to diffuse world interest for support.

A second reason the sequence took hold in the South was that the movement in the 1960s was consistent with the deepest values of the nation, including the values of white Southerners. Racial injustice, against both black and Native Americans, has persistently been the principal moral blight on our nation. With its religious base and its focus on non-violent protest, the Civil Rights Movement appealed directly to this value conflict. Gunnar Myrdal's "American dilemma"[15] is, then, a major ally of the cause of racial justice. Notice how this factor explains why the institutional-to-behavioral-to-attitude change sequence did not fully take hold for prohibition. In addition to being only sporadically enforced, prohibition did not fit comfortably with the basic values of most Americans. While complete alcoholic abstinence was consistent with the values of many evangelical Protestants, this was not the case for the majority of Americans. By contrast, America's dilemma over racial injustice runs across religious and regional lines.

A third factor contributing to the relative success of the racial change sequence in the South is sometimes overlooked but is critically important. In large part, black and white Southerners basically share a common culture. Their institutions, lives, even speech patterns have been intertwined for three-and-a-half-centuries. To be sure, there are real and vital differences, as Jim Jones reminds us, many of them caused by their contrasting racial experiences. But black and white Southerners are far more culturally similar than blacks and whites in any other region of the country. As a white Southerner, I have been repeatedly surprised by the ignorance and distortions about black Americans than can characterize the racial thinking of even educated whites in the North and West. Often these distortions relate to cultural differences that are far less vast in the South, such as differences in religion, food, and speech. It is not necessary to romanticize the point. However, it seems clear that greater cultural similarity helped to make possible racial change in the South with less intergroup conflict than observers back in the 1950s had dared hope.

Let a positive point be added, too, for much maligned social science. It is sometimes said the social sciences can explain everything after the fact, but are rarely able to predict important social trends in advance. The phenomenon just described, however, was repeatedly predicted by sociologists and social psychologists throughout the 1950s. Indeed, I gave an address in 1960 in Atlanta to the Southeastern Psychological Association that made most of the points just given.[16] The terms then of the social science debate involved the relative causal importance of individual factors (antiblack "prejudice") or social structural factors (direct antiblack discrimination). Those who favored prejudice as the central problem tended to be pessimistic about the white South's acceptance of racial change. In arguing the same structure-to-situation-to-individual causal sequence advanced here, I predicted, more optimistically, major attitude changes in the white South as a function of the desegregation process without the need for individual therapy and other micro-remedies.[17]

Six years earlier, even before the 1954 Supreme Court ruling, Professor Guy Johnson of the University of North Carolina had made a similar argument in his presidential address to the Southern Sociological Society.[18] Johnson's speech in Atlanta, given on March 26, 1954, is truly remarkable for the specificity, as well as accuracy, of its nine forthright predictions. "1. It will be a period of tension, of evasive actions and experiments . . . [It was indeed!] 2. The initial period is likely to see an increase in race rumors, an increase in aggression against Negroes, and occasional violence . . . [Again on target; but note Johnson did not predict that mass and continuous violence would erupt—which was the then popular prediction.] 3. . . . [N]ot more than ten percent of the total Negro and white pupils will be attending schools together for a long-time to come . . . [It took two decades.] 4. In rural farming areas the proportion of mixed school units will be somewhat higher . . . I would estimate that within twenty to twenty-five years as many as half of the rural school units may be composed of student bodies of both races . . . [Close to accurate if the all-white private schools are included in the count.] 5. The only areas to have complete racial integration in the schools will be those areas which have very low Negro population rates . . . [This proved true in the first years with school desegregation largely confined to the border states.] 6. Official norms of 'equal treatment' of all students will soon develop . . . [Few, if anyone else, was making this prediction in 1954; but once again it was correct.] 7. Equal-status social contacts will be very rare . . . [Regretfully, Johnson was again on target.] 8. Negro teachers will probably suffer some loss of jobs, at least temporarily . . . [This became a major problem.] 9. The financial cost of the public schools in the South will increase quite heavily." [Right again.][19]

Modern Racial Prejudice and Discrimination Is More Subtle and Indirect

Before we can apply these lessons from the past, we must first recognize the changed nature of racial prejudice and discrimination in the 1980s that Jack Dovidio and Steven Gaertner describe. The current extent of American prejudice today is often underestimated, because many people think of white resistance to racial change only in terms of raw, overt bigotry. This is misleading. To be sure, old-style bigotry is still often involved. But majority-group resistance to racial change today is generally more subtle, indirect, and ostensibly nonracial. The changes of the sixties and seventies gave overt, traditional antiblack prejudice a disreputable image. Modern forms are typified by several noteworthy characteristics.[20]

(1) Gross and global stereotypes (such as blacks being genetically less intelligent) and blatant forms of racial discrimination (such as open refusal to hire qualified blacks on racial grounds alone) are now generally rejected.[21]

(2) But white opposition to racial change is now often cloaked in ostensibly nonracial concerns. Thus, school desegregation is not attacked directly, but the necessary student transportation to achieve desegregation is singled out for attack.[22]

(3) Moreover, white American attitudes about racial policy are deeply intertwined with individualistic conceptions of opportunity in America.[23]

(4) At the behavioral level, these attitudes are reflected in acts that betray compliance without internalization of the new norms of equal racial treatment together with both ambivalence toward and avoidance of blacks.

Schuman and his colleagues document the attitude changes in their comprehensive review of American survey data on racial attitudes gathered over the past forty years.[24] They note major shifts in white stereotypes of blacks and in matters of abstract principle. In 1942, 42 percent of surveyed whites believed that blacks had the same intelligence as whites; but by 1956 the percentage had risen to 80 percent, where it has remained. This is the critical 20 percent Jack Dovidio discussed previously. More striking are the large majorities of whites who now favor equal racial treatment in a variety of settings. Only 42 percent of whites surveyed in 1942 thought blacks "should have as good a chance as white people to get any kind of job," but 97 percent did so by 1972. In addition, over 80 percent of white Americans now say they would also support having "the same schools" for black and white children, the same public transportation and accommodations for the races, and a "qualified" black candidate of their own political party for President.

The annual rates of change on these questions were greatest between 1963 and 1972, especially the two-year period 1970–72.[25] We have noted that these were the years of the most sweeping institutional changes in American society, particularly in the schools. It is this intimate connection between structural and individual changes that is the essence of this analysis. Note also that these questions are broad, hypothetical items that avert personal involvement and threat. The questions do not specify the precise schools or jobs the races will share. Yet the hypothetical quality of these often-used survey questions does not render their data meaningless. These dramatic trends are important indicators of a major alteration in white American thinking about the abstract principles of black-white relations. The point is to not over-interpret these data, for they can be and often have been misread to mean that antiblack prejudice has now eroded to the point of near-disappearance.

The reality of modern antiblack prejudice is revealed by current white views concerning actual governmental implementation of nondiscrimination. Only white minorities favor governmental intervention to secure black entry into jobs (36 percent in 1974), open housing (46 percent in 1983), and public schools (25 percent in 1978).[26] It is this gap between high principle and low inclination to implement these principles that is the hallmark of modern white American thinking about their black fellow citizens.[27]

The behavioral counterparts of this apparent discrepancy in the current racial attitudes of whites have been uncovered in a variety of social psychological experiments. In a broad range of situations, most whites and blacks (though not all) comply with the new racial norms but without full internalization. Often, too, American whites evince either ambivalence or avoidance of black people. A revealing field study at a midwestern supermarket illustrates this research.[28] Black and white women, matched for social class appearance and age, dropped their groceries as they left the supermarket in the path of oncoming white customers. The dependent variable was how much help the women received. Old-style racist norms would dictate that whites help the white woman but ignore the black woman. This did not happen. In compliance with the new norms, approximately the same proportion of whites stopped to help each woman. But the "new" pattern is revealed by the unequal help they provided after stopping. On 64 percent of the occasions with the white woman, the white passersby picked up all the dropped groceries. But 70 percent of the time they gave only perfunctory help to the black woman by picking up just a few packages—suggesting a failure to internalize the new norms. Forty-three such helping studies reveal varying degrees of discrimination.[29] Nineteen (44 percent) noted that subjects gave more aid to their own race than to the opposite race. Consistent with compliance but not internalization, whites were less likely to discriminate in face-to-face than in non-contact situations.

Nonverbal research, with its focus on behaviors that lie largely beyond awareness, offers additional evidence. These studies often find that white American college students sit farther away, use a less friendly voice tone, make less eye contact and more speech errors, and terminate the interview faster when interacting with a black than a white.[30]

Precisely because of their subtlety and indirectness, these newer forms of prejudice and avoidance are hard to eradicate. Often only blacks are in a position to draw the conclusion that prejudice is operating in an interracial situation. Whites usually observe only a subset of the incidents, any one of which can be explained away by a nonracial account. Consequently, many whites remain unconvinced of the reality of subtle prejudice and discrimination, and think of their black colleagues as "overly sensitive" to the issue. Hence, the modern forms of prejudice typically remain invisible even to its perpetrators.

Applying the Past Lessons to the Changed Future

The Southern process of first structural change followed by new racial behavior and attitudes is the key lesson of the past era that should guide future racial action. The many remaining institutional barriers to full black participation in American society must be addressed directly, with structural changes throughout the nation comparable to those that have begun to transform the South. And we cannot and need not wait for further white attitude change before initiating such institutional alterations. Ending housing segregation and opening economic opportunities are prime targets for such future efforts. These linchpins of modern racism serve nationally the similar functions of racial separation to those once served in the South by legal segregation.

In discussing past structural gains, we have noted the importance of four underlying social psychological processes. Applying these processes to the present helps to explain the current retreat in U.S. race relations. The Reagan Administration has worked for eight years to undercut the national perception of the inevitability of full racial justice. With little recent institutional change, limited behavioral change has occurred to further attitude change. Nor has there been the needed focus on the conditions of intergroup contact. Problems of desegregated institutions are typically attributed to the process itself rather than to the far-less-than-optimal conditions that exist in such institutions. It is as if a return to legal racial segregation is sought by such critics—including, incredibly, much of the U.S. Civil Rights Commission together with the Attorney General of the United States and his chief of the Justice Department's Civil Rights Division. Finally, in a time of entrenchment, the disconfirmation of racial fears process is constrained. Indeed, situations have emerged this past decade where the worst fears of both races risk confirmation.

Adding to this bleak perspective is the more subtle nature of modern racial problems in America.[31] These ostensibly nonracial, yet effective, barriers to racial justice are more difficult to combat than the earlier gross forms. These newer barriers will also require extensive structural initiatives, such as affirmative action policies in education, employment, and housing. And given our political system, such initiatives require strong support from the federal government.

Can such changes be accomplished? Undoubtedly, it will once again require political will importantly bolstered by black American pressure for change. But it seems appropriate to venture a not-so-obvious prediction for the future: namely, that these needed institutional alterations will evolve more rapidly in the South than elsewhere. Thus, in the 21st Century, the South—long the nation's negative bellwether—could in time become the positive bellwether of American race relations.

We can take heart that the Reagan Administration has had considerable difficulty in undoing the structural gains of previous decades. For example, despite unrelenting Administration efforts under Attorney General Meese to end affirmative action programs, there is growing evidence of the institutionalization of the effort. The increasing number of supporting decisions—with some exceptions, to be sure—by the current conservative U.S. Supreme Court offers formal evidence. And several revealing rebuffs of opportunities to overturn affirmative action hiring programs offer informal evidence. In March 1985, the U.S. Department of Justice asked more than fifty states, cities, and counties throughout the nation to modify or eliminate their affirmative action hiring plans. These plans had been established earlier by Federal courts following suits brought by the Justice Department under previous Administrations. The request attempted to exploit a 1984 Supreme Court decision involving the Memphis firefighters (*Firefighters* v. *Stotts*), which ruled in favor of seniority over affirmative action rights.[32] Only a handful took up the offer.

We can take heart, too, from the general reception of Jesse Jackson's second presidential campaign, particularly in comparison to his first. To be sure, symptomatic of our transitional period, the mass media have shown considerable awkwardness in how to cover Jackson and his campaign. But that is the point. His effort has proved a learning experience for the whole nation. An anecdote from Jackson's campaign illustrates this point and at the same time provides a fitting close for this chapter. The Reverend Jackson was in Beaumont, Texas, and a white man asked if he would pose with him while his wife took a picture of them together. As they stood for the snapshot, the man mentioned that he had marched in Selma.

"Glad to be with you again, brother," replied Jackson.

"No, you don't understand," the man said. "I marched with the Klan. I just don't want to be on the wrong side of history again."[33]

10

PIERCING THE VEIL

Bi-cultural Strategies for Coping
with Prejudice and Racism

James Jones

It is a bittersweet privilege for me to share in the commemoration of Governor Wallace's schoolhouse stand. It is sweet to read about the progress that has been made at The University of Alabama with a steady state of some 9 percent black enrollment since 1976 (this compares with my University of Delaware at about 4 percent); black homecoming queens numbering five and on a roll; illustrious black alumni; successful black student recruitment and retention programs in the academic disciplines, not to mention athletic accomplishments.

It is bitter to realize, however, that the state of black America, by the accounts of members of the Kerner Commission and social political science scholars, is in real terms worse than twenty-five years ago. It is bitter also to commemorate the twenty-fifth anniversaries of the tragedies of the assassinations of Dr. Martin Luther King, Jr. and Robert F. Kennedy. It is bitter indeed to reflect on that year, 1963, when the political and moral leadership of the White House stood firm in support of humanity of all colors, and its leader too was gunned down.

It is bitter to witness the resurgence of black-white campus confrontations, the retrenchment on affirmative action and civil rights in the Justice Department and the Commission on Civil Rights, and the steady decline of black students' participation in higher education since 1976. In the late 1970s, we were advised that race was no longer the most critical determinant of opportunity, but economic circumstance was. This was possible because of the wide-ranging effects of Great Society programs of the Lyndon Johnson era. However, in the late 1980s, we are told that

179

race is now intertwined with economic circumstance to create a calcified black underclass with, at best, vague prospects for escape.

In 1903, the great black scholar and activist W. E. B. DuBois wrote that "the problem of the twentieth century was the problem of the color line."[1] In 1986, Secretary of Education William Bennett offered an Alice-in-Wonderland solution: a colorblind society! Mr. Bennett observed that

> People of good will disagree about the means [but] I don't think anybody disagrees about the ends . . . I think the best means to achieve the ends of a colorblind society is to proceed as if we were a colorblind society . . . I think the best way to treat people is as if their race did not make any difference.[2]

Alas, the problem is not so easily solved. Sociologist Pierre vanden Berghe defined race as "a group that is socially defined on the basis of physical criteria."[3] If race is a social definition, how can we act if it didn't make any difference? If it is meaningful enough to provide a basis for social categorization, it is inexorable that it provide a basis for social judgments and corresponding social behaviors. Social psychology has documented these basic human tendencies with increasing precision and sophistication for over fifty years.

But there is more. Even though we now agree that race has very little meaning biologically, we do have a history of treating people differently on the basis of their physical attributes. Moreover, we treat people differently on the basis of their cultural attributes as well. The intersection of race and culture is itself a critical variable in race relations, but one that eludes the simple proscription of Mr. Bennett, which seemed to be, "Ignore it and maybe it will go away!"

Du Bois also perceived the critical consequences of being black in America. He went on in his remarkable *Souls of Black Folk* to detail the deep psychological double-bind that gripped black Americans in these stirring terms:

> After the Egyptian and Indian, the Greek and Roman, the Teuton and mongolian, the Negro is a sort of seventh son, born with a veil, and gifted with second-sight in this American world—a world which yields him no true self-consciousness, but only lets him see himself through the revelation of the other world. It is a peculiar sensation, this double-consciousness, this sense of always looking at one's self through the eyes of others, of measur-

ing one's soul by the tape of a world that looks on in amused contempt and pity. One ever feels his twoness—an American, a Negro; two warring ideals in one dark body, whose dogged strength alone keeps it from being torn asunder.[4]

The problem is not only a problem of color, it is a problem of culture. The experience of being black is different from the experience of being white in America. In 1987 Jimmy the Greek Snyder and Al Campanis distinguished themselves with *ad hominem* social science analyses of race and culture and, subsequently, were dropped from their respective highly visible positions in the sports establishment. Not so well known, but perhaps even more illustrative is the following observation by then New York Football Giants quarterback, Fran Tarkenton:

As for quarterback, it doesn't take more than a few seconds of glancing at the NFL roster to figure out that the cast majority of them are Anglo-Saxons . . . By tradition, Anglo-Saxons have been prideful, explorative, curious men with a powerful strain of self-confidence. These characteristics have been developed over centuries of family life and schooling, and Anglo-Saxons seem to be ethnically well-equipped to operate as leaders. On the other hand, the hatred and cultural isolation meted out to the Black man over the past centuries seem to have provided an environment far removed from that in which cocky quarterback types are fostered. Therefore, as the Black community gains confidence in itself (which is happening at an ever accelerating rate), it should begin to raise the fund of whip-cracking personalities who can ramrod around a collection of diverse personalities like a football team. So far, for better or for worse, the Anglo-Saxon seems best equipped—culturally, not physically—for this job.[5]

In 1987 there were three starting black quarterbacks in the NFL, one of whom was the Most Valuable Player in that year's SuperBowl. Does this mean that the black community has gained sufficient self-confidence to produce such 'leader' personalities, or that, as in 1947, the time has come when suppressing conspicuous talent is no longer profitable or psychologically necessary?

My point in reviewing these perspectives is this: race relations in this country are complex and symbiotic. In the early seventies Tarkenton would have us believe that it was the debilitating effects of centuries of racism that obstructed black psychological development and produced weakened psyches. Today, Bennett would have us believe that there are no racial differences that matter, and that policies should reflect this fact. The first view seems to imply that the only response to oppression is weakness. This is the prevailing perspective of Kardiner and Ovesy in their classic *Mark of Oppression*.[6] The second view sees no merit in difference, presumably because all meaningful merit rests in the Western intellectual tradition. Thus we have tended to focus our analyses on weaknesses in blacks in response to adversity of racism, and on evidence of capabilities by demonstration that blacks are or can be no different from whites.

We have, however, missed one of the pervasive issues in understanding race relations. The double-consciousness proposed by Du Bois is a very real dilemma that has real psychological implications for all black people in this country. Being black in America is a political reality. It is no more evident than in the contemporary political process. For example, during the 1988 presidential primary campaign I noted a headline in *USA Today* that read, "Jackson, 'hurts' ticket!" The *USA Today*/CNN poll of 1,253 voters showed Michael Dukakis would beat George Bush head to head 45 to 38 percent. When Dukakis's possible running mates other than Jackson were listed, this advantage was little changed (48 to 40 percent with John Glenn, 45 to 39 percent with Bill Bradley). However, when Dukakis was paired with Jackson, Dukakis was a *loser* to Bush by 47 to 40 percent! A majority of white voters did not feel Jackson's strong primary showing earned him any special consideration in a Dukakis administration (60 percent said he should NOT be guaranteed a cabinet post; 59 percent said he should NOT be promised a major policy-making role; and 52 percent said he earned NO guarantees at all). Black voters saw things very differently. A majority of black voters felt Jackson had indeed earned a major role in the Dukakis administration with 57 percent saying he earned the vice presidency; 54 percent a cabinet post; and 58 percent a major policy role!

The point of this example is profound: whites and blacks were diametrically opposite in their experience of this campaign and the meaning they attached to specific outcomes. This opposition is, I submit, at the heart of the race relations problem in this country. In a society with a history of racial antagonism and oppression, the mistrust of blacks and the self-aggrandizement of whites continue to drive a wedge between them. As long as blacks and whites maintain different beliefs about this society and derive fundamentally different meaning from important socio-economic and political events, there will continue to be racial disharmony in this country.

It is amusing to consider Dukakis's dilemma. If I offer the vice presidency to Jackson, I'll lose because whites won't vote for me. If I don't offer the vice presidency, I'll lose because blacks won't vote for me. Woe is me. This dilemma was perceived in another way by Marvin Kalb four years ago. His confusion was put forth on national network television on *Meet the Press* in 1984 in the following way:

> Kalb: The question . . . [is] are you a black man who happens to be an American running for the presidency, or are you an American who happens to be a black man running for the presidency?

> Jackson: Well, I'm both an American and a black at one and the same time. I'm both of these . . .

After a lengthy reply from Jackson detailing the issues he has addressed in his candidacy and asserting that they are fundamentally national issues that should be of concern to any American citizen, Kalb is still searching for an answer to the question that perplexes *him*:

> Kalb: What I'm trying to get at is something that addresses a question no-one seems able to grasp and that is, are your priorities deep inside yourself, to the degree that anyone can look inside himself, those of a black man who happens to be an American, or the reverse?

> Jackson: Well I was born black in American, I was not born American in black! You're asking a funny kind of Catch-22 question. *My* interests are *national* interests.[7]

Kalb is confused, Bennett is confused, and America is confused. They are confused because black Americans are black and different, but at the same time are citizens with a history albeit different in fundamental respects, that is as long and significant as that of whites. Are you black OR American? Kalb seems to be asking. I am black AND American, Jackson answers. Kalb views the consideration of racial and national issues as EITHER/OR, which is implicitly divisive and absolute. Jackson, perhaps speaking for the bi-cultural resolution of black Americans, substitutes

AND for Kalb's EITHER/OR. This substitution is means to be di-unital (after Vernon Dixon[8]), inclusive, and comprehensive.

What whites must understand is that blacks can be and are both different and the same. In trying to understand race relations and project a smoother course of action, we so frequently focus on whites and their reluctance, ignorance, meanness. But we must recognize with Du Bois that this confusion in America is the source of the double-consciousness for black people of whom he spoke. It is part and parcel of the political reality of black psychological development. It is the ever-present Veil that hangs between us creating, in increasingly subtle ways, barriers as great as the Iron Curtain. Indeed, perhaps greater, for President Reagan seemed to have become more comfortable with Mr. Gorbachev than any black leader one could name.

Prejudice, Racism, and Culture

In 1972, I published *Prejudice and Racism*. There were two notable points in that effort. First, I sought to distinguish between prejudice, which is a characteristic way of perceiving one's social world without regard to the facts revealed by it, and racism, which is a set of beliefs one has about people as well as a systematic pattern of institutional intentions, behaviors, and outcomes. Individual racism, in this view, is like prejudice, except that it rests on a set of fundamental beliefs about the biological inferiority of persons of another race.[9] Institutional racism came into view with the Kerner commission,[10] and the Knowles and Prewitt[11] and Carmichael and Hamilton[12] analyses of the late 1960s. It is this view that produced the set of strategies associated with affirmative action and equal opportunity. For the most part, these perspectives and strategies for amelioration are based on race or color. There is some notion that when the strategies are successful there will be no statistical difference associated with race and that the programs and prescriptions can be dismantled.

I offered another perspective in 1972, that of Cultural Racism. This idea was meant to suggest that when groups differ in their cultural heritage, and when one group uses its power advantage to exploit the disadvantage of the other group, then cultural racism is an appropriate explanation for the results. I will not go into the details of this analysis here, but will note two things. First, the concept of cultural racism acknowledges the overlap and confusion of race and culture. Africans came to this country with a clearly distinct and different cultural ethos. This difference was exacerbated by systematically different treatment that created a subtext for an evolving and adapting cultural development that did not serve to create opportunities for mainstream involvement in American life. So discrimination, prejudice and racism on the basis of color or physical characteristic both followed from cultural difference as well as produced them.

The second point is that the notion of a colorblind society necessarily is one in which standards of competence and appropriateness are subtly linked to cultural styles that are Anglo-Saxon in origin and character. That is, there are those in our society who may well want a colorblind modus operandi, but they do not similarly want a culture blind strategy. It is the same proponent of a colorblind society, Mr. Bennett, who advocates the Western Intellectual tradition over any and all other cultural forms of thought and expression.

I have concentrated much of my recent work on understanding aspects of black life and culture that have significance for this analysis. I have arrived at set of five intertwined and somewhat overlapping concepts I refer to as TRIOS.

TRIOS is an acronym standing for five dimensions of human experience, Time, Rhythm, Improvisation, Oral Expression, and Spirituality. The concepts emerged from an analysis of racial differences in sports performance,[13] African religion and philosophy,[14] Trinidadian culture,[15] and psychotherapy with black clients.[16]

These five dimensions reflect basic ways in which individuals and cultures orient themselves to living. They refer to how we experience and organize life, make decisions, arrive at beliefs, and derive meaning. TRIOS is important because we will find divergences between the Euro-American and Afro-American perspective on these dimensions of human experience. The culture in which we live has evolved from the Euro-American perspective, but because it interacts with the Afro-American culture both necessarily share in the fabric of contemporary culture. The matter is, in part, one of emphasis and of preference.

Time is the cornerstone of TRIOS. There are several reasons why time is crucial to our analysis here.

1. Cultures differ significantly in how they organize, perceive and

value time. One of the enduring findings in psychology is the relationship between future time perspective (FTP) and achievement attitudes and behaviors. One of the reasons for this relationship is that achievement is itself often defined as setting goals in the future and adopting behavioral strategies for meeting them. Such goal setting and attainment behavior is sustained by two fundamental beliefs:

a. There is a sufficiently high probability that the behaviors one chooses to engage in at the present will increase the likelihood of attaining a goal set in the future; and

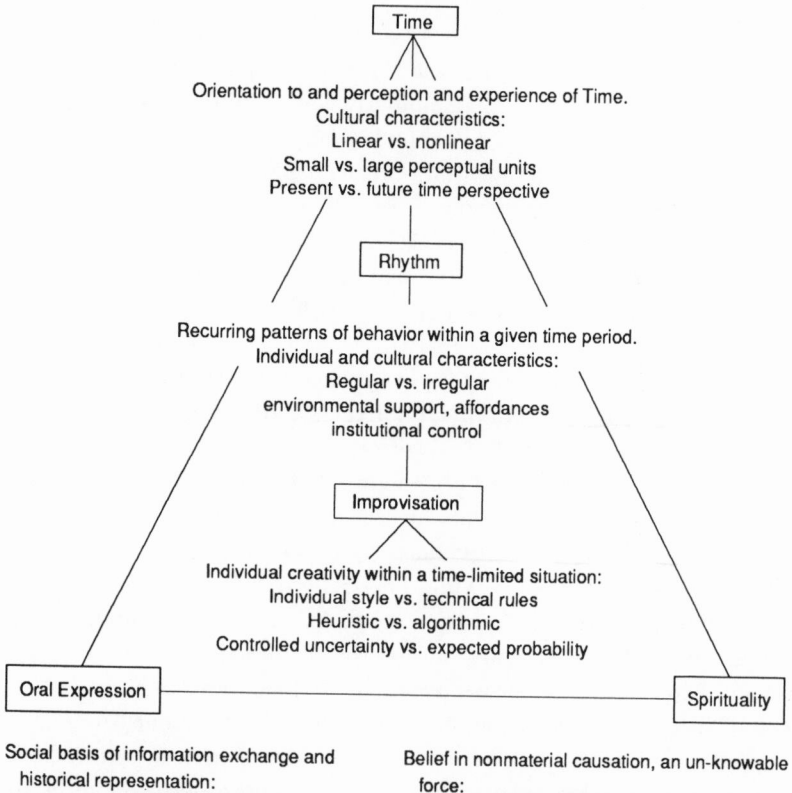

Figure 10.1. Trios: A quintet of cultural concepts. From Figure 1 in Jones (1988) reprinted with permission of Plenum Publishing Corporation.

b. Goals that are set in the future are inherently more valuable than those that do not require sustained effort over time.

In this society, racism has largely severed the probabilistic link between present behaviors and specific goal attainments for black people. That is, arbitrary and capricious obstacles have been inserted that make future projections for black people more complicated and less automatic. This is not to say that goals cannot or are not set and attained. But the process is necessarily different and requires other facilities (such as Improvisation, which will be mentioned later).

There is also a cultural legacy that does not value the future goals any more than present or proximal goals. The concept of "Progress" is not a universally positive one in cultures around the world. The point is that we have taken little time to understand the psychological benefits to be gained from a present time perspective, and have spent a great deal of time documenting the virtues of focusing on the future.

2. Future time perspective is also predicated on a linear view of time. Time marches on, inexorably forming a substrate against which achievement and accomplishment are measured. By contrast, many people and cultures adopt a non-linear or cyclical view of time characterized by what Ornstein calls the extended present.[17] "Any time is Trinidad time," describes a cultural phenomenon in which one gains functional control over one's life, making behavioral decisions that flow from how one feels now. This is in contrast to decisions that follow from structural requirements of the situation such as what time it is, or what others expect one to do.

Interesting work by Levine and his colleagues[18] and Zimbardo and his colleagues[19] have shown that differences in temporal perspective are associated with different value systems, behavioral preferences, and cultural expectations for achievement.

The point of this discussion of time is that people whose values and experiences appear to place them at opposite ends of the FTP spectrum, and attempt to interact or communicate, will likely bring different assumptions to the interaction, interpret behaviors differently, derive different meanings from certain events, and evaluate the other person differently. The future oriented, time conscious person is more likely to draw negative conclusions about the other person, and, moreover, is likely to have institutional support for his or her view of things. In this society, linear perspectives are valued and normative, while deviations often prove to be disadvantageous.

My belief that time carries the fundamental dimensions of culture that make a difference in this society causes me to consider this concept in more detail. Let me briefly mention the other dimensions of the TRIOS scheme.

Rhythm refer to a recurring pattern of behavior within a given time frame. Rhythm is associated with a flow of energy which drives behavior. Building energy or rhythm requires that effort or behavior is synchronized with environmental forces through which it must operate. Thus synergy is a positive state associated with movement and flow between person and environment. Asynchronous rhythms often have the effect of inhibiting psychological and behavioral flow and undermining performance.

Improvisation is defined as expressive creativity under pressures of immediacy. The expressive aspect gives improvisation its personal mark or character, while inventiveness must be problem-solving or goal directed. This is crucial because we tend to think of improvisation as a free for all. In jazz music, many mistake the disciplined inventions as capricious fancy. The intellectual underpinnings of successful improvisation are often missed so that negative cultural comparisons of jazz and Western classical music are common among cultural-centric people. Here, Wynton Marsalis typifies the popular manifestation of the Jackson "AND." In this characterization, improvisation is an achievement behavior that requires a prior level of skill and discipline to be accomplished. Improvisation is a cultural legacy for black Americans as well as a cultural necessity when survival in a capricious and oppressive society demands creative problem-solving and inventiveness.

Oral expression is the social basis of information exchange. When important information is communicated orally between people over time, then interpersonal relationships, social knowledge, and judgment will be important. This leads to a social foundation of culture that can be contrasted with a literate foundation in which written expressions of intelligence, opinion, ability, and accomplishment tend to define merit. In fact, with massive computer communications, it is possible to maintain regular communication with many people without ever seeing them. Moreover, langugage and all of its context-based characteristics play a central role in communication and imply the social reality of culture.

Finally, the oral tradition is more than mere language. Anthropologist Janheinz Jahn describes the concept of the word, or *nommo*, as life itself.[20] With this profound significance of the word, and the social foundation of culture, of speaking meaning into actions and products, it is important to trace the form and functions of such origins in the evolution of culture.

Spirituality is the belief in nonmaterial causation. In African philosophy all being can be placed into four categories: *Muntu*—human being; *Kintu*—thing; *Hantu*—place and time; and *Kuntu*—modality. Muntu is the one force in the world that affects human beings and it includes the dead as well as the living, orishas, loas, and ancestors. This force is present in all things, in all places and time and modalities. That is the meaning of spirituality. If force is causation, and causation is control, then individuals have a relatively smaller degree of control in the grand scheme of things. In this society, personal control or causation is seen as a fundamental virtue, even to the point where people will create illusions of control when engaging in clearly chance activities.[21]

TRIOS, then, stands as a set of conceptualized dimensions of human perception and experience organized as a clustered 'culture/personality' orientation. In considering the question of cultural differences, the dimensions of TRIOS are represented as two poles of possibility. On one extreme is the materialistic, future-oriented, iconographic, individualistic profile of the hard-working, narrowly driven high achiever. On the other extreme is the spiritual, present-oriented, orally expressive, socially responsive profile of the gregarious, flexible, easy-going, effectively driven person. These idealized polarities form the dialectical basis of cultural and personality synthesis. One model of this synthesis is biculturalism.

Bi-Cultural Strategies for Piercing the Veil

To be black in America is to live a life of personal psychological politics. To understand race relations in America is to understand, in part, how these psychological politics guide the behavior of black Americans. Robert Blauner pointed out that an enduring and inescapable feature of black life and culture is the persistence of a political, moral, and psychological struggle against a system of oppression, denigration, denial, and disadvantage.[22] How shall I face the struggle, what shall be the means by which my personal politics will be enacted? Every black person must confront this choice, consciously or unconsciously.

The president of an eastern university recently announced the creation of a scholarship for black South African students as an alternative to divestment in South African businesses. In announcing the scholarship program, the president suggested it would be similar to two current programs for black students in engineering at the University which, according to the president were ". . . designed to aid underprivileged students and ensure their academic success." Black students took significant exception to the characterization of the programs as for "underprivileged" students. A confrontation with the president ensued and it seemed from all accounts that he did not understand their problem. The president reaffirmed his commitment to black hiring and affirmative action; the students demanded required courses in Black Life and Culture for all students in the University. The rub here was the implication of deficiency based on inadequacy of resources that appear to be unavailable in one's environment. The concept of "culture of poverty" or "cultural disadvantage" was suggested, a benign form of blaming the victim that is, alas, a political statement of causality.

The president surely was well-intentioned, but he may not have understood the political dimensions of the term "underprivileged." He may have considered the new program an elightened and far more effective response to the moral conflict represented by apartheid and the United States involvement in that system. However, he must know that blacks cannot give whites the benefit of the doubt, that at this time blacks cannot trust good intentions, cannot trust white decisions as to the best way to go. This is, for blacks, a matter of continuing struggle for self from which all else emanates.

I have suggested that bi-culturalism is a means of piercing the veil, a way to join the Euro- and Afro-traditions in one dark body and mind. There are two ways of viewing this bi-cultural merger: one I call the Central Tendency approach, which is represented by the Melting Pot concept; the second is the Variance approach and is represented by the Ethnicity concept. Let us consider each in turn.

Bi-Culturalism as Central Tendency—The Melting Pot

The central tendency approach to bi-culturalism assumes that blacks adapt or acculturate to prevailing norms of performance, accomplishment, attitude, and behavior by incorporating aspects of the *Afro* and

American features outlined above into a single constellation of ethnic/personality traits. The melting pot view suggests that prevailing norms guide the incorporation of traits and behaviors toward a common instrumental purpose.[23] Thus, if American-ness is considered to include individualistic, future-oriented, goal-directed behavior, nuclear family constellations, cognitive and intellective expressions of intelligence and so on, then this view suggests any and all ethnic groups should assimilate to these beliefs, values, and practices as a condition for advancement. The American overshadows the Afro in this case, and assimilationist strategies seem to be the inevitable outcome.

What is here referred to as the central tendency approach is equivalent to the "nomothetic" approach to measurement. Its basic principle is that experience or capacity can be ordered across all people such that a single underlying dimension can be extracted. Thus, people may be compared one to the other on the degree to which they possess a given attribute. Trait psychology, indeed scientific psychology, rests on the nomothetic properties of measurement and comparison.

The central tendency or nomothetic approach operates on three basic premises: (1) One can and does assign value to dimensions of human character and ability, based on the norms or values of society; (2) one can assess the standing of *every* citizen along those dimensions; and (3) one can evaluate the *merit* of citizens on the basis of the value assigned to the behavior and the standing one attains in its expression. This merit then becomes the basis for allocation of rewards.

The central tendency approach represents a majority rule strategy by which normative expectancies often define acceptability. The most constantly enjoined expression and operation of such a central tendency is the testing movement, particularly the IQ test. It is assumed that intellective ability (IQ) is a major dimension of value, that IQ tests are valid measures of that ability, and that one can assign opportunity and allocate rewards on the basis of one's standing on that measure. The onging battles over testing point out, often in dramatic form, the operation of this approach and its negative as well as positive consequences.

Bi-Culturalism as Variance—Ethnicity

In contrast to the central tendency approach, the variance model does not limit a person or group to a single expression of its standing on a dimension of value. Rather, one may be located at different places at different times depending on situational dispositional and related factors. This approach to bi-culturality assumes that the normative values and attributes are instrumental in the society and necessarily must be incorporated into any plan of advancement. It does not, however, assume that those culturally valued attributes must be expressed at all times, are enduring and permanent features of one's makeup, and govern the behavior of people across situations.

Writing a decade later, Glazer and Moynihan acknowledged that the ethnic foundation seems to have assumed more importance in recent years, that ethnicity represents a strong statement of identity which is expressed by ". . . sudden increase in tendencies by people in many countries and in many circumstances to insist on the significance of their group distinctiveness and identity and on new rights that derive from this group character." They also stipulated that "doing without ethnicity in a society as its subgroups assimilate to the majority group may be as utopian and as questionable an enterprise as the hope of doing without social classes in a society."[24]

The strong insistence of ethnicity for black Americans came in the late 1960s as the "Black Power" or "Black is Beautiful" movement. The important point to note is that the melting pot or central tendency approach presents a central option, apparently adopted by both sides. As Cleaver noted in 1968, you were either part of the problem or part of the solution![25] Thus ethnicity was opposed to the melting pot. Black pride was opposed to assimilation. Integration was equated with assimilation and the loss of ethnic identity.

The variance approach is equivalent to the *idiographic* route to knowledge. It is predicated on the idea that detailed analysis of individual experience can reveal important information about a person that cannot be obtained through some normative comparison. If the nomothetic analysis is deductive, the idiographic approach is basically inductive. Whereas the former suggests the kind of person one ought to be to become successful in society, the latter suggests the kind of society that would evolve from the kind of people who make it up.

The *problem* of being a minority person in this society follows from the nomothetic or central tendency bias which defines positive values by comparison with normative features of society's majority people. Whereas the idiographic approach builds a view of society as the aggregate diversity of its members, the nomothetic approach dictates uniformity by its comparison of all to a common standard.

The idiographic approach identifies the aspects of traditional culture or ethnicity as those which are *expressive* of one's identity. It also takes into account those features of the broader society that consistently get rewarded and hence define the *meritocracy*.[26] The strategy, then, for an Afro-American bicultural person, is to identify and develop those instrumentalities, and select the situations and contexts in which their expression may serve instrumental goals.

The Chinese in Hong Kong similarly draw a distinction between Modernity and Westernization. Modernity refers to the need to develop technologies that are instrumental for collective development and advancement in a modern technological world. Acknowledging the need for modernization is distinctly different from accepting the cultural values of individualism and competitiveness that are associated with modernity in the Western world. Therefore, the Hong Kong Chinese reject westernization while embracing modernity.[27]

The salient point to make regarding the central tendency versus variance approach is that the latter requires a contextual or situational analysis to be appropriate and effective.

When we discuss group differences, we must be clear that these two approaches offer different accounts of observed group differences. If we consider a concept like temporal orientation, then to the extent that future orientation is valued positively, and one's capacity or tendency measurable, then rewards will be allocated in response to behaviors that reflect that tendency. Thus by a central tendency analysis, members of a group that did not score high on the measure of that attribute would either fare poorly in competition for rewards, or be obliged to make a *fundamental* change in their character over a period of time. Cultural assimilation seems to be a necessary consequence of the central tendency approach.

By contrast, while there might be a measurable difference in future orientation between two groups, in the variance model the distributions are largely overlapping. That is, members of both groups behave in both future and present orientation ways. It may be that over time more members of one group behave in present-oriented ways than do members of another group. However, for any given situation, the large majority of persons in both groups have the capacity to make future oriented decisions and benefit from the consequences. Thus, individuals within these distributions have a bi-directional possibility that is situationally determined. Attempts to measure or assess one's standing on the dimension may fail to capture this behavioral flexibility if it is done in a context that is judged inappropriate for its expression.

The broad questions of acculturation often take on political urgency as they seem to pit giving up one's heritage against making it in the system. In many respects, the central tendency approach does tend to require this choice (I do not, however, consider this necessarily to be a conscious choice.). Thus, in this view, as one moves toward the mainstream values and behaviors, one necessarily moves away from the prevailing cultural orientation. This movement is not required in the variance or idiographic model. One might further assume that other things equal, natural expression occurs within one's 'primary' culture, while the majority culture may hold the key to instrumental behaviors. It may be, further, that aspects of one's own expressive culture take on instrumentality in the majority culture (e.g., Richard Pryor and Eddie Murphy have successfully exploited their indigenous cultural experiences for great public gain). The variance model allows one to move back and forth across cultures to develop and maintain a duality in terms of both values and behavioral styles. Thus, the prevailing tendency in social and behavioral science to take a nomothetic approach to racial/ethnic differences fails to capture the more subtle complexity of the situationally-based, variance model of biculturalism.

Conclusion—Beyond Either/Or

The primary assumption of cultural racism is that one way is the best way, majority rules, and tradition prevails. The antidote to this approach is the implementation of the principles of diversity which recognize the biological idea that diversity promotes adaptability and increases genetic fitness and evolutionary success. There are two basic elements in this approach.

First, we must reduce discrimination against blacks because they are perceived as different and possessing competing motivations, values, and goals. Kalb's comments reflect this we/they, either/or perspective. There is important and exciting work in social psychology that helps us get a handle on how we might reduce discrimination. The basic problem can be conceived as follows: Human tendencies toward social categorization lead to ingroup preference which results in outgroup discrimination. Thus, the basic tendency for human beings to make social categorical judgments leading to an ingroup preference combines with a power and control to create racial inequalities. The research literature has demonstrated convincingly two ways in which one may reduce the social categorization effects:

(1) By reducing the salience of group boundaries, we can create a wider conception of ingroup and a correspondingly smaller sense of outgroup. Work by Gaertner and Dovidio has shown that intergroup processes that emphasize ways in which people are similar can capitalize on ingroup biasing effects to strengthen relationships among people previously thought to be part of different groups.[28]

(2) By increasing the salience of individual variability, we can show that individuating information about specific people serves to reduce the use of category (or group level) information and thereby diminishes the operation of group-based bias. This approach emphasizes the differences between people, in contrast to the previous approach that builds upon similarities among them. Research by Lockesley and her colleagues[29] and by Miller and Brewer[30] has offered empirical and theoretical support for the ability of individuating information to reduce category-based social judgments.

A second approach to the problem is to acknowledge directly the fact of group differences and to understand ways in which such differences contribute to the cultural fabric of a multicultural society. To do this we must think more clearly about human diversity and differently from how we do now. We readily accept in principle the notion that diversity is good, but when we are pressed to answer "what's good about it?" we often are lost for an acceptable answer. An acceptable answer is always framed in terms of instrumental advantages in a cultural system driven by socio-economic materialistic success.

The approaches to living envisioned by the TRIOS model represent not simply a basis for describing racial-cultural differences between black and white Americans. Rather, it is an attempt to systematically review aspects of racial difference in which the orienting premise does not put blacks at a deficient starting point, and, further, to elaborate the range of human behaviors deemed important in this society. In fact, I argue, the dimensions of TRIOS are important to any functioning society. Biculturality, thus, is a two-way street. While blacks have and must necessarily develop the same skills that whites must and do in this society, whites should recognize the salience of the flip side of traditional cultural truisms. In this regard it would be a worthwhile exercise to make a list of positive and negative expressions of characteristics assumed to be traditional in the Euro-American and Afro-American adaptations of living in the United States.

We can also learn from the experiences of people who are socialized and forced to adapt to fundamentally different environmental circumstances. How does a person, born and raised in an urban ghetto of the northeast or a barrio of the southwest or an Appalachian mountain town of West Virginia convert an ecological-economic disadvantage to an occasion for growth and development? What skills and abilities go into converting expressive qualities and localized instrumentalities into a wider set of opportunities and accomplishments? Do we have any understanding, and how might we advance our own appreciation of differences by learning of what they consist? It is often argued that increased tolerance for others often accompanies the experience of intolerance at the hands of others. Learning, therefore, to understand and truly appreciate cultural diversity and the variety of circumstances from which individuals and groups evolve in this society is a backdrop for both the means of reducing social categorization and its corresponding discriminatory effects.

TRIOS is offered as a set of ideas that may have currency for such an expanded appreciation of cultural diversity. It is not meant as a simple portrayal of black people as African people—rather, it looks at dimensions of human experience that are real, evolutionary, and valid as legitimate human responses to survival in an oppressive environment undergoing the inexorable processes of evolution.

It is an important task to develop ways of incorporating diversity not only in the development of intergroup attitudes, but in the determination of a system for the allocation of resources. Here I would suggest we develop the goal of *Affirmative Diversity*. We speak often and easily about the values of cultural diversity, but do not yet have an operational model of how to construct meaningful ways of incorporating this value into everyday life. Affirmative Action is always seen, even among proponents, as a short-term remedy. But how do we weave cultural diversity into the monolith of goal-oriented capitalism? This system has already decided what matters. While it is easy to reject color as a basis for the allocation of resources, having committed to a "colorblind" society does not solve the problem. In reality, it is far more difficult to incorporate cultural differences in personality and behavioral style among agreed upon standards of reward. Affirmative diversity must attack this problem head-on.

The critical question of racism must go beyond biological roots to confront cultural issues. The multi-dimensional model of human character and conduct is demanded in a multi-cultural society. Those who are and have been culturally different know this fact very well. Those who have enjoyed the advantage of defining the norm still have this lesson to learn.

NOTES

1. HELLHOUND ON MY TRAIL: Race Relations in the South from Reconstruction to the Civil Rights Movement
LEON F. LITWACK

1. Willard B. Gatewood, Jr., *Black Americans and the White Man's Burden, 1898–1903* (Urbana: University of Illinois Press, 1975), 117–18.

2. Sgt. [deleted], Troop [deleted], Cavalry, Gibara, Cuba, June 22, 1899, to John E. Bruce, John E. Bruce Papers, Schomburg Center for Research in Black Culture, New York Public Library. In concluding his letter, the sergeant wrote, "I must caution you on the necessity of secrecy in this letter as it would hurt me a great deal should it ever come under the eyes of the authorities."

3. Theodore Rosengarten, *All God's Dangers: The Life of Nate Shaw* (New York, 1974), 161.

4. Mary E. Mebane, *Mary* (New York: Fawcett, 1982), 5.

5. Pauli Murray, *Proud Shoes* (New York: Harper & Row, 1987), 270.

6. Margaret Walker, "Growing Out of Shadow," in Dorothy Abbott, ed., *Mississippi Writers: Reflections of Childhood and Youth* (2 vols., Jackson, Miss., 1985–86), 2: Nonfiction, 601, 602.

7. James Weldon Johnson, *Along This Way* (New York, 1933), 85–86; George P. Rawick, ed., *The American Slave: A Composite Autobiography*, Supplement, Series 1 (12 vols., Westport, 1977), 1: Alabama Narratives, 4.

8. Ralph Ellison, *Shadow and Act* (New York, 1964), 116.

9. W. E. B. Du Bois, *The Souls of Black Folk: Essays and Sketches* (Chicago: A. C. McClurg, 1903), 68; John Temple Graves, "The Problem of the Races," in *The Possibilities of the Negro in Symposium: A Solution of the Negro Problem Psychologically Considered* (Atlanta, Ga., 1904), 30.

10. Southern Society for the Promotion of the Study of Race Conditions and Problems in the South, *Race Problems of the South: Report of the Proceedings of the First Annual Conference . . . at Montgomery, Ala., May 8–10, A.D. 1900* (Richmond, Va., 1900), 36.

11. Rebecca Felton, Palmer House, Chicago, to William H. Felton, March 15, 1893, Rebecca Felton Papers, University of Georgia, Athens, Ga.

12. Ray Stannard Baker, *Following the Colour Line* (New York, 1908), 28.

13. Quoted in Edward L. Ayers, *Vengeance & Justice: Crime and Punishment in the 19th-Century American South* (New York, 1984), 236.

14. William Archer, *Through Afro-America: An English Reading of the Race Problem* (London, 1910), 60.

15. Rosengarten, *All God's Dangers*, 36.

16. Booker T. Washington, *Future of the American Negro* (Boston, 1899), 176; Robert L. Factor, *The Black Response to America* (Reading, Mass., 1970), 253; Francis L. Broderick, *W. E. B. Du Bois: Negro Leader in a Time of Crisis* (Stanford, 1955), 66.

17. See, for example, Silas X. Floyd, *Floyd's Flowers or Duty and Beauty for Colored Children* (Atlanta, Ga., 1905); William Henry Harrison, Jr., *Colored Girls and Boys' Inspiring United States History and a Heart to Heart Talk about White Folks* ([Bethlehem, Pa.], 1921); T. L. Haines and L. W. Yaggy, eds., *Getting On In The World: Or Aids and Helps to Success Under Difficulties* (Chicago, n.d.).

18. Loyle Hairston, "Growing Up in Mississippi," in Abbott, ed., *Mississippi Writers*, 2: Nonfiction, 313.

19. Baker, *Following the Colour Line*, 242.

20. Clifton Johnson, *Highways and Byways of the South* (New York, 1904), 82.

21. Myrta Lockett Avary, *Dixie After the War* (New York, 1906), 410–2.

22. Graves, "The Problems of the Races," and Willis B. Parks, "A Solution of the Negro Problem Psychologically Considered," in *The Possibilities of the Negro in Symposium*, 21, 147–53.

23. Isaiah T. Montgomery, Mound Bayou, Miss., to Booker T. Washington, September 6, 1904, in Louis R. Harlan and Raymond W. Smock, eds., *The Booker T. Washington Papers* (13 vols., Urbana, Ill., 1971–84), 8:61–63.

24. Quoted in Robert T. Kerlin, *The Voice of the Negro* (New York, 1920), 131.

25. C. Vann Woodward, *Origins of the New South, 1877–1913* (Baton Rouge, La., 1951), 218; letter to the editor, *Chicago Defender*, April 28, 1917; "'The Money Ralley' at Sweet Gum: The Story of a Visit to a Negro Church in the Black Belt, Alabama," typescript, n.d. (circa 1912), Robert Park Papers, box

1, folder 10, p. 11, University of Chicago. I am grateful to Dr. James Grossman for bringing the last two items to my attention.

26. Fannie Lou Hamer, "To Praise Our Bridges," in Abbott, ed., *Mississippi Writers*, 2: Nonfiction, 321.

27. *Report of the Joint Select Committee To Inquire Into the Condition of Affairs in the Late Insurrectionary States* (13 vols., Washington, D.C., 1872), 2: Mississippi, 891–92. See also, for example, J. Sternfeld, Montgomery, Ala., to W. S. Reese, November 12, 1903; George Randolph, Memphis, to Attorney General of the United States, November 3, 1904, May 9, 1905; W. M. Hanson, Galveston, Texas, to Attorney General, November 10, 1904; W. S. Reese, Jr., Montgomery, Ala., to Attorney General, February 25, 1905; T. Brady, Jr., Brookhaven, Miss., to Attorney General, May 9, 1906; Records of the Attorney-General's Office, Department of Justice, National Archives, Washington, D.C.; *The Crisis: Record of the Darker Races*, 1 (December 1910): 27.

28. Quoted in Jacquelyn Dowd Hall, *Revolt Against Chivalry* (New York, 1979), 140.

29. Rosengarten, *All God's Dangers*, 544, 193, 264, 27, xxi.

30. "Arthur Raper, 1899–1979—A Life Looking 'for the Heart of the Thing': Interview by Cliff Kuhn," *Southern Changes*, 9 (June/July 1987): 6.

31. Hamer, "To Praise Our Bridges," In Abbott, ed., *Mississippi Writers*, 2: Nonfiction, 323.

32. Charles Evers, "Evers," in Abbott, ed., *Mississippi Writers*, 2: Nonfiction, 196.

33. Little Rock *Daily News*, quoted in *The Crisis*, 15 (April 1918): 289.

34. Quoted in Gatewood, *Black Americans and the White Man's Burden*, 2.

35. For the depiction of blacks and African-American history in textbooks, the best sources are the texts themselves, both on the secondary public school and college level. See also Lawrence D. Reddick, "Racial Attitudes in American History Textbooks of the South," *Journal of Negro History*, 19 (July 1934): 225–65; Ruth Miller Elson, *Guardians of Tradition: American Schoolbooks of the Nineteenth Century* (Lincoln, 1964), 87–100; Frances FitzGerald, *America Revised: History Schoolbooks in the Twentieth Century* (Boston, 1979), 64–65, 83–89; Marie E. Carpenter, *The Treatment of the Negro in American History School Textbooks* (Menasha, Wisc., 1941).

36. Hairston, "Growing Up in Mississippi," in Abbott, ed., *Mississippi Writers*, 2: Nonfiction, 319.

37. Archer, *Through Afro-America*, 234.

38. Richard Wright, *Black Boy: A Record of Childhood and Youth* (New York, 1945), 65, 171.

39. Ellison, *Shadow and Act*, 83.

40. Lawrence W. Levine, *Black Culture and Black Consciousness: Afro-American Folk Thought from Slavery to Freedom* (New York, 1977), 407–20.

41. Richard Wright, "How Bigger Was Born," in Abraham Chapman, ed., *Black Voices: An Anthology of Afro-American Literature* (New York, 1968), 542; Charles W. Chesnutt, Manuscript Journal II, entry for March 16, 1880, Charles W. Chesnutt Papers, Fisk University, Nashville.

42. David Evans, "Charley Patton: The Conscience of the Delta," in Robert Sacre, ed., *The Voice of the Delta: Charley Patton and the Mississippi Blues Traditions* (Liege, Belgium, 1987), 143.

43. Willie Brown, "Future Blues," in Michael Taft, comp., *Blue Lyric Poetry: An Anthology* (New York, 1983), 41, and on *The Mississippi Blues No. 1, 1927–1940* (Origin Jazz Library, OJL-5).

44. Robert Johnson, "Preaching Blues," in Eric Sackheim, comp., *The Blues Line: A Collection of Blues Lyrics* (New York, 1969), 225, and on *Robert Johnson: King of the Delta Blues Singers* (Columbia Records CL 1654).

45. Furry Lewis, "Furry's Blues," in Taft, comp., *Blues Lyric Poetry*, 169, and on *Furry Lewis: In His Price, 1927–1928* (Yazoo Records 1050).

46. Greil Marcus, *Mystery Train: Images of America in Rock 'n' Roll Music* (New York, 1975), 33.

47. Charley Patton, "Down the Dirt Blues," in Taft, comp., *Blues Lyric Poetry*, 211, and on *Charley Patton: Founder of the Delta Blues* (Yazoo Records L-1020).

48. Bertha "Chippie" Hill, "Trouble in Mind," in Paul Oliver, comp., *Early Blues Songbook* (London, 1982), 103.

49. Levine, *Black Culture and Black Consciousness*, 418.

50. Robert Johnson, "Me and the Devil Blues," in Sackheim, comp., *Blues Line*, 224, and on *Robert Johnson: King of the Delta Blues Singers*.

51. Paul Oliver, *Blues Fell This Morning: The Meaning of the Blues* (New York, 1960), 23.

52. Du Bois, *The Souls of Black Folk*, 5.

53. Theodore Roosevelt to Owen Wister, April 27, 1906, in Elting E. Morison et al., eds., *The Letters of Theodore Roosevelt* (8 vols., Cambridge, Mass., 1951–54), 5: 226.

54. Ralph Ellison, *Going to the Territory* (New York, 1986), 287–88.

55. Rosengarten, *All God's Dangers*, 309.

56. Howard Zinn, *SNCC: The New Abolitionists* (Boston, 1964), 136–37.

57. David J. Garrow, *Bearing the Cross: Martin Luther King, Jr., and the Southern Christian Leadership Conference* (New York, 1986), 562.

58. Robert Johnson, "Hellhound on My Trail," in Sackheim, comp., *Blues Line*, 223, and on *Robert Johnson: King of the Delta Blues Singers*.

3. THE SCHOOLHOUSE DOOR: An Institutional Response to Desegregation
E. CULPEPPER CLARK

1. J. E. Chappell to Chauncy Sparks, April 8, 1943, and Raymond R. Paty, "Notes on the Report Titled 'A Study of Higher Education for Negroes in Alabama,'" in John Moran Gallalee papers, University of Alabama Library (cited hereafter as Gallalee papers, UAL). For the original report see Edgar W. Knight, "A Study of Higher Education for Negroes in Alabama" (Montgomery, June 1940), in State Department of Archives and History, Montgomery, Alabama (cited hereafter as State Archives, Montgomery). For Sparks's speeches see "Founders' Day Speech," Tuskegee, April 4, 1943, and "Message of Governor Chauncy Sparks to Legislature of Alabama," Reg. Session, May 4, 1943, in Governor's Files, State Archives, Montgomery.

2. Nathaniel S. Colley to The Registrar, March, 11, 1946, Gallalee papers, UAL.

3. Ralph E. Adams to Nathaniel S. Colley, March 21, 1946, ibid.

4. William H. Hepburn to Marion Smith, March 23, 1946, and Smith to Hepburn, March 25, 1946; John E. Adams to Ralph E. Adams, April 4, 1946, and R. Adams to J. Adams, April 18, 1946. Ibid.

5. John E. Adams to Ralph E. Adams, April 20, 1946, ibid.

6. John B. Scott to Rufus Bealle, July 14, 1953, ibid.

7. Memorandum, Frontis H. Moore to Board of Trustees, October 19, 1954, Burr and Forman Files.

8. New York Times, August 22, 1948. Original "Student Opinion Survey" in Gallalee papers, UAL.

9. For discussion of Morrison Williams's role see J. Tyra Harris, "Alabama Reaction to the Brown Decision, 1954–1956: A Case Study in Early Massive Resistance," Ph.D. diss., Middle Tennessee State University, 1978, 251–52. Harvey's comments appeared in the Birmingham Post-Herald, October 5, 1950, and those of the Auburn editor in the Birmingham Post-Herald, October 31, 1950; Noble B. Hendrix, Dean of Students, to Gallalee, October 31, 1950, Gallalee papers, UAL.

10. O. C. Carmichael to Wilton B. Persons, March 1, September 8, 1954, January 1, 1955; persons to Carmichael, February 14, 1955, Oliver Cromwell Carmichael papers, University of Alabama Library (cited hereafter as Carmichael papers, UAL).

11. "Memorandum for the President," March 1, 1954, ibid.

12. O. C. Carmichael to John Temple Graves, July 23, 1954, and Graves to Carmichael, July 24, 25, 1954, ibid.

13. O. C. Carmichael to Hill Ferguson, June 27, 1955, ibid. Carmichael's

record at Vanderbilt indicates a history of weakness in the face of a crisis and inordinate deference to a board of trustees. See Paul K. Conkin, *Gone with the Ivy: A Biography of Vanderbilt University* (Knoxville: University of Tennessee Press, 1985), 403, 423–29.

14. University News Bureau, University of Alabama, February 9, 1956, report on remarks filed by Robert S. Bird, February 8, 1956, Carmichael papers, UAL.

15. The board meeting of February 29, 1956, was an adjourned meeting from the traditional homecoming meeting and was held at the Tutwiler Hotel in Birmingham at 6:30 P.M. All were present except for Governor Folsom, State Superintendent of Education Austin Meadows, and Gordon Palmer. Also attending the meeting were President Carmichael, Dean Adams, Frontis Moore, Andrew Thomas, and Rufus Bealle. It was on a motion by William Key, seconded by Eris Paul, that the board authorized the admission of Peters should she be qualified. On March 9, 1956, Ferguson continued his opposition to Peters in a telegram to Carmichael, "With all the tension and unrest that now prevails, I think it would be suicide to provoke another incident. Hence I urge no action on the Peters case." Quoted material in Hill Ferguson letters to Judge Clarence W. Allgood and to James A. Green, March 19, 1956, ibid.; interview with Henry McCain, December 1985.

16. Alan Knight Chalmers to Arthur Gray, March 9, 21, 1956; Chalmers to O. C. Carmichael, Trustees File, Talladega College Historical Collections; Chalmers, "Situation on University of Alabama—August, 1956," A. K. Chalmers papers, Boston University Library; Brewer Dixon to O. C. Carmichael, June 11, 1956, and Carmichael to Chalmers, August 7, 1956, Carmichael papers, UAL; Birmingham *World*, May 18, 1956.

17. Brewer Dixon to O. C. Carmichael, June 11, 1956, Carmichael papers, UAL.

18. R. E. Steiner to Carmichael, June 2, 6; Brewer Dixon to Carmichael, June 8; Thomas S. Lawson to Carmichael, June 5, 11, 1956, ibid.

19. O. C. Carmichael to R. E. Steiner, June 5, 9, 1956, ibid.

20. John Rutland interview, November 18, 1985; A. K. Chalmers to Billy Joe Nabors with blind copy to Arthur Gray, August 22, 1956, Trustee Files, Talladega College Historical Collections.

21. Notes recorded to Jefferson Bennett, September 6–12, 1956, James Jefferson Bennett Papers, University of Alabama Library (cited hereafter as Bennett papers, UAL); notes from Jefferson Bennett for Governor Folsom as recorded by Ralph Hammond, Governors Papers, University of Alabama File, October 1, 1955–September 30, 1956, State Archives, Montgomery, Alabama.

22. Frank Rose to W. R. Jones, January 16, 1963, Frank Rose papers, University of Alabama Library.

23. Burke Marshall to Robert F. Kennedy, June 26, 1963, Robert F. Kennedy papers, John Fitzgerald Kennedy Presidential Library.

24. Gessner T. McCorvey to Andrew Thomas, March 30, 1964, Bennett papers, UAL.

25. Gessner T. McCorvey to Frank Rose, Jefferson Bennett, Alex S. Pow, and Rufus Bealle, June 12, 1963, ibid.

4. FROM FOSTER AUDITORIUM TO SANDERS AUDITORIUM: The "Southernization" of American Politics
DAN T. CARTER

1. Mrs. Charles Ash to Lister Hill, April 11, 1963, in Lister Hill Papers, Box 499; C. J. Long to Armistead Selden, May 28, 1963, in "Segregation File, 1963–1964," Armistead I. Selden, Jr., Congressional Collection, W. Stanley Hoole Special Collections Library, The University of Alabama.

2. Marshall Frady, *Wallace* (New York: World Publishing Co., 1968), 170–71.

3. Montgomery *Advertiser,* November 5, 1963.

4. Art Wallace to George Wallace, August 13, 1963; George Wallace to Art Wallace, September 13, 1963, "Segregation" File, Box 399, Alabama Governors' Papers, Alabama Department of Archives and History, Montgomery, Alabama.

5. George Santayana, *Life of Reason* (New York: Charles Scribner's Sons, 1905), 1:284.

5. A PSYCHOANALYTIC APPROACH TO THE PROBLEMS OF PREJUDICE, DISCRIMINATION, AND PERSECUTION
MORTIMER OSTOW

1. Yosef Yerushalmi, "Assimilation and Racial Anti-Semitism: The Iberian and the German Models," Leo Baeck Memorial Lecture 26 (1982).

2. Mortimer Ostow, "A Contribution to the Study of Antisemitism." Presented on the Occasion of the 50th Anniversary of the Israel Psychoanalytic Society, *Israel Journal of Psychiatry and Related Disciplines,* 20, 1–2 (1983): 95–118.

3. F. W. Eickhoff, "Identification and Its Vicissitudes in the Context of the Nazi Phenomenon," *International Journal of Psycho-Analysis,* 67 (1986): 33–44.

4. Mortimer Ostow, "The Psychodynamics of Apocalyptic: Discussion of Papers on Identification and the Nazi Phenomenon," *International Journal of Psycho-Analysis,* 67, (1986) 1:277–85.

5. Robert Waelder, *Progress and Revolution* (New York: International Universities Press, 1967).

6. Sigmund Freud, *The Standard Edition of the Complete Psychological Works of Sigmund Freud*, 23: *Moses and Monotheism* (London: Hogarth Press, 1939).

6. SCHOOL DESEGREGATION: Short-Term and Long-Term Effects
WALTER G. STEPHAN

1. Marshall Frady, *Wallace* (New York: World, 1968), 153–63.

2. Richard Kluger, *Simple Justice* (New York: Knopf, 1976), 424.

3. David J. Armor, "White Flight and the Future of Desegregation," in Walter G. Stephan and Joe R. Feagin, *School Desegregation: Past, Present, and Future* (New York: Plenum, 1980), 187–226.

4. *Griffin v. County School Board of Prince Edward County*, 377 U.S. 218 (1964).

5. Thomas F. Pettigrew, *Racial Discrimination in the United States* (New York: Harper & Row, 1975), 225–28, 231–33.

6. Alvis V. Adair, *Desegregation: The Illusion of Black Progress* (New York: Lanham, 1984); Walter G. Stephan, "School Desegregation: An Evaluation of Predictions Made in *Brown* vs. *The Board of Education*," *Psychological Bulletin*, 85 (1978): 217–38.

7. Adair, *Desegregation;* Harrell R. Rodgers and Charles S. Bullock III, *Coercion to Compliance* (Lexington, Mass.: Heath, 1976), 126, 150; Gary Orfield, *Must We Bus? Segregated Schools and National Policy*, (Washington, D.C.: The Brookings Institution, 1978), 298.

8. Orfield, *Must We Bus?* 319.

9. U.S. Commission on Civil Rights, *The New Evidence on Civil Rights on School Desegregation* (Washington, D.C.: U.S. Government Printing Office, 1987), 11.

10. Charles S. Bullock III and Charles M. Lamb, *Implementation of Civil Rights* (Monterey, Calif.: Brooks/Cole, 1984); James McPartland, "Desegregation and Equity in Higher Education and Employment: Is Progress Related to Desegregation of Primary and Secondary Schools?" *Law and Contemporary Problems*, 43 (1978), 108–32.

11. *Chronicle of Higher Education*, April 6, 1988, 1.

12. Ibid., March 9, 1988, 33.

13. Ibid., February 3, 1988, 1.

14. Ibid., January 6, 1988, 6.

15. Ibid., January 20, 1988, 21.

16. David J. Armor, "White Flight," 187–226; U.S. Commission on Civil Rights, *The New Evidence*, 37–68.

17. Christine H. Rossell, "School Desegregation and Community Social Change," *Law and Contemporary Problems*, 42: (1978), 133–83; U.S. Commission on Civil Rights, *The New Evidence*, 37–68.

18. U.S. Commission on Civil Rights, *The New Evidence*, 13–14.

19. U.S. Commission on Civil Rights, *Fifteen Years Ago . . . Rural Alabama Revisited* (Washington, D.C.: U.S. Government Printing Office, 1983), 43–82.

20. Armor, "White Flight"; U.S. Commission on Civil Rights, *The New Evidence*, 206–209.

21. Orfield, *Must We Bus?*, 31–30; Derrick Bell, "Civil Rights Commitment and the Challenge of Changing Conditions in Urban School Cases," in Adam Yarmolinsky, Lance Liebman, and Corinne S. Schelling, eds., *Race and Schooling in the City* (Cambridge: Harvard University Press, 1981), 194–203.

22. U.S. Commission on Civil Rights, *Statement of the United States Commission on Civil Rights on School Desegregation* (Washington, D.C.: U.S. Government Printing Office, 1982), 17.

23. Walter G. Stephan, "School Desegregation: An Evaluation of Predictions Made in *Brown* vs. *The Board of Education*," *Psychological Bulletin 85* (1978), 217–38.

24. Lawrence A. Bradley and Gifford W. Bradley, "The Academic Achievement of Black Students in Desegregated Schools: A Critical Review," *Review of Educational Research*, 47 (1977): 377–449; Robert L. Crain and Rita E. Mahard, "Desegregation and Black Achievement: A Review of the Research," *Law and Contemporary Problems*, 42 (1978): 17–56; R. A. Krol, "A Meta-Analysis of Comparative Research on the Effects of Desegregation on Academic Achievement," *The Urban Review*, 12 (1980): 211–24; Nancy H. St. John, *School Desegregation Outcomes for Children* (New York: Wiley, 1975), 7, 17–19, 79, 111; Meyer Weinberg, *The Search for Quality Integrated Education* (Westport, Conn.: Greenwood Press, 1983), 146–72; Paul M. Wortman, C. King, and F. B. Bryant, *Meta-Analyses of Quasi-Experiments: School Desegregation and Black Achievement* (Ann Arbor, Mich.: Institute for Social Research, 1982), 1–23.

25. Walter G. Stephan, "Effects of School Desegregation: An Evaluation 30 Years after *Brown*," in L. Saxe and M. Saks, *Advances in Applied Social Psychology*, (New York: Academic Press, 1986), 181–206.

26. Robert L. Crain and Rita E. Mahard, "School Racial Composition and Black College Attendance and Achievement Test Performance," *Sociology of Education*, 51 (1978): 81–101; Stephan, "Effects of School Desegregation," 191.

27. St. John, *School Desegregation Outcomes for Children*, 34–36.

28. Stephan, "Effects of School Desegregation," 187–89.

29. Stephan, "Effects of School Desegregation"; Walter G. Stephan and D. Rosenfield, "Black Self-Rejection: Another Look," *Journal of Educational Psychology*, 70 (1979): 708–16.

30. Morris Rosenberg, "Self-Esteem Research: A Phenomenological Corrective," in J. Prager, D. Longshore, and M. Seeman, eds., *School Desegregation Research: New Approaches to Situational Analyses* (New York: Plenum, 1986), 175; Roberta G. Simmons, "Blacks and High Self-Esteem: A Puzzle," *Social Psychology*, 41 (1978): 57–67.

31. Stephan, "School Desegregation: An Evaluation of Predictions," 221–26.

32. Rossell, "School Desegregation and Community Social Change," 173–74.

33. John B. McConahay and Willis D. Hawley, "Attitudes of Louisville and Jefferson County Citizens Toward Busing for Public School Desegregation," unpublished report (Durham, N.C.: Duke University, 1976); Margaret A. Parsons, "Attitude Changes Following Desegregation in New Castle County, Delaware," in Robert L. Green, ed., *Metropolitan Desegregation* (New York: Plenum, 1986), 194–98.

34. Rossell, "School Desegregation and Community Social Change," 143–48.

35. Willis D. Hawley, *Effective School Desegregation* (Beverly Hills: Sage, 1981); Orfield, *Must We Bus*, 102–118; Martin Patchen, *Black-White Contact in the Schools: Its Academic and Social Effects* (West Lafayette, Ind.: Purdue University Press, 1982), 154–55.

36. Robert L. Crain, J. A. Hawes, R. L. Miller, and J. A. Peichert, "Finding Niches: Desegregated Students 16 Years Later," Report R3243–NIE (The Rand Corporation, 1985); Crain and Mahard, Desegregation and Black Achievement; Jomills H. Braddock II, Robert Crain, and James McPartland, "A Long-Term View of Desegregation: Some Recent Studies of Graduates as Adults," *Phi Delta Kappan*, 66 (1984): 259–64; K. Green, "Integration and Achievement: Preliminary Results from a Longitudinal Study of Educational Attainment among Black Students," paper presented at the American Educational Research Association, 1981; Kenneth L. Wilson, "The Effects of Integration and Class on Black Educational Attainment," *Sociology of Education*, 52 (1979): 84–98.

37. Jomills H. Braddock II, "The Impact of Segregated School Experiences on College and Major Field Choices of Black High School Graduates: Evidence from the High School and Beyond Survey," paper presented at the National Conference on School Desegregation, University of Chicago, 1987; Jomills H. Braddock II and James McPartland, "Assessing School Desegregation Effects: New Directions in Research," *Research in Sociology of Education and Socialization*, 3 (1982): 259–82.

38. Braddock and McPartland, "Assessing School Desegregation Effects," 263–70.

39. Robert L. Crain, "School Integration and Occupational Achievement of

Negroes," *American Journal of Sociology,* 75 (1970): 593–606; Robert L. Crain and Jack Strauss, "School Desegregation and Black Occupational Attainments: Results from a Long-Term Experiment," unpublished report (Baltimore: Johns Hopkins University, 1982); Robert L. Crain and Carol Sachs Weisman, *Discrimination, Personality and Achievement* (New York: Seminar Press, 1972), 161–64, 210–15.

40. Jomills H. Braddock II and James McPartland, "The Social and Academic Consequences of School Desegregation," *Equity and Choice* (February 1988): 5–10, 63–73.

41. Reynolds Farley, "Three Steps Forward and Two Back? Recent Changes in the Social and Economic Status of Blacks," in R. D. Alba, ed., *Ethnicity and Race in the U.S.A.* (Boston: Routledge & Kegan Paul, 1985), 4–28; Thomas F. Pettigrew, "Racial Change and Social Policy," *Annals,* 441 (1979): 114–31.

42. Robert L. Crain, "School Integration and Occupational Achievement of Negroes," *American Journal of Sociology,* 75 (1970): 593–606; Crain, et al., "Finding niches," 596–606.

43. Braddock, "The Impact of Segregated School Experiences," 14–20.

44. Crain, et al., "Finding Niches," 15–19; Marvin P. Dawkins, "Black Students' Occupational Expectations: A National Study of the Impact of School Desegregation," *Urban Education,* 18 (1983): 83–113.

45. Jomills H. Braddock II, Robert Crain, James McPartland, and R. L. Dawkins, "Applicant Race and Job Placement Decisions: A National Field Experiment," *International Journal of Sociology and Social Policy,* 6 (1984): 3–24.

46. Alexander W. Astin, *Minorities in American Education* (San Francisco: Jossey-Bass, 1982): 85–88, 184; Braddock and McPartland, *More Evidence on the Social-Psychological Processes,* 1–24.

47. R. Scott and Jomills H. Braddock II, "Desegregation as a National Policy: Correlates of Racial Attitudes," *American Educational Research Journal,* 19 (1982): 397–414.

48. Crain and Weisman, *Discrimination, Personality and Achievement;* Green, "Integration and Achievement," 167.

49. Jomills H. Braddock II, James McPartland, and William T. Trent, "Desegregated Schools and Desegregated Work Environments," paper presented at American Educational Research Association, 1984.

50. Crain, "School Integration and Occupational Achievement," 166.

51. Braddock, et al., "Long-Term View of Desegregation," 262; Orfield, "School Desegregation and Residential Segregation"; D. Pearce, *Breaking Down Barriers: New Evidence on the Impact of Metropolitan School Desegregation on Housing Patterns* (Washington, D.C.: National Institute of Education, 1980), 25–36; Gary Orfield, "School Desegregation and Residential Segregation: A Social Science Statement," in Walter Stephan and J. Feagin, *School Desegregation: Past, Present, and Future* (New York: Plenum, 1980), 227–47.

52. Susan L. Greenblatt and Charles V. Willie, "The Serendipitous Effects of Desegregation," in Walter Stephan and Joe R. Feagin, *School Desegregation: Past, Present, and Future* (New York: Plenum, 1980), 51–68.

53. John F. Dovidio and Samuel L. Gaertner, "The Aversive Form of Racism," in John F. Dovidio and Samuel L. Gaertner, eds., *Prejudice, Discrimination and Racism* (New York: Academic Press, 1986), 61–89; Walter G. Stephan and Cookie W. Stephan, "Intergroup Anxiety," *Journal of Social Issues*, 41 (1985): 157–75.

54. Pettigrew, "Racial Change and Social Policy," 118–20.

55. Howard Schuman, Charlotte Steeh, and Lawrence Bobo, *Racial Attitudes in America* (Cambridge: Harvard University Press, 1985), 79; Armor, "White Flight"; *Time*, March 7, 1988, 23.

56. U.S. Commission on Civil Rights, *Statement*, 7.

57. Orfield, *Must We Bus?*, 134–35.

58. Harris poll cited in U.S. Commission on Civil Rights, *Statement*, 48.

59. *Time*, March 7, 1988, 23.

60. Donal E. Muir and Donald McGlamery, "Trends in Integration Attitudes on a Deep-South Campus during Two Decades of Desegregation," *Social Forces*, 62 (1984): 963–72.

61. Pettigrew, "Racial Change and Social Policy," 119; Rossell, "School Desegregation," 172–75.

62. Goodwin Watson, *Action for Unity* (New York: Harper, 1947), 54–75; Robin Murray Williams, Jr., *The Reduction of Intergroup Tensions* (New York: Social Science Research Council, 1947), 15–19, 69–71.

63. Floyd J. Allport, et al., "The Effects of Segregation and the Consequences of Desegregation: A Social Science Statement," *Minnesota Law Review*, 37 (1953): 429–40.

64. Walter G. Stephan, "The Contact Hypothesis in Intergroup Relations," in C. Hendrick, ed., *Group Processes and Intergroup Relations* (Beverly Hills: Sage, 1987), 13–40.

65. Jennifer Crocker, Darlene B. Hannah, and Renée Weber, "Person Memory and Causal Attributions," *Journal of Personality and Social Psychology*, 44 (1983): 55–56; M. Rothbart and O. P. John, "Social Categorization and Behavioral Episodes: A Cognitive Analysis and the Effects of Intergroup Contact," *Journal of Social Issues*, 41 (1985): 81–104; Thomas K. Srull, "Person Memory: Some Tests of Associative Storage and Retrieval Models," *Journal of Experimental Psychology: Human Learning and Memory*, 7 (1981): 440–63; Walter G. Stephan, "A Cognitive Approach to Stereotyping," in D. Barl-Tal, C. F. Graumman, A. W. Kruglanski, and W. Stroebe, eds., *Stereotypes and Prejudice: Changing Conceptions* (New York: Springer-Verlag, 1989), 37–57; Walter G. Stephan and D. Rosenfield, "Racial and Ethnic Stereotypes," in A. Miller, ed., *In the Eye of the Beholder* (New York: Praeger, 1982), 92–136; Renée Weber and Jennifer

Crocker, "Cognitive Processes in the Revision of Stereotypic Beliefs," *Journal of Personality and Social Psychology,* 45 (1983): 961–77.

66. Jomills H. Braddock II and James M. McPartland, Jr., "How Minorities Continue to Be Excluded from Equal Employment Opportunities: Research on Labor Market and Institutional Barriers," *Journal of Social Issues,* 43 (1987): 5–39; Crain and Weisman, *Discrimination, Personality, and Achievement,* 161–71.

67. Walter G. Stephan and Cookie W. Stephan, "The Role of Ignorance in Intergroup Relations," in Marilyn B. Brewer and N. Miller, *Groups in Contact: The Psychology of Desegregation* (New York: Academic Press, 1984), 229–51.

68. Miles Hewstone and Rubert Brown, *Contact and Conflict in Intergroup Encounters* (Oxford: Basil Blackwell, 1986), 50, 94–96, 116.

69. Stephan and Stephan, "The Role of Ignorance," 229–51.

70. Walter G. Stephan, "Intergroup Relations," in G. Lindzey and Elliot Aronson, eds., *Handbook of Social Psychology* (New York: Addison-Wesley, 1985), 3: 599–658.

71. Elliot Aronson, Cookie Stephan, Jev Sikes, Nancy Blaney, and Matthew Snapp, *The Jigsaw Classroom* (Beverly Hills: Sage, 1978), 125–34.

7. CHANGES IN THE EXPRESSION AND ASSESSMENT OF RACIAL PREJUDICE

JOHN F. DOVIDIO AND SAMUEL L. GAERTNER

1. John F. Dovidio and Samuel L. Gaertner, "Prejudice, Discrimination, and Racism: Historical Trends and Contemporary Approaches," in John F. Dovidio and Samuel L. Gaertner, eds., *Prejudice, discrimination, and racism* (Orlando, Fla.: Academic Press, 1986), 4–8; Marvin Karlins, T. L. Coffman, and Gary Walters, "On the Fading of Social Stereotypes: Studies in Three Generations of College Students," *Journal of Personality and Social Psychology,* 13 (1969): 5.

2. Howard Schuman, Charlotte Steeh, and Lawrence Bobo, *Racial Attitudes in America: Trends and Interpretations* (Cambridge, Mass.: Harvard University Press, 1985), 123–25.

3. *Newsweek,* February 26, 1979, "A New Racial Poll," 49.

4. James R. Kluegel and Elliot R. Smith, *Beliefs about Inequality: Americans' Views of What Is and What Ought To Be* (New York: Adline de Gruyter, 1986), 189.

5. Paul M. Sniderman and Michael Gray Hagen, *Race and Inequality: A Study in American Values* (Chatham, N.J.: Chatham House, 1985), 30.

6. *Newsweek,* March, 7, 1988, "Black and White: How Integrated Is America?" 23.

7. Keith Cox, "Changes in Stereotyping of Negroes and Whites in Magazine Advertisements," *Public Opinion Quarterly*, 33 (1969–70): 605; Robert Humphrey and Howard Schuman, "The Portrayal of Blacks in Magazine Advertisements: 1950–1982," *Public Opinion Quarterly*, 48 (1984): 555; Audrey Shuey, "Stereotyping of Negroes and Whites: An Analysis of Magazine Pictures," *Public Opinion Quarterly*, 17 (1953): 286.

8. Lawrence Plotkin, *The Frequency of Appearance of Negroes on Television* (New York: The Committee on Integration, New York Society for Ethical Culture, 1964), 12.

9. S. Dominick and Bradley Greenberg, "Three Seasons of Blacks on Television," *Journal of Advertising Research*, 10 (1970): 31–32; Bradley Greenberg and S. L. Mazingo, "Racial Issues in the Mass Media," in P. A. Katz, ed., *Towards the Elimination of Racism* (New York: Pergamon, 1976), 325; Russell H. Weigle, Julia Wolfe Loomis, and M. J. Soja, "Race Relations on Prime Time Television," *Journal of Personality and Social Psychology*, 39 (1980): 888.

10. Ibid.

11. Robert M. Liebert, Joyce N. Sprafkin, and Emily S. Davidson, *The Early Window: Effects of Television on Children and Youth*, 2nd ed. (New York: Pergamon, 1982), 162.

12. Schuman, et al., *Racial Attitudes in America*, 74–75.

13. Ibid., 130–31; D. G. Taylor, Paul B. Sheatsley, and Andrew M. Greeley, "Attitudes toward Racial Integration," *Scientific American*, 238 (1978): 42–49.

14. Schuman, et al., *Racial Attitudes in America*, 78.

15. *Newsweek*, March, 7, 1988, 23.

16. James R. Kluegel and Elliot R. Smith, *Beliefs about Inequality*, 202.

17. Lee Sigelman and S. Welch, "Race, Gender, and Opinion toward Black and Female Presidential Candidates," *Public Opinion Quarterly*, 48 (1984): 471; Thomas Woodward Smith and G. N. Dempsey, "The Polls: Ethnic Social Distance and Prejudice," *Public Opinion Quarterly*, 47 (1983): 599.

18. Russell H. Weigel and P. W. Howes, "Conceptions of Racial Prejudice: Symbolic Racism Revisited," *Journal of Social Issues*, 41 (1985): 124–32.

19. John Harding, Harold Proshansky, B. Kutner, and Isidor Chein, "Prejudice and Ethnic Relations," in G. Lindzey and Elliot Aronson, eds., *The Handbook of Social Psychology*, 2nd ed., (Reading, Mass.: Addison-Wesley, 1969), 17–39.

20. H. Sigall and Rufus Page, "Current Stereotypes: A Little Fading, a Little Faking," *Journal of Personality and Social Psychology*, 18 (1981): 250–54.

21. Smith and Dempsey, "The Polls," 588–89.

22. *Newsweek*, March 7, 1988, 23.

23. D. Colfax and S. Sternberg, "The Perpetuation of Racial Stereotypes: Blacks in Mass Circulation Magazine Advertisements," *Public Opinion Quarterly*, 36 (1982), 13.

24. Greenberg and Mazingo, "Racial Issues in the Mass Media," 326.

25. Weigel, et al., "Race Relations on Prime Time Television," 889.

26. D. P. G. McNally, "Blacks and Television: A Comparsion of the Portrayal of Black and White Characters on Television" (Ph.D. diss., University of Maryland, College Park), 84.

27. Leibert, et al., *The Early Window*, 162.

28. Weigel, et al., "Race Relations on Prime Time Television," 884.

29. Schuman, et al, *Racial Attitudes in America*, 88–89.

30. Seymour Martin Lipset and William Schneider, "The Bakke Case: How Would It Be Decided at the Bar of Public Opinion?" *Public Opinion*, 1 (1978): 39.

31. *Newsweek*, March 7, 1988, 23.

32. Kluegel and Smith, *Beliefs about Inequality*, 202–205.

33. Irving Katz, J. Wackenhut, and Robert G. Hass, "Racial Ambivalence, Value Duality, and Behavior," in John F. Dovidio and Samuel L. Gaertner, eds., *Prejudice, Discrimination, and Racism* (Orlando, Fla.: Academic Press, 1986), 44–46.

34. Theodor W. Adorno, E. Frenkel-Brunswik, Daniel J. Levinson, and R. N. Sanford, *The Authoritarian Personality* (New York: Harper, 1950), 337–89.

35. Marilyn B. Brewer and Ralph M. Kramer, "The Psychology of Intergroup Attitudes and Behavior," *Annual Review of Psychology*, 36 (1985): 220–27; Samuel L. Gaertner and John F. Dovidio, "The Aversive Form of Racism," in John F. Dovidio and Samuel L. Gaertner, eds., *Prejudice, Discrimination, and Racism* (Orlando, Fla.: Academic Press, 1986), 61–66; David L. Hamilton and T. K. Trolier, "Stereotypes and Stereotyping: An Overview of the Cognitive Approach," in John F. Dovidio and Samuel L. Gaertner, eds., *Prejudice, Discrimination, and Racism* (Orlando, Fla.: Academic Press, 1986), 127–37; David M. Messick and D. M. Mackie, "Intergroup Relations," in M. R. Rosenweig and L. W. Porter, eds., *Annual Review of Psychology*, 40 (1989): 42–65; Walter G. Stephan, "Intergroup Relations," in G. Lindzey and Elliot Aronson, eds., *The Handbook of Social Psychology*, 3rd ed., (New York: Random House, 1985): 599–636.

36. Hamilton and Trolier, "Stereotypes and Stereotyping," 128–33.

37. Marilyn B. Brewer, "In-Group Bias in the Minimal Intergroup Situation: A Cognitive-Motivational Analysis," *Psychological Bulletin*, 86 (1979): 319–22.

38. Dorothy D. Stein, J. A. Hardyck, and M. Bentick Smith, "Race *and* Belief: An Open and Shut Case," *Journal of Personality and Social Psychology*, 1 (1965): 284–89.

39. David Byrne, *The Attraction Paradigm* (New York: Academic Press, 1971), 47–57.

40. Harvey A. Hornstein, *Cruelty and Kindness: A New Look at Aggression*

and Altruism (Englewood Cliffs, N.J.: Prentice-Hall, 1976), 98–112; Ralph M. Kramer and Marilyn B. Brewer, "Effects of Group Identity on Resource Use in a Simulated Commons Dilemma," *Journal of Personality and Social Psychology,* 46 (1984): 1055; Jane A. Piliavin, John F. Dovidio, Samuel L. Gaertner, and R. D. Clark III, *Emergency Intervention* (New York: Academic Press, 1981), 145–50.

41. M. G. Frank and T. Gilovich, "The Dark Side of Self- and Social Perception: Black Uniforms and Aggression in Professional Sports," *Journal of Personality and Social Psychology,* 54 (1988): 83–84; J. E. Williams, R. D. Tucker, and Franklin Y. Dunham, "Changes in the Connotations of Color Names among Negroes and Caucasians," *Journal of Personality and Social Psychology,* 19 (1971): 225–28.

42. Thoma Ashby Wills, "Downward Comparison Principles in Social Psychology," *Psychological Bulletin,* 90 (1981): 255–57.

43. William J. Wilson, *The Declining Significance of Race,* 2nd ed. (Chicago: University of Chicago Press, 1980), 42–61.

44. Joe R. Feagin and Clairece Booher Feagin, *Discrimination American Style: Institutional Racism and Sexism* (Englewood Cliffs, N.J.: Prentice-Hall, 1978), 102–23.

45. Sigall and Page, "Current Stereotypes," 253–54; Irving Katz and Robert G. Hass, "Racial Ambivalence and American Value Conflict: Correlational and Priming Studies of Dual Cognitive Structures," *Journal of Personality and Social Psychology,* 55 (1988): 894–95.

46. Kluegel and Smith, *Beliefs about Inequality,* 21–30; Lipset and Schneider, "The Bakke case," 39.

47. Thomas F. Pettigrew and J. Martin, "Shaping the Organizatonal Context for Black American Inclusion," *Journal of Social Issues,* 43 (1987): 46–50.

48. Mary R. Jackman, "General and Applied Tolerance: Does Education Increase Commitment to Racial Integration?" *American Journal of Political Science,* 22 (1978): 320–23.

49. John B. McConahay, "Modern Racism, Ambivalence, and the Modern Racism Scale," in John F. Dovidio and Samuel L. Gaertner, eds., *Prejudice, Discrimination, and Racism* (Orlando, Fla.: Academic Press, 1986), 91–93; David O. Sears and Helen Mary Allen, "The Trajectory of Local Desegregtaion Controversies and Whites' Opposition to Busing," in Marilyn B. Brewer and N. Miller, eds., *Groups in Contact: The Psychology of Desegregation* (New York: Academic Press, 1984), 126–34.

50. Joel Kovel, *White Racism: A Psychohistory* (New York: Pantheon, 1970), 54–55.

51. Gaertner and Dovidio, "The Aversive Form of Racism," 66–86.

52. Samuel L. Gaertner and John F. Dovidio, "The Subtlety of White Racism,

Arousal, and Helping Behavior," *Journal of Personality and Social Psychology*, 35 (1977): 694–98.

53. John M. Darley and Bibb Latane, "Bystander Intervention in Emergencies: Diffusion of Responsibility," *Journal of Personality and Social Psychology*, 8 (1968): 379–81.

54. Samuel L. Gaertner and J. P. McLaughlin, "Racial Stereotypes: Associations and Ascriptions of Positive and Negative Characteristics," *Social Psychology Quarterly*, 46 (1983): 28–29.

55. Sigall and Page, "Current Stereotypes," 253–54.

56. Gaertner and McLaughlin, "Racial Stereotypes," 24–26.

57. D. E. Meyer and R. W. Schvaneveldt, "Facilitation in Recognizing Pairs of Words: Evidence of Dependence between Retrieval Operations," *Journal of Experimental Psychology*, 90 (1971): 229–30.

58. Ibid.

59. Gaertner and McLaughlin, "Racial Stereotypes," 24–26.

60. Eleanor Rosch, "Cognitive Representations of Semantic Categories," *Journal of Experimental Psychology: General*, 104 (1975): 197–224.

61. Messick and Mackie, "Intergroup Relations," 49–51.

62. J. A. Bargh and P. Pietromonaco, "Automatic Information Processing and Social Perception: The Influence of Trait Information Presented Outside of Conscious Awareness on Impression Formation," *Journal of Personality and Social Psychology*, 43 (1982): 440–42.

63. Burton B. Kline and John F. Dovidio, "Effects of Race, Sex, and Qualifications on Predictions of a College Applicant's Performance," paper presented at the annual meeting of the Eastern Psychological Association, Baltimore, (April 1982), 3–4.

64. John F. Dovidio and Samuel L. Gaertner, "The Effects of Race, Status, and Ability on Helping Behavior," *Social Psychology Quarterly*, 44 (1981): 194–99.

65. *Regents of the University of California* v. *Bakke, U.S. Law Weekly*, 46 (1978): 4896.

66. Jackman, "General and Applied Tolerance," 320–23.

67. Mary R. Jackman and M. J. Muha, "Education and Intergroup Attitudes: Moral Enlightenment, Superficial Democratic Commitment, or Ideological Refinement?" *American Sociological Review*, 49 (1984): 751.

68. Jackman, "General and Applied Tolerance," 309–19; Jackman and Muha, "Education and Intergroup Attitudes," 755–58.

69. D. T. Campbell, "Social Attitudes and Other Acquired Behavioral Dispositions," in S. Koch, ed., *Psychology: A Study of a Science* (New York: McGraw-Hill, 1963), 6: 157–62.

70. Faye Crosby, S. Bromley, and Leonard Saxe, "Recent Unobtrusive Stud-

ies of Black and White Discrimination and Prejudice: A Literature Review," *Psychological Bulletin*, 87 (1980): 558–59.

71. Kleugel and Smith, *Beliefs About Inequality*, 212.

72. Sears and Allen, "The Trajectory of Local Desegregation," 126–34; Donald R. Kinder and David O. Sears, "Symbolic Racism versus Threats to 'the Good Life,'" *Journal of Personality and Social Psychology*, 40 (1981): 416; John B. McConahay and Joseph C. Hough, Jr., "Symbolic Racism," *Journal of Social Issues*, 32 (1976): 23–28; David O. Sears, Carl P. Hensler, and L. K. Speer, "Whites' Opposition to 'Busing': Self-Interest or Symbolic Politics?" *American Political Science Review*, 73 (1979): 370–71.

73. McConahay, "Modern Racism, Ambivalence," 91–93.

74. Ibid., 93–98.

75. Kinder and Sears, "Symbolic Racism," 421–27.

76. Sears, et al., "Whites' Opposition to 'Busing,'" 374–78; John B. McConahay, "Self-Interest versus Racial Attitudes in Louisville: Is It the Buses or the Blacks?" *Journal of Politics*, 44 (1982): 700–14.

77. John B. McConahay, "Modern Racism and Modern Discrimination: The Effects of Race, Racial Attitudes, and Context on Simulated Hiring Decisions," *Personality and Social Psychology Bulletin*, 9 (1983): 555–57.

78. C. K. Jackobson, "Resistance to Affirmative Action: Self-Interest or Racism?" *Journal of Conflict Resolution*, 29 (1985): 326–28.

79. Samuel L. Gaertner, "Helping Behavior and Discrimination among Liberals and Conservatives," *Journal of Personality and Social Psychology*, 25 (1973): 337–40; Samuel L. Gaertner, "Nonreactive Measures in Racial Attitude Research: A Focus on 'Liberals,'" in P. Katz, ed., *Toward the Elimination of Racism* (New York: Pergamon Press, 1976), 337–40.

80. McConahay and Hough, "Symbolic Racism," 23.

81. Kluegel and Smith, *Beliefs about Inequality*, 212.

82. Harding, et al., "Prejudice and Ethnic Relations," 12.

83. Walter Lippmann, *Public Opinion* (New York: Harcourt, Brace, 1922), 79–94.

84. D. Katz and K. W. Braly, "Racial Stereotypes of 100 College Students," *Journal of Abnormal and Social Psychology*, 28 (1933): 284.

85. Harding, et al., *The Authoritarian Personality*, 102–50.

86. Gardner Murphy and Rensis Likert, *Public Opinion and the Individual* (New York: Harper, 1938), 14–67.

87. Adorno, et al., *The Authoritarian Personality*, 222–79.

88. Howard Schuman and John Harding, "Sympathetic Identification with the Underdog," *Public Opinion Quarterly*, 27 (1963): 231–33.

89. Weigel and Howes, "Conceptions of Racial Prejudice," 124–32.

90. John Carl Brigham, J. J. Woodmansee, and Stuart Welford Cook, "Di-

mensions of Verbal Racial Attitudes: Interracial Attitudes and Approaches to Racial Equality," *Journal of Social Issues,* 32 (1976): 11–12; J. J. Woodmansee and Stuart Welford Cook, "Dimensions of Verbal Racial Attitudes: Their Identification and Measurement," *Journal of Personality and Social Psychology,* 7 (1967): 244–249.

91. Ibid., 128–32.

92. Adorno, et al., *The Authoritarian Personality,* 222–79.

93. Gaertner and Dovidio, "The Aversive Form of Racism," 67.

94. Stuart Oskamp, *Attitudes and Opinions* (Englewood Cliffs, N.J.: Prentice-Hall, 1977), 57–73.

95. McConahay and Hough, "Symbolic Racism," 28–36; David O. Sears and John B. McConahay, *The Politics of Violence: The New Urban Blacks and the Watts Riot* (Boston: Houghton Mifflin, 1973), 7–89.

96. McConahay, "Modern Racism, Ambivalence," 92.

97. Ibid., 93–115.

98. Sears and Allen, "The Trajectory of Local Desegregation," 134–39; McConahay, "Modern Racism, Ambivalence," 93–115.

99. Lawrence Bobo, "Whites' Opposition to Busing: Symbolic Racism or Realistic Group Conflict?" *Journal of Personality and Social Psychology,* 45 (1983): 1208–1209.

100. C. K. Jacobson, "Resistance to Affirmative Action," 321–28.

101. Irving Katz and Robert G. Hass, "Racial Ambivalence and American Value Conflict: Correlational and Primary Studies of Dual Cognitive Structures," *Journal of Personality and Social Psychology,* 47 (1988): 895–903; Irving Katz, J. Wackenhut, and Robert G. Hass, "Racial Ambivalence, Value Duality, and Behavior," in John F. Dovidio and Samuel L. Gaertner, eds., *Prejudice, Discrimination and Racism* (Orlando, Fla.: Academic Press, 1986), 50–54.

102. Katz and Hass, "Racial Ambivalence and American Value Conflict," 905.

103. Irving Katz, *Stigma: A Social Psychological Analysis* (Hillsdale, N.J.: Erlbaum, 1981), 23–29; Katz, et al., "Racial Ambivalence, Value Duality," 50–54.

104. Jackman and Muha, "Education and Intergroup Attitudes," 759–62.

105. Ronald W. Rogers and Steven Prentice-Dunn, "Deindividuation and Anger-Mediated Interracial Aggression: Unmasking Regressive Racism," *Journal of Personality and Social Psychology,* 41 (1981): 67–71.

106. Jomills H. Braddock II and James M. McPartland, Jr., "How Minorities Continue to Be Excluded from Equal Employment Opportunities: Research on Labor Market and Institutional Barriers," *Journal of Social Issues,* 43 (1987): 24–28.

107. Stuart Welford Cook, "Experimenting on Social Issues: The Case of School Desegregation," *American Psychologist,* 40 (1985): 459–60.

108. Donald G. Dutton, "Tokenism, Reverse Discrimination, and Egalitarianism in Interracial Behavior," *Journal of Social Issues*, 32 (1976): 93–94.

109. A. J. Buonocore and D. R. Crable, "Equal Opportunity: An Incomplete Evolution," *Personnel Journal*, 65 (August 1986): 34.

110. McConahay, "Modern Racism, Ambivalence," 123.

8. MAKING A STAND FOR CHANGE: A Strategy for Empowering Individuals

RHODA E. JOHNSON

1. Paula S. Rothenberg, *Racism and Sexism* (New York: St. Martin's Press, 1988), 178.

2. Ibid., 177.

3. Ibid., 178–79.

4. Aldon D. Morris, *The Origins of the Civil Rights Movement* (New York: Free Press, 1984), 286–87.

5. William J. Wilson, *The Declining Significance of Race* (Chicago: University of Chicago Press, 1978).

6. William J. Wilson, *The Truly Disadvantaged* (Chicago: University of Chicago Press, 1987).

7. Harvey Kline, Patrick Cotter, William Stewart, and Mylon Winn, "Political and Economic Change in Black Belt Alabama Since the Voting Rights Act of 1965: A Preliminary Report," paper presented at Southern Political Science Association, Atlanta, Georgia, 1986.

8. Robert J. Norrell, *Reaping the Whirlwind: The Civil Rights Movement in Tuskegee* (New York: Vintage Books, 1986), 208–209.

9. John F. Dovidio and Samuel L. Gaertner, *Prejudice, Discrimination, and Racism: Historical Trends and Contemporary Approaches* (Florida: Academic Press, 1986), 61–89; John F. Dovidio and Samuel L. Gaertner, "The Subtlety of White Racism: Helping Behavior and Stereotyping by Whites Toward Black and White Supervisors and Subordinates" (Office of Naval Research, Organizational Effectiveness Programs), 1977a.

10. Samuel L. Gaertner and John F. Dovidio, "Racism Among the Well-Intentioned," in E. Clausen and J. Bermingham, eds., *Pluralism, Racism, and Public Policy: The Search for Equality* (Boston: G. K. Hall, 1981), 208–222.

11. Ellen Cantarow, *Moving the Mountain* (New York: Feminist Press, 1980).

12. Paulo Freire, *Pedagogy of the Oppressed* (New York: Continuum, 1970).

13. Audre Lorde, "Age, Race, Class, and Sex: Women Redefining Difference,"

in P. Rothenberg, *Racism and Sexism* (New York: St. Martin's Press, 1988), 352–59.

14. Judy H. Katz, *White Awareness* (Norman: University of Oklahoma Press, 1978).

15. *NOW Guidelines for Feminist Consciousness-Raising*, rev. (Washington, D.C.: National Organization for Women, 1983).

16. Unpublished document (1983) available from FOCAL, P.O. Box 214, Montgomery, Alabama 36106.

17. Sarah Evans, *Personal Politics* (New York: Alfred A. Knopf, 1979), 219–20.

18. *Encyclopedia of Sociology* (Guilford, Conn.: Dushkin Publishing Group, 1974).

19. Judy H. Katz, *White Awareness* (Norman: University of Oklahoma Press, 1978), 46–47.

20. Ibid., 17.

21. Rupert G. John, *Racism and Its Elimination* (New York: United National Institute for Traning and Research, 1981).

9. ADVANCING RACIAL JUSTICE: Past Lessons for Future Use
THOMAS F. PETTIGREW

1. Howard Schuman, Charlotte Steeh, and Lawrence Bobo, *Racial Attitudes in America: Trends and Interpretations* (Cambridge, Mass.: Harvard University Press, 1985).

2. Reynolds Farley, *Blacks and Whites: Narrowing the Gap?* (Cambridge, Mass.: Harvard University Press, 1984); Gary Orfield, *Must We Bus?* (Washington, D.C.: Brookings, 1978).

3. R. H. Forbes, "Test Score Advances among Southeastern Students: A Possible Bonus of Governmental Intervention?" *Phi Delta Kappan* (1981), 332–34, 350.

4. L. V. Jones, "Trends in School Achievement of Black Children," unpublished address to Institute for Research in Social Science, University of North Carolina–Chapel Hill, March 17, 1987, 11; L. V. Jones, "White-Black Achievement Differences: The Narrowing Gap," *American Psychologist*, 39 (1984): 1207–1213.

5. Forbes, "Test Score Advances," 333.

6. Jones, "Trends in School Achievement," 11.

7. Ibid.

8. United States Bureau of the Census, *Census of Population and Housing: 1980* (Washington, D.C.: U.S. Government Printing Office, 1982); United States

Bureau of the Census, *America's Black Population: 1970–1982* (Washington, D.C.: U.S. Government Printing Office, 1983).

9. Orfield, *Must We Bus?*

10. Elliot Aronson, "The Theory of Cognitive Dissonance: A Current Perspective," in L. Berkowitz, ed., *Advances in Experimental Social Psychology* (New York: Academic Press, 1969), vol. 4; D. J. Bem, "Self-Perception Theory," in L. Berkowitz, ed., *Advances in Experimental Social Psychology* (New York: Academic Press, 1972), 6; L. Festinger, *A Theory of Cognitive Dissonance* (Stanford, Calif.: Stanford University Press, 1957); Thomas F. Pettigrew, "Social Psychology and Desegregation Research," *American Psychologist*, 16 (1961): 105–112.

11. Gordon W. Allport, *The Nature of Prejudice* (Reading, Mass.: Addison-Wesley, 1954).

12. Thomas F. Pettigrew, "The Intergroup Contact Hypothesis Reconsidered," in Miles Hewstone and Rupert Brown, eds., *Contact, Conflict and Intergroup Relations* (Oxford, England: Blackwell, 1987).

13. Thomas F. Pettigrew, E. L. Useem, C. Normand, and M. S. Smith, "Busing: A Review of 'the Evidence,'" *The Public Interest*, 30 (1973): 88–118.

14. D. L. Hamilton, S. Carpender, and G. D. Bishop, "Desegregation of Suburban Neighborhoods," in N. Miller and M. B. Brewer, eds., *Groups in Contact: The Psychology of Desegregation* (New York: Academic Press, 1984).

15. Gunnar Myrdal, *An American Dilemma: The Negro Problem and Modern Democracy* (New York: Harper and Brothers Publishers, 1944).

16. Pettigrew, "Social Psychology and Desegregation Research," 105–112.

17. Ibid.

18. G. B. Johnson, "A Sociologist Looks at Racial Desegregation in the South," *Social Forces*, 33 (1954): 1–10.

19. Ibid.

20. Thomas F. Pettigrew, "New Black-White Patterns: How Best to Conceptualize them?" in R. Turner, ed., *Annual Review of Sociology* (Palo Alto, Calif.: Annual Reviews, 1985), 329–46; Thomas F. Pettigrew, *Modern Racism: American Black-White Relations Since the 1960s* (Cambridge, Mass.: Harvard University Press, 1989).

21. Howard Schuman, et al., *Racial Attitudes in America*, pp.; Thomas Woodward Smith and Paul B. Sheatsley, "American Attitudes toward Race Relations," *Public Opinion*, 7 (1984): 14–15, 50–53; D. Garth Taylor, Paul B. Sheatsley, and Andrew M. Greeley, "Attitudes toward Racial Integration," *Scientific American*, 238 (1978): 42–51.

22. John B. McConahay, "Is It the Buses or the Blacks? Self-Interest versus Symbolic Racism as Predictors of Opposition to Busing in Louisville," *Journal of Politics*, 44 (1982): 692–720; Schuman, et al., *Racial Attitudes in America*.

23. James R. Kluegel and Elliot R. Smith, *Beliefs About Inequality: Americans' Views of What Is and What Ought to Be* (New York: Aldine de Gruyter, 1986).

24. Schuman, et al., *Racial Attitudes in America.*

25. Smith and Sheatsley, "American Attitudes," 50; Taylor, et al., "Attitudes toward Racial Integration," 42–51.

26. Schuman, et al., *Racial Attitudes in America*, 88–90.

27. Thomas F. Pettigrew, "Racial Change and Social Policy," *Annals of American Association of Political and Social Science*, 441 (1979): 114–31.

28. Lauren G. Wispe and H. G. Freshley, "Race, Sex, and Sympathetic Helping Behavior: The Broken Bag Caper," *Journal of Personality and Social Psychology*, 17 (1971): 59–65; Samuel S. Gaertner, "Nonreactive Measures in Racial Attitude Research: A Focus on Liberals," in P. A. Katz, ed., *Towards the Elimination of Racism* (New York: Pergamon, 1976).

29. F. Crosby, S. Bromley, and Leonard Saxe, "Recent Unobtrusive Studies of Black and White Discrimination and Prejudice: A Literature Review." *Psychological Bulletin*, 87 (1980): 546–63.

30. Stephen Orlofsky, ed., *Facts on File Yearbook, 1985*, 45 (New York: Facts on File Publications, 1986); M. Hendricks and Richard Bootzin, "Race and Sex as Stimuli for Negative Affect and Physical Avoidance," *Journal of Social Psychology*, 98 (1976): 111–20; S. Weitz, "Attitude, Voice and Behavior: A Repressed Affect Model of Interracial Interaction," *Journal of Personality and Social Psychology*, 24 (1972): 14–21.

31. Pettigrew, "New Black-White Patterns," 329–46; Pettigrew, *Modern Racism.*

32. C. O. Word, Mark P. Zanna, and J. Cooper, "The Nonverbal Mediation of Self-Fulfilling Prophecies in Interracial Interaction," *Journal of Experimental Social Psychology*, 10 (1974): 109–20.

33. David S. Broder, "Why Jackson Believes We Are Winning Every Day," *International Herald-Tribune*, No. 32 (April 30, 1988): 714, 4.

10. PIERCING THE VEIL: Bi-Cultural Strategies for Coping with Prejudice and Racism
JAMES JONES

1. W. E. B. Du Bois, *The Souls of Black Folk: Essays and Sketches* (Chicago: A. C. McClurg, 1903), 23–24.

2. K. Sawyer, "King Scholars Steal Bennett's Lines," *Washington Post*, January 15, 1986, A8.

3. Pierre L. vanden Berghe, *Race and Racism: A Comparative Perspective* (New York: Wiley, 1967), 9.

4. Du Bois, *Souls*, 23–24.

5. Paul Zimmerman, "The Ethnologist," *New York Post*, August 24, 1971.

6. Abram Kardiner and L. Ovesy, *The Mark of Oppression* (New York: Norton, 1951).

7. Excerpted from *Meet the Press*, February 13, 1984.

8. Vernon Dixon, "World Views and Research Methodology," in L. King, V. Dixon, and W. Nobles, eds., *African Philosophy: Assumptions and Paradigms for Research on Black Persons* (Los Angeles: Fanon Center Publications, 1976).

9. James M. Jones, *Prejudice and Racism* (Reading, Mass.: Addison Wesley Publishers, 1972), 118–21.

10. O. Kerner, *Report of the National Advisory Commission on Civil Disorders* (New York: Bantam Books, 1968).

11. Louis L. Knowles and Kenneth Prewitt, *Institutional Racism in America* (Englewood Cliffs, N.J.: Prentice-Hall, 1969), 1–7.

12. Stokely Carmichael and Charles V. Hamilton, *Black Power: The Politics of Liberation in America* (New York: Vintage Books, 1967), 4–6.

13. James M. Jones and A. R. Hochner, "Racial Differences in Sports Activities: A Look at the Self-Paced versus Reactive Hypothesis," *Journal of Personality and Social Psychology*, 27 (1973): 86–95.

14. James M. Jones, "Conceptual and Strategic Issues in the Relationship of Black Psychology to American Social Science," in A. W. Boykin, A. J. Franklin, and J. F. Yates, eds., *Research Directions of Black Psychologists* (New York: Basic Books, 1979), 390–432; J. Mbiti, *African Philosophy and Religions* (New York: Doubleday, 1970), 19–36.

15. James Morgan Jones and H. Liverpool, "Calypso Humor in Trinidad," in A. Chapman and H. Foot, eds., *Humour: Theory and Research* (London: John Wiley, 1976), 259–86.

16. James Morgan Jones and C. B. Block, "Black Cultural Perspectives," *The Clinical Psychologist*, 37 (1984): 58–62.

17. Robert E. Ornstein, *The Psychology of Consciousness* (New York: Harcourt, Brace Jovanovich, 1977), 89.

18. R. V. Levine and K. Bartlett, "Pace of Life, Punctuality, and Coronary Heart Disease in Six Countries," *Journal of Cross-Cultural Psychology*, 15 (1984): 233–55; R. V. Levine, L. West, and H. Reis, "Perceptions of Time and Punctuality in the United States and Brazil," *Journal of Personality and Social Psychology*, 38 (1980): 541–50.

19. Phillip G. Zimbardo, Gary Marshall, and Christina Maslach, "Liberating Behavior from Time-Bound Control: Expanding the Present through Hypnosis," *Journal of Applied Social Psychology*, 1 (1971): 305–23.

20. Janheinz Jahn, *Muntu: An Outline of the New African Culture*, (New York: Grove Press, 1961), 121–55.

21. Ellen J. Langer, *The Psychology of Control* (Beverly Hills, Calif.: Sage, 1983), 23–27.

22. Robert Blauner, "Black Culture: Myth or Reality?" in Norman E. Whitten and J. Szwed, eds., *Afro-American Anthropology* (New York: Free Press, 1970), 347–66.

23. Nathan Glazer and Daniel P. Moynihan, *Ethnicity: Theory and Experience* (Cambridge, Mass.: Harvard University Press, 1976), 282.

24. Nathan Glazer and Daniel P. Moynihan, *Beyond the Melting Pot* (Cambridge, Mass.: Harvard University Press, 1976), 24–85.

25. Eldridge Cleaver, *Soul on Ice* (New York: McGraw Hill, 1968), 3.

26. Richard Herrnstein, "I.Q.," *Atlantic Monthly*, 228, No. 3 (1971): 43–64.

27. Michael Harris Bond and A. Y. C. King, "Coping with the Threat of Westernization in Hong Kong," *International Journal of Intercultural Relations*, in press.

28. Samuel L. Gaertner and John F. Dovidio, "The Aversive Form of Racism," in John F. Dovidio and Samuel L. Gaertner, eds., *Prejudice, Discrimination and Racism* (Orlando, Fla.: Academic Press, 1986), 61–66; Samuel L. Gaertner and John F. Dovidio, "Prejudice, Discrimination and Racism: Problems, Progress and Promise," in John Dovidio and Samuel Gaertner, eds., *Prejudice, Discrimination and Racism* (Orlando, Fla.: Academic Press, 1986).

29. A. Locksley, Victoria Ortiz, and C. Hepburn, "Social Categorization and Discrimination Behavior: Extinguishing the Minimal Intergroup Discrimination Effect," *Journal of Personality and Social Psychology*, 39 (1980): 773–83; A. Locksley, C. Hepburn, and Victoria Ortiz, "Social Stereotypes and Judgments of Individuals: An Instance of the Base-Rate Fallacy," *Journal of Experimental Social Psychology*, 18 (1982): 23–42.

30. N. Miller, Marilyn B. Brewer, and K. Edwards, "Cooperative Intersection in Desegregated Settings: A Laboratory Analogue," *Journal of Social Issues*, 41 (1985): 63–80.

SELECTED BIBLIOGRAPHY

Abbott, Dorothy. *Mississippi Writers: Reflections of Childhood and Youth*, (2 vols.). Jackson, Miss.: 1985–86.

Adair, Alvis, V. *Desegregation: The Illusion of Black Progress.* New York: Lanham, 1984.

Astin, Alexander W. *Minorities in American Education.* San Francisco: Jossey-Bass, 1982.

Ayers, Edward L. *Vengeance & Justice: Crime and Punishment in the 19th-Century American South.* New York: Oxford University Press, 1984.

Braddock, Jomills H., II, and James McPartland, "The social and academic consequences of school desegregation." *Equity and Choice.* Feb., 1988.

Brewer, Marilyn B. and N. Miller. *Groups in Contact: The Psychology of Desegregation.* New York: Academic Press, 1984.

Brown v. Board of Education. 347 U.S. 483, 1954.

Bullock, Charles S., III, and Charles M. Lamb, *Implementation of Civil Rights.* Monterey, Cal.: Brooks/Cole, 1984.

Crosby, F. S. Bromley, and Leonard Saxe. "Recent unobtrusive studies of black and white discrimination and prejudice: A literature review." *Psychological Bulletin,* 87, (1980): 546–563.

Dovidio, John F. and Samuel L. Gaertner. *Prejudice, Discrimination, and Racism: Historical Trends and Contemporary Approaches.* Orlando, Florida: Academic Press, 1986.

Du Bois, William Edward Burghardt. *The Souls of Black Folk: Essays and Sketches.* Chicago: A. C. McClurg, 1903.

Ellison, Ralph. *Shadow and Act.* New York: Random House, 1964.

Evans, Sarah, *Personal Politics.* New York: Alfred A. Knopf, Inc., 1979.

Frady, Marshall. *Wallace* New York: World Publishing Co., 1968.

223

Hendrick, C. *Group Processes and Intergroup Relations.* Beverly Hills: Sage, 1987.

Hewstone, Miles and Rupert Brown. *Contact and Conflict in Intergroup Encounters.* Oxford, U.K.: Blackwell, 1986.

Hewstone, Miles and Rupert Brown. *Contact, Conflict and Intergroup Relations.* Oxford, U.K.: Blackwell, 1987.

Jones, James Morgan. *Prejudice and Racism.* Reading, Mass.: Addison Wesley Publishers, 1972.

Katz, P. A. *Towards the Elimination of Racism.* New York: Pergamon, 1976.

Kerner, O. *Report of the National Advisory Commission on Civil Disorders.* New York: Bantam Books, 1968.

Kluegel, James R. and Elliot R. Smith. *Beliefs about Inequality: Americans' Views of What Is and What Ought To Be.* New York: Aldine de Gruyter, 1986.

Kluger, Richard. *Simple Justice.* New York: Knopf, 1976.

Knowles, Louis L. and Kenneth Prewitt, *Institutional Racism.* Englewood Cliffs, N.J.: Prentice-Hall, 1969.

Morris, Aldon D. *The Origins of the Civil Rights Movement.* New York: The Free Press, 1984.

Norrell, Robert J. *Reaping the Whirlwind: The Civil Rights Movement in Tuskegee.* New York: Vintage Books, 1986.

Orfield, Gary. *Must We Bus?: Segregated Schools and National Policy.* Washington, D.C.: The Brookings Institution, 1978.

Pettigrew, Thomas F. *Modern Racism: American Black-White Relations Since the 1960s.* Cambridge, Mass.: Harvard University Press, 1989.

Pettigrew, Thomas F. *Racial Discrimination in the United States.* New York: Harper & Row, 1975.

Pettigrew, Thomas F. "Social psychology and desegregation research." *American Psychologist,* 16 (1961): 105–112.

Rawick, George P. *The American Slave: A Composite Autobiography,* Supplement, Series 1. 1: Alabama Narratives, 4. Westport: 1977.

Rodgers, Harrell R. and Charles S. Bullock, III. *Coercion to Compliance.* Lexington, Mass.: Heath, 1976.

Rosengarten, Theodore. *All God's Dangers: The Life of Nate Shaw.* New York: Alfred A. Knopf, 1974.

Rothenberg, Paula S. *Racism and Sexism.* New York: St. Martin's Press, 1988.

St. John, Nancy H. *School Desegregation Outcomes for Children.* New York: Wiley, 1975.

Schuman, Howard, Charlotte Steeh, and Lawrence Bobo. *Racial Attitudes in America: Trends and Interpretations.* Cambridge, Mass.: Harvard University Press, 1985.

Sniderman, Paul M. and Michael Gray Hagen. *Race and Inequality: A Study in American Values.* Chatham, N.J.: Chatham House, 1985.

Stephan, Walter G. "Effects of school desegregation: An evaluation 30 years after *Brown.*" In L. Saxe and M. Saks, *Advances in Applied Social Psychology,* (Vol. 4) New York: Academic Press, 1986.

Stephan, Walter G. "Intergroup relations." In G. Lindzey and Elliot Aronson (Eds.), *Handbook of Social Psychology.* (Vol. III) New York: Addison-Wesley, 1985.

Stephan, Walter G. "School desegregation: an evaluation of predictions made in *Brown vs. The Board of Education.*" *Psychological Bulletin,* 85 (1978): 217–238.

Stephan, Walter and J. Feagin. *School Desegregation: Past, Present, and Future.* New York: Plenum, 1980.

U.S. Commission on Civil Rights. *Statement of the United States Commission on Civil Rights on School Desegregation.* Washington, D.C.: U.S. Government Printing Office, 1982.

U.S. Commission on Civil Rights. *The New Evidence on Civil Rights on School Desegregation.* Washington, D.C.: U.S. Government Printing Office, 1987.

Weinberg, Meyer. *The Search for Quality Integrated Education.* Westport, Conn.: Greenwood, Press, 1983.

Wilson, William J. *The Declining Significance of Race.* Chicago: The University of Chicago Press, 1978.

Wilson, William J. *The Declining Significance of Race,* 2nd ed. Chicago: The University of Chicago Press, 1980.

Wilson, William J. *The Truly Disadvantaged.* Chicago: The University of Chicago Press, 1987.

Wortman, Paul M., C. King, and F. B. Bryant. *Meta-Analyses of Quasi-Experiments: School Desegregation and Black Achievement.* Ann Arbor, Mich.: Institute for Social Research, 1982.

CONTRIBUTORS

DAN T. CARTER is a noted historian serving as the Andrew W. Mellon professor in the humanities at Emory University. His books, *Scottsboro: A Tragedy of the American South* and *When the War was Over: The Failure of Self-Reconstruction in the South,* have won many national awards. A work in progress is titled "The Life and Times of George Corley Wallace."

E. CULPEPPER CLARK, professor and chair of speech communication and professor of history at The University of Alabama, is presently working on a book to be titled "The Schoolhouse Door: From Lucy to Malone." His writings include essays on historical method and communication history with special emphasis on Southern demagoguery.

JOHN F. DOVIDIO, professor and former chair of the Psychology Department at Colgate University, is co-author of *Prejudice, Discrimination, and Racism,* among other books. He shared the 1985 Gordon Allport Intergroup Relations Prize awarded by Division 9 of the American Psychological Association for his work on subtle forms of racism. He is a fellow of the American Psychological Association.

SAMUEL L. GAERTNER, professor of psychology, University of Delaware, is co-author of *Prejudice, Discrimination, and Racism,* among other books. He shared the 1985 Gordon Allport Intergroup Relations Prize awarded by Division 9 of the American Psychological Association for his work on subtle forms of racism. He is a fellow of the American Psychological Association.

226

RHODA E. JOHNSON is chair and associate professor of the Women Studies Program at The University of Alabama. She participated in a project on the culture of southern black women which was funded by the Fund for the Improvement of Post-Secondary Education. Her publications include a study of post-secondary baccalaureate careers of black graduates.

JAMES JONES serves as executive director for public interest, director of the Office on AIDS, and director of the Minority Fellowship Program at the American Psychological Association. Also a professor of psychology at the University of Delaware, he has written many articles and book chapters on racism, culture, and personality, and a book *Prejudice and Racism* (1972).

HARRY J. KNOPKE is Executive Assistant to the President and Associate Professor of Behavioral and Community Medicine at The University of Alabama. He has published extensively in the areas of primary health care, medical education, and the behavioral sciences. He has been active in developing and implementing intergroup programs on the University campus and in communities through the University's BioPrep Program.

LEON F. LITWACK is the Alexander F. and May T. Morrison professor of history at The University of California, Berkeley. Among his books is *Been in the Storm So Long: The Aftermath of Slavery,* which won the Pulitzer Prize, the American Book Award, and the Parkman Prize. He is a member of the American Academy of Arts and Sciences.

FANNIE ALLEN NEAL was appointed field director for the Committee on Political Education, AFL-CIO, in 1960, and has organized voter registration and voter education programs nationally. In 1977 she was named AFL-CIO's southern director of Volunteers in Politics, serving 11 southern states. She has received a number of awards for her leadership in the labor movement and in voter registration. She retired in 1987.

ROBERT J. NORRELL is currently associate professor of history and director of The Center for Southern History and Culture at The University of Alabama. Author of *Reaping the Whirlwind: The Civil Rights Movement in Tuskegee,* which won the 1986 Robert F. Kennedy Book Award, Norrell was a Mellon Research Fellow at the University of Cambridge in 1984–85.

MORTIMER OSTOW, M.D., is Edward T. Sandrow visiting professor of pastoral psychiatry at the Jewish Theological Seminary of America. He is also the attending psychiatrist at Montefiore Hospital and president of the Psychoanalytic Research and Development Fund, as well as chairman of its study group on antisemitism. His writings include works on neurology, psychiatry, psychoanalysis, religion, and antisemitism.

THOMAS F. PETTIGREW is professor of social psychology at The University of California, Santa Cruz, and The University of Amsterdam. A foremost authority on race relations, Pettigrew has authored or edited some 12 books on the topic and has received The Sydney Spivack Fellowship for Race Relations Research, awarded by the American Sociological Association, and The Kurt Lewin Award of the Society for the Psychological Study of Social Issues.

RONALD W. ROGERS is a professor of psychology and assistant dean of the Graduate School at The University of Alabama. He is a Fellow of the American Psychological Association and has served on advisory panels at the National Science Foundation and the National Institutes of Health. Dr. Rogers's research on intergroup relations has received several regional and national awards.

WALTER G. STEPHAN specializes in the study of intergroup relations. He has published a number of articles on the effects of school desegregation on achievement, self-esteem, and prejudice and coauthored the book *Desegregation: Past, Present, and Future*. He is a professor of psychology at New Mexico State University.

INDEX

229